A Blackwater Press book

First published in the United States of America by
Blackwater Press, LLC

Copyright © Robert A. Ford, 2025

All rights reserved. No part of this publication may be reproduced, stored in a retrieval system, or transmitted, in any form or by any means, electronic, mechanical, photocopying, recording or otherwise, without the prior permission of the publishers.

Library of Congress Control Number: 2025930009

ISBN: 978-1-963614-10-7

Blackwater Press
120 Capitol Street
Charleston, WV 25301
United States

blackwaterpress.com

The Battle of Cowpens, Reexamined

ROBERT A. FORD

Preface

Reexamining the Battle of Cowpens may seem like a novel idea. After all, what remains to reexamine? Cowpens presented heroic actions against a backdrop of desperate fighting. The heroism and the desperation are firmly settled and need no reexamination. Cowpens gained fame as a tactical masterpiece. Brigadier General Daniel Morgan earned his spurs as one of the most brilliant tacticians born on American soil. Cowpens was his master stroke, the most extraordinary exercise of a genius in the full bloom of his powers.

If all this is true, what will this book reexamine? As things developed, the tactics themselves became the subject of a great deal of misunderstanding. Those familiar with the history of the Revolutionary War have been told many times that Morgan was a great tactical innovator. This, of course, is completely accurate. But the nature of his innovation became obscured through time and the accretions of legend.

In the traditional narrative of the battle, Morgan devised a plan deploying his forces into three lines: militia skirmishers with rifles in front, conventional militia with muskets in the second line, and Continental regulars in the third. This, we are told, was a brilliant twist on the idea of the defense in depth. As the British moved forward, they moved into deeper trouble. There was a certain bait-and-switch aspect to the plan. The British had no fear, indeed little regard, for the militia. British opinion was justified; the militia usually performed poorly in conventional battles fought in straight lines. Placing them in front allowed the British to believe their performance represented the abilities of the entire army. Falsely confident, the British would charge the Continentals, to be brought up short by hardened professional soldiers.

Examining the battle yields a renewed appreciation for the genius and hard work that went into the astounding American victory. Reexamining the battle generates an entirely new view of Morgan's tactics. They were brilliant; his genius was a constant. His innovation, however, had nothing to do with a defense in depth. A close reexamination, focused on a critical reading of the eighteenth-century source materials, reveals his innovation was exactly the opposite of a defense in depth. Rather than three lines of increasing deadliness, Morgan formed his army into two lines. Skirmishers armed with rifles manned the first line. Continentals formed behind the skirmishers, with conventional militia guarding the regulars' flanks. Of all the many innovations present on the ground, depth was blatant in its absence.

The key to Morgan's tactical thinking was his background of military service. He had served long years in rifle regiments, eventually commanding one. Most commanders at the time spurned the rifle for a number of reasons, most of which seem tenuous to modern eyes. Uniquely among his contemporaries, Morgan realized its potential at the time. He knew how to capitalize on its major strong point: accuracy at long distances. At Cowpens, he massed riflemen in the first rank of his formation, with orders to target British officers. This was new, exciting, and deadly. The riflemen, most of them backwoodsmen who had grown up honing their marksmanship, were murderously accurate sharpshooters. British officers paid dearly in blood.

Morgan's innovation with the rifle went further. As well as the rifle's advantages, he understood its disadvantages. Most importantly, the rifle required a significantly longer reloading time than the musket. A proficient infantryman could reload a musket four times a minute. A proficient rifleman might manage one shot in a minute, sometimes one in two minutes. Morgan, aware of the problem, ordered the riflemen to fire as many rounds as time allowed, then withdraw behind the main battle line.

The actual nature of Morgan's tactics ran directly counter

to any idea of a defense in depth on the field at Cowpens. The traditional narrative of Cowpens stood in the tradition of conventional eighteenth-century tactics: straight lines of infantry in a set-piece formation. Morgan, the narrative went, added the idea of hiding the Continentals behind the militia, luring the British forward, stepwise, into increasing levels of American power. The narrative took advantage of the reputation of the British commander, Lieutenant Colonel Banastre Tarleton, an avatar of aggression. Tarleton, a bull seeing a red cape, charged recklessly into the American lines, his aggression lubricating the springs of the trap set by Morgan.

In actuality, Morgan deployed his forces in two lines, not three. Morgan massed riflemen on the first line, ordering them to shoot as many British officers as circumstances permitted, then withdraw before the British drew close enough to threaten with their bayonets. Behind the riflemen stood the main line of Continental regulars. Militia riflemen guarded one flank of the regulars, conventional militia armed with muskets guarded the other. Rather than acting as a separate and deadly line facing the British, their post was simply to guard the flanks of the regulars.

This was news, and for many, not favorable. In the traditional narrative, the conventional militia had occupied the second line of battle, all by themselves, the final barrier shielding the Continentals. Morgan's actual deployment represented a significant demotion. The militia tradition runs deep in our history. Americans grow up on the legends of the minutemen, the citizen-soldiers who wrested liberty from the redcoated professionals and Hessian mercenaries sent by the British government. At Cowpens, the militia's legendary accomplishments far exceeded the role Morgan assigned them on the ground. The bulk of the fighting was done by the Continental regulars.

Reexamining the battle generated an understanding of the true nature of Morgan's innovative thinking. At the same time, it exposed the vast gulf between the actual tactics used on the field, and the accumulated misconceptions lurking within the traditional narrative of the battle. Where did this divergence originate?

Henry Lee, better known to the world as "Light-Horse Harry," was the commander of the 2nd Partisan Corps., a mixed unit of infantry and cavalry, intended for warfare considered unconventional by eighteenth-century standards. Lee was a spirited, aggressive commander whose days of military service formed a high point in his life. Long after the war, he put pen to paper and wrote a memoir of his experiences that has proved immensely popular.[1] Rightfully so; his skill as a *raconteur* closely paralleled his ability as a field commander. Lee was a brilliant writer whose prose retains the ability to grab the reader's attention, two hundred years after he wrote it. Lee's unit formed part of the southern army at the time of the fighting at Cowpens. Lee, however, attended to duties many miles east. As it related to Cowpens, his book was not a memoir in any sense. Lee never disclosed his sources, and there is no way to know where he learned his version of events. At worst, Lee read popular histories of the day and reconstructed what he thought must have happened. At best, Lee reported a series of stories he gleaned from soldiers who fought the battle. Not a memoir, it was not history in any real sense, either. There has been no suggestion Lee endeavored to research the battle, check his facts, or perform any of the other, myriad tasks associated with writing history. In its most advantageous light, Lee on Cowpens was simply hearsay. Riveting to read, but hearsay nonetheless.

Lee was an early exponent of the three-level defense in depth at Cowpens. His memoir rapidly achieved tremendous prominence after its publication in 1812. With the popularity of the book spread Lee's version of Cowpens. Lee was more than an early exponent of the defense in depth; he was a persuasive and influential advocate of his version of events.

There were other writers, credentialed and influential, who attempted to analyze Morgan at Cowpens. All failed. David Ramsay wrote a popular history of the Revolutionary War that gained great regard immediately after the war.[2] Ramsay, a physician by training, was enchanted by Morgan's victory but

---

[1] Henry Lee, *Memoirs of the War in the Southern Department of the United States*, 2 vols. (Philadelphia, 1812).

[2] David Ramsay, *History of the American Revolution*, 2 vols. (Philadelphia, 1789).

unable to appreciate the tactics that created it. His version of Cowpens correctly put the Americans into two lines of battle. He made no mention of the true innovation, massed rifle fire, and his account suffers from the absent explanation of the way Morgan was able to defeat Tarleton. Similarly, William Moultrie was a hero of the war in South Carolina. He was not involved at Cowpens. His memoir related a version of the battle almost identical to that told by Ramsay.[3] Although it divided the Americans properly into two lines of battle, Moultrie depicted the tactics entirely as a classic eighteenth-century chessboard encounter, with nothing remarkable other than the astounding victory itself. The reader may search Moultrie's book in vain for any analysis of the reasons motivating Morgan's achievement.

Lee stood out in the period following the war in his ability to leverage his experience on the battlefield into an analysis of the battles discussed in his book. He achieved great recognition for this achievement, prominent at the time for its uniqueness. As this book moves through the battle, it will refer to the three-line defense in depth as "the Lee version" as a necessary shorthand, understanding that a legend as deeply imbued as this one has a complex, multifaceted origin. For example, William Johnson was another historian writing in the very early nineteenth century. His two-volume biography of Nathanael Greene first saw light in 1822.[4] Johnson, a trained jurist, became another exponent of the three-line defense in depth at Cowpens.[5] His book, popular in its day, like Lee's cultivated the idea of Morgan's genius, but misdirected its praise.

Reexamination of the tactics at Cowpens leads to a further, deeper inquiry. Despite its deep-seated popularity, the idea of

---

[3] William Moultrie, *Memoirs of the American Revolution, So Far as It Related to the States of North and South Carolina, and Georgia*, 2 vols. (New York, 1802).

[4] William Johson, *Sketches of the Life and Correspondence of Nathanael Greene*, 2 vols. (Charleston, 1822).

[5] This fact was remarkable in that while he acknowledged Lee as a source, he also credited Moultrie, Ramsay, and Tarleton, all of whom attested to two lines of battle. More remarkable was the fact that Johnson had access to all of Greene's papers, including Morgan's original after-action report, which he failed to reference as a source for his narrative of Cowpens, Johnson, *Life*, 1:377. Johnson's work is a testament to the persuasive force of Lee's prose.

Americans in three lines at Cowpens, awaiting the British *seriatim*, lacks foundation in the memoirs of the true witnesses to the battle. Morgan was the commander on the field. He clearly and unambiguously reported that he deployed a two-line formation, riflemen in the front, regulars in the rear.[6] The British, weakened by massed rifle fire, crashed into the Continental line like a ripe watermelon on a rock. With all this in mind, one must ask how Morgan's rendition of his own battle vanished into the ether of history, replaced by Lee's version, authored by a man who was not there.

Morgan originated the tactics under discussion. Morgan commanded the troops on the battlefield. Morgan authored the report documenting his deployment into two lines of battle. His report was very clear: riflemen in front with orders to shoot and withdraw; a single main battle line; no pretense of any defense in depth. It could not have been simpler, but when Lee's version appeared in 1812, Morgan's disappeared as if it were never there. Among American historians, subscribing to Lee's version of events has been a universal prerequisite to credentials as an expert on Cowpens.

Morgan, brilliant in command, lacked spark as a wordsmith. Cowpens was one of the most thrilling events to take place in a theater of excitement. In tragic contrast, Morgan's report was dry as dust. One might read it and wonder why people were so enthralled with the events he described. Lee's version presented the opposite face. His version surged with the emotion of hard fighting and hair's-breadth escapes, larger-than-life heroes and contemptible villains. Not intentionally, Morgan's and Lee's versions were placed in competition, and Lee's won, unquestionably. Lee, not an eyewitness but a marvelous writer, won the day, and his version has dominated the landscape ever since.

Just as the traditional narrative of a three-line defense in depth—what this book will call the Lee version—has many roots, so with the Morgan version. Morgan was not the only

---

[6] Daniel Morgan to Nathanael Greene, 19 January 1781, in Richard K. Showman, Dennis M. Conrad, Roger N. Parks, Elizabeth C. Stevens, eds., *The Papers of General Nathanael Greene, vol. 7: 26 December 1780–29 March 1781* (Chapel Hill: University of North Carolina Press, 1994), 7: 153.

writer to report the facts accurately. The British, less impressed with Lee, universally reported an American two-line formation, exactly as described by Morgan. Even so, hundreds of years later, Lee's magic with the pen has been able to convince some very smart people that Morgan deployed a three-level defense in depth.

Chronology provides a testament to the power of the Lee tradition. Before his *Memoirs* appeared in 1812, authors on both sides of the Atlantic correctly reported the American formation. The *Annual Register* in 1781,[7] and works by Tarleton in 1787, Gordon in 1788,[8] Ramsay in 1789, Stedman in 1794, and Moultrie in 1802, documented two American lines and shunned any notion of a defense in depth. With Lee's memoirs in 1812, the curtain dropped. As early as 1816, the second volume of McCall's *History of Georgia* recorded three American lines.[9]

Does this mean that everything one believed about the Battle of Cowpens was incorrect? Almost certainly. A search of histories written in the past two hundred years will reveal many well-written, thoroughly researched renditions of narratives in the Lee tradition. The Morgan version proved much less noteworthy. This was unfortunate on many levels. Consider this: Morgan defied the straight-line conventions of his day to allow riflemen to use cover and concealment for protection, maximizing damage to the enemy and minimizing their own casualties. In this idea, he forecast the tactics of a later century, when all armies abandoned chessboard formations in favor of adaptation to the advantages presented by natural terrain. Morgan's genius transcended decades. Adherence to the Lee narrative has hindered his recognition as the true predictor of infantry tactics of the mid-twentieth century.

In its reexamination of the Battle of Cowpens, this book will look in depth at the Lee and Morgan traditions. They pre-

---

7 *The Annual Register* was a highly influential London publication that provided an accurate record of the point of view of the British establishment at the time.

8 William Gordon, *The History of the Rise, Progress, and Establishment of the Independence of the United States of America*, 4 vols. (London, 1788).

9 Hugh McCall, *The History of Georgia, Containing Brief Sketches of the Most Remarkable Events Up to the Present day (1784)*, vol. 2 (Savannah, 1816).

sented different tactics, and at the same time, emphasized different qualities. In concrete terms, Morgan and Lee presented conflicting notions of Morgan's genius. A forecast may provide clarity. Lee emphasized Morgan's gut-level skill as a battlefield commander. To this end, in his version, Morgan allowed the flanks of his lines to dangle freely in the wind, unprotected and vulnerable to a British flanking attack. Lee's point was that Morgan was the kind of no-nonsense battlefield general who could meet any challenge, plug any hole, do whatever it took, to win. In painting this picture of Morgan, Lee said much about himself. More, in fact, than he said about Morgan. Lee, famous as a cavalry commander, was a great improviser, glad to accept challenges as they arose. He admired the same quality in others.

Morgan, in contrast, made it very clear that he put great emphasis on guarding his flanks. He secured his main battle line with ample flank protection. Morgan's point opposed the one made by Lee. Morgan insisted he was a careful and methodical planner. The victory at Cowpens was not the random product of a coin toss by the fickle gods of war. It was the predictable result of hard work and reasoned preparation.

Further questions lie in the path of a reexamination of Cowpens. The traditional battlefield narrative—the Lee version—is the most apparent of the many legends adhering to the nucleus of the battle. There are others. At this point, a forecast of two will illustrate the whole. In praising Morgan's genius, many suggested he achieved an envelopment of the British forces on the field. An envelopment has long enjoyed the reputation of the ultimate battlefield coup. An enveloped army finds the enemy surrounding it on all sides. Any general achieving such a feat truly belongs in the pantheon of heroes, not just national, but universal. Did Morgan reach such an apotheosis at Cowpens? This book will examine, or better stated, reexamine, the evidence.

The most famous legend to arise out of Cowpens concerns the near-death of Lieutenant Colonel William Washington, Morgan's cavalry commander. The traditional narrative held that in the final melee of the battle, Washington was surrounded and in deep trouble. At the last minute, a young person of color, perhaps a waiter, perhaps a bugler, fired the final shot, saving the heroic Washington from a tragic death at the bloody hands of Tarleton's dragoons. How much faith may we place in this admittedly fascinating story? The evidence, reexamined, will tell us.

And, so with the battle as a whole. This reexamination will follow all the evidence. We will see where it takes us.

Prologue

Lee was wrong about Morgan's battle plan. He was wrong about the nature of Morgan's innovation. Like most military thinkers of his generation, he failed to comprehend the potential of the rifle. Like most writers in his and the following generations, he failed to understand that Morgan had grasped it. Nevertheless, Lee demonstrated a keen understanding of something Morgan never conceived: the importance of narrative. Lee understood that good history must tell a story. Lee's work demonstrated that history resonates with us more deeply when we receive it with the trappings of narrative: characters good and bad, protagonists and antagonists, plot, climax, and *dénouement*. Lee's rendition of the Battle of Cowpens achieved greatness as a perfect example of the value of narrative in history. The battle is an important piece of what made America possible. As important as it is, if we are to grasp its meaning, we will do so better if it comes to us as a story.

Fortunately, when told correctly, Cowpens is a fascinating tale. It has everything one looks for in a story. The main characters provide outstanding examples. The battle brought forward Daniel Morgan, a backwoodsman with humble beginnings made general of the Revolution, and pitted him against Banastre Tarleton, spoiled scion of the mother country who achieved notoriety in a later century as the model for the villainous antagonist in the film *The Patriot*.

Before introducing the characters in the story in more detail, the plot requires attention. The narrative of Cowpens began months before the engagement of 17 January 1781. To find the roots of the battle, one must return to the events of the previous late winter and early spring.

At the time the story began, Major General Benjamin Lincoln commanded the American southern army, a force of several thousand Continental regular soldiers, plus a measure of militiamen. Lincoln maintained his headquarters in Charleston, South Carolina, and in the late winter of 1780, he manned the city with the bulk of his forces.

On 11 February, General Henry Clinton, the British commander-in-chief in America, landed a huge invasion force on John's Island, thirty miles from Charleston.[10] Clinton had tried and failed to take Charleston by force in 1776. Clinton, commanding 12,200 soldiers,[11] intended a different result in 1780.

Charles Stedman was an officer in the British Army, and is a name that will arise often as the story works its way to its conclusion. He performed dual services as an eyewitness and a historian. For now, the point from Stedman's work is his estimate of the size of Lincoln's army.

Stedman asserted Lincoln commanded seven thousand men in Charleston.[12] If true, a force of this magnitude evinced a huge American commitment to defend the city. Compare more famous engagements: Bunker Hill saw three thousand British soldiers fighting 2400 Americans; Trenton mustered 1500 British against 2400 Americans. Saratoga, the turning point in the war, saw six thousand British defeated by 1500 Americans. The size of the forces arrayed against each other in Charleston spoke to the perceptions of worth of the city on adjoining sides of the

---

10 C. Stedman, *History of the Origin Progress, and Termination of the American War,* 2 vols. (London, 1794), 2:177; Henry Lee, *Memoirs of the War in the Southern Department of the United States* (Washington, D.C., 1827), 62. Unless noted, all citations to Lee will be to the one-volume 1827 edition.

11 Bernard Uhlendorf, trans. and ed., *The Siege of Charleston With an Account of the Province of South Carolina: Diaries and Letters of Hessian Officers from the von Jungkenn Papers in the William L. Clements Library* (Ann Arbor: University of Michigan Press, 1938), 108–109; William B. Willcox, ed., *The American Rebellion: Sir Henry Clinton's Narrative of His Campaigns, 1775–1782, With an Appendix of Original Documents* (New Haven: Yale University Press, 1954), 167n14.

12 Stedman, *History,* 2:179.

battle line. To both, Charleston was the ultimate goal, the jewel in the southern crown. The city sang its siren song, and neither side was immune to its allure. The importance of the city, psychologically and militarily, will imprint the events that follow the British landing in February.

There was another fact hidden in the troop numbers. In the eighteenth-century texts, even the most trustworthy, the troop counts and casualty figures were inherently malleable. Several reasons underscored this phenomenon. In many cases, the author labored under a lack of good information. In other cases, an author might abandon good information in an effort to further an argument.

Lee asserted that Stedman was unquestionably, almost laughably, wrong in his assessment of the American force at Charleston. Lee's position was demonstrably thin, in that Stedman served as a staff officer with the British Army in South Carolina during the invasion, while Lee was on duty several states distant, in the northern theater of the war. Unhindered, Lee insisted Lincoln's army contained two thousand Continentals and a few hundred militia of the city.[13]

A British tally of American and French fighting men captured at Charleston documented over five thousand soldiers and one thousand sailors, largely confirming Stedman's number and disavowing any support for Lee. Both authors wrote with full knowledge of the troop count.[14] What explains the difference? The two authors cannot be reconciled. As a last resort, one can only look to their respective agendas for a resolution. Stedman, fighting with the British, had every incentive to sculpt the battle over Charleston in high relief. In Stedman's work, one sees large formations of great men battling over the lynchpin to the southern war. In contrast, Lee, an enthusiastic Whig, at the time he wrote knew that the battle for Charleston had gone badly. His memoir presented the opportunity to minimize the loss. Lee was an admirer of the city, and his book grieved its loss to the British.

---

13 Lee, *Memoirs*, 75.
14 Carl P. Borick, *Relieve Us of This Burthen: American Prisoners of War in the South, 1780–1782* (Columbia: University of South Carolina Press, 2012), 4, 46, 85; Stedman, *History*, 2:186; Lee, *Memoirs*, 75.

But, militarily, he found a means to describe the American loss as less overwhelming and less pervasively adverse to the cause of liberty. So, as Lee told the story of the battle for Charleston, the American effort was significant, but not an epic disaster.

Lee was more successful in advancing his agenda with Cowpens. In discussing Charleston, Lee's version has gained little traction over the years. When seen today, it is usually to quote his sneer at the official troop count: it included not only men under arms within the city, but, "no doubt, all the inhabitants capable of bearing arms."[15]

Lee's efforts to modify the legacy of Charleston told later generations much about the plasticity of facts in the eighteenth century when authors confronted developments on the ground. At the same time, his efforts highlighted the importance of the battle's outcome. Charleston was the key to the deep south, just as its loss was the key to everything that followed.

Clinton made slow, deliberate progress from John's Island toward the city. Lincoln, under tremendous pressure from Whig officials, abandoned freedom of movement and blockaded his army inside the city, a rash and dangerous decision. The militia from the countryside saw the folly in this move. Several authors reported these men declined to confine themselves in what soon became a besieged city.[16]

Both commanders had believed Charleston impervious to naval attack. Both were mistaken. The British fleet crossed the sand bar at the mouth of the harbor on 20 March. By 30 March, Clinton invested the city in a siege. The Americans fought hard, but acceded to the consequences of their confinement. On 12 May, Lincoln surrendered the city and his army to the British.

Clinton, finally achieving the prize that had eluded him four years earlier, retired to New York to resume his duties as commander-in-chief. He left Lieutenant General Charles Cornwallis in command of British forces in the southern theater.

At the time Cornwallis assumed command in the south, the British star was ascendant. Georgia and South Carolina were

---

15 Lee, *Memoirs*, 75.
16 Lee, *Memoirs*, 62–64; Stedman, *History*, 2:178–179.

beaten and out of the war. The Continentals in the south, almost to a man, were prisoners of war. Cornwallis demonstrated no willingness to rest on the British laurels. A commander combining measures of caution and aggression, he believed it possible that pockets of resistance persisted in the countryside.

The American loss at Charleston cast the Patriot cause in the south into shadow. Many factors played into the sense of magnitude of the disaster: the numbers of soldiers on both sides; the emotional significance of Charleston; the irreplaceable loss of an entire Continental army. The Tories, emboldened by the British victory, accepted more responsibilities and acted more visibly in the service of the royal government. The Whigs, radically disheartened, withdrew into inaction.

In the midst of the universal gloom overhanging the Patriots, and the unleavened delight among the British and Loyalists, there was one point of distinction. A small force of Continentals escaped the surrender of Charleston. The commander was Lieutenant Colonel Abraham Buford. His force consisted of about three hundred infantry, a detachment of cavalry, and two six-pound artillery pieces. Buford was moving quickly toward North Carolina to join with another American force near Salisbury.[17]

In ordinary times, Cornwallis might have allowed Buford to retreat unmolested. By his actions, Buford intended no threat to British installations or Cornwallis's field army in South Carolina. But, in the heady days following the surrender of Charleston, Cornwallis saw the seductive vision of a complete rout of the entire Continental Army in the deep south. In this new south of absolute British mastery, Buford could not survive.

Cornwallis set out to catch this final American force. He made a late start from Charleston, then stopped at the British northwestern strong point at Camden. By this time, Buford had made great gains toward North Carolina and freedom. Defeated by the mechanics and logistics of moving a large army, Cornwallis detached Tarleton with a highly mobile, mixed force of

---

17 Stedman, *History*, 2:190; Lee, *Memoirs*, 78. There are variant spellings, "Burford" appearing in Stedman's book.

270 cavalrymen and mounted infantrymen drawn from several units. Tarleton, a model of aggression, force-marched his men relentlessly, covering 105 miles in fifty-four hours. On 29 May, Tarleton caught Buford at the Waxhaws, a region in north-central South Carolina near the North Carolina border.[18]

At this point in the story, the legacy of Charleston intervened. While still in Charleston, Clinton issued a series of proclamations in his capacity as military governor. Clinton believed, with some justification, that he had purged the spirit of rebellion from South Carolina. In an era of uncontested royal government, Clinton envisioned conciliation as the proper means to bring the populace into cooperation. His three proclamations provided mechanisms for everyone, including Whigs formerly under arms in rebel militias, to return to compliance with colonial officials.[19]

As Continentals, Buford and his men were ineligible for the amnesty contemplated by Clinton's proclamations. Clinton, however, had injected conciliation into the air. By the time Tarleton reached Buford, Clinton had accepted the surrender of thousands of Continentals, and had provided amnesty for uncounted Whig militiamen. Tarleton found himself trapped between conflicting objectives. He enjoyed a reputation cemented in the slash and burn school of warfare. His commander, however, had mandated conciliation as his preferred means to deal with subjects of the crown who had strayed into rebellion. Tarleton, as ambitious as he was aggressive, knew that the path to honors in the army lay in obeying the spirit as well as the letter of orders from the commander-in-chief. He had no real choice but to entertain talk of surrender with Buford.

Buford wrote an official report, but no popular accounting of the engagement at the Waxhaws. There was no counterweight to Tarleton's memoir, written not just from the British side, but from Tarleton's personal point of view. While one may properly enumerate the disadvantages of relying exclusively on Tarleton, this paradigm presented one huge advantage: Tarleton

---

18 Stedman, *History*, 2:193.
19 Stedman, *History*, 2:190–192; Lee, *Memoirs*, 77–82.

was a marvelous writer. Tarleton had the rare ability to put the reader into the thick of the action, to feel what happened. Much like Lee's writing, and for many of the same reasons, Tarleton's memoir remains a core resource for the war in the south.[20]

Tarleton began his story several days preceding, when Cornwallis gave him the mission to stop Buford. As Tarleton told the story, Cornwallis impressed him with the dire nature of the situation. Buford had to be stopped. Cornwallis put no limits on his eager subordinate: "the attempt could only be guided by discretionary powers, and not by any antecedent commands."[21] In short, Tarleton was free to do as he pleased. With Cornwallis's orders, Tarleton's dilemma became more acute. Clinton, still commander in the south, wanted reconciliation. Cornwallis, in command of the field army and due to take overall command in the south within days, knew Tarleton well, and turned him loose on the Americans, unrestrained. On the road, Tarleton decided "no time was to be lost," and "a vigorous effort" was the only way to prevent Buford from reaching North Carolina and safety.

A difficult calculation presented when he came face to face with Buford. If we accept Tarleton's narrative, and here we should, Cornwallis's orders were almost directly contrary to Clinton's mandates. Conciliation or unrestricted warfare? Tarleton's inclinations pushed him toward the latter.

Reading Tarleton's memoir on this encounter, one feels the tension in the British officer as he decided to follow Clinton's lead and discuss terms of surrender with Buford. He sent Buford a summons calling on him to surrender.[22] Tarleton inflated his numbers in the summons, threatening Buford with seven hundred British soldiers in his immediate front, backed by Cornwallis "within a short march" with nine battalions of redcoated professionals.

Tarleton offered Buford essentially the same terms Lincoln had received in the surrender of Charleston. Clinton would have been gratified. Buford, however, was in no mood for con-

---

[20] Banastre Tarleton, *History of the Campaigns of 1781 and 1781, in the Southern Provinces of North America* (Dublin, 1787).
[21] Tarleton, *Campaigns*, 28–29.
[22] Tarleton, *Campaigns*, 29–30, 78–79.

ciliation. Tarleton asserted that Buford dismissed any talk of surrender, proposed no counteroffer for a bloodless resolution, and ordered his troops into a defensive line. At this point in the story, Tarleton had satisfied Clinton's mandates. Unrestrained warfare would follow.

Tarleton emphasized an odd point that would gain importance very shortly. After recounting the long forced march, he wrote that the British soldiers were "totally worn out." British soldiers, exhausted, fell to the rear. The horses drawing the artillery could go no further. Tarleton saw no facts calling for a reconsideration of his battle plans. He "made his arrangements for the attack with all possible expedition." Those readers finding a pattern in Tarleton's conduct are correct. He earned his reputation for ruthless aggression. His soldiers worn out and his horses collapsing, Tarleton deployed his force into three divisions, right, center, and left, with those too exhausted to move forming a reserve in the rear.

The engagement was brief and hard-hitting. Buford's strategy defied analysis. Tarleton formed his line three hundred yards in front of the Americans. The British stood outside of musket range, but well within range of the American artillery. Nevertheless, the British deployed unmolested by artillery fire.[23] Tarleton charged. He waited for the American musket volley. At fifty yards' distance, he wrote that he heard the American officers ordering the men to wait until the British were 10 yards from them before firing. At 10 yards' distance, the Americans fired their first, and only, volley. There were British casualties, but too few and too late to matter. The British cavalry decimated the American infantry line. Tarleton's horse was shot from under him, and by the time he remounted, the battle was largely concluded.

This minor engagement of a few hundred soldiers gained great importance for the manner in which it concluded. Stedman left tantalizing clues of the matter in his work. Writing in 1794, long after the encounter, and long after it had achieved notoriety on both sides of the Atlantic, he asserted:

---
23 Tarleton, *Campaigns*, 31.

> The execution done in this action was severe: One hundred and thirteen were killed on the spot, and two hundred and three made prisoners, of whom one hundred and fifty were badly wounded. Buford made his escape by a precipitate flight on horseback. The king's troops were entitled to great commendation for their activity and ardor on this occasion, but the virtue of humanity was totally forgot.[24]

Stedman had no use for Tarleton, believing him the tragic mixture of too much aggression and too little skill.[25] Even so, Stedman acquired the reputation of absolute equanimity, and his bemoaning lost humanity was serious. Although aware of the reputation of the encounter at the Waxhaws, Stedman saw fit to say nothing further. Given this lack even in the British sources, the only recourse is a return to Tarleton.

Tarleton wrote that his riders crashed into the American line of battle, which was "totally broken." Buford's decision to wait until the British were ten yards distant explained this aspect of the battle's conclusion. Infantry in the open was ripe wheat to the cavalry's scythe. The British, not weakened by American musket fire, made short work of the opposing infantry. It was at this point that Tarleton lost his horse.

He wrote that before he could remount, "slaughter was commenced." The word *slaughter* resonated with eighteenth-century readers much as it does today. If Tarleton, not squeamish, believed there was slaughter on the field at the Waxhaws, one should take him at this word.

Tarleton made no comment on his course of action after remounting. This lacuna in his narrative screamed at the reader. He gave no insight into his reaction. He may equally well have encouraged the slaughter as ordered a halt to it. He added only that "thus in a few minutes ended an affair which might have had a very different termination." The ambiguity is tense and frustrating. While he acknowledged that Americans were slaughtered, he hinted that things might have gone much worse.

What Tarleton wrote did not respond to Stedman in any realistic manner. Stedman suggested the British committed an

---

24 Stedman, *History*, 2:193.
25 Stedman, *History*, 2:324, 2:354n.

atrocity at the Waxhaws. His recounting of the American casualties emphasized his point: 113 killed, another 150 severely wounded. Tarleton replied only that his men, force-marched beyond toleration, lost their discipline and gave vent to their exhaustion and frustration. Stedman, saddened and outraged at the outcome, said otherwise.

Both British officers failed to confront the problem foursquare. A sense of its magnitude lay in the fact that Tarleton's nickname among the Americans, "Bloody Ban," derived largely from this engagement. Tarleton and Stedman wrote within a few years after the war, and both were acutely aware of the terrible reputation the British Army gained at the Waxhaws. Neither could afford to ignore it. Each acknowledged the matter in his own way, but neither offered a satisfactory explanation.

In contrast, the Americans grabbed the problem, unhesitatingly, with both hands. Lee stood out as a powerful voice in the conversation about the Waxhaws. As with his views on Cowpens, his position on the Waxhaws spread with the popularity of his book.

Lee fought Tarleton directly for much of the southern campaign. Lee could be a harsh critic of his British counterpart. Lee's criticism, as with all his thoughts on Tarleton, welled up from month after month of front-line contact. Of all the Americans in the field, Lee was the most familiar with Tarleton, his tactics, and his predilections. Overall, his view of Tarleton closely mirrored that expressed by Stedman: Tarleton was "more distinguished for courage and activity than for management and address;" "his mode of operation was to overtake and fight."[26]

Lee wrote thirty years after the conclusion of hostilities. With respect to the Waxhaws, thirty years was enough time to circulate and dissect every proposition on the matter. As with Cowpens, Lee was not an eyewitness to any aspect of the engagement at the Waxhaws. The value of his writing on the Waxhaws was not as memoir, or even as history. With thirty years of experience on which to draw, the position in his book was a fair distillation of the American views on the matter. Once more, as a matter of shorthand, this book will refer to Lee's narrative of the events

---

26 Lee, *Memoirs*, 78.

at the Waxhaws as "the Lee version," again understanding its roots were more complex.

Lee approached the Waxhaws from a perspective alien to the two British officers. Lee wanted the world to know exactly what happened, and most of all, why it happened. Lee was not a subtle, nuanced thinker, and he expressed his thoughts in black and white clarity: what happened was an atrocity, and why it happened boiled down to the single word *Tarleton*.

Lee introduced a new fact into the mix that changed everything. As Lee told the story, Buford offered to surrender, and Tarleton refused. Lee tacitly accused Tarleton of the worst sort of subterfuge. While pretending to negotiate with Buford, Tarleton aligned his forces for attack. When he ended the negotiations, he assaulted "the still unprepared Americans."[27]

Lee, still feeling the outrage thirty years later, stormed that Tarleton's decline of Buford's offer to surrender was "inexplicable," and could only have come from deceit. Lee spewed invective: the British were "barbarous;" their conduct a "disgrace."[28] If we accept that Lee's version accurately reflected American opinion, and we should, his strong words tell us a great deal about the depth of feeling about the Waxhaws in America.

The story of Lee's writing took a dramatic, reverse turn. The first edition saw print in 1812. A revised edition appeared in 1827, several years after Lee's death in 1818. In the 1827 edition, Lee's editors left the original narrative intact, but in footnotes explained that the old man had erred. Tarleton was right: it was Buford who declined surrender.[29]

The amendment to Lee's version worked no changes in public opinion. As matters developed, which officer made or declined the offer to surrender was a sideshow. Lee had not wasted invective on a question of military protocol. He was outraged, as was the rest of the country, about the way in which the engagement at the Waxhaws concluded.

Lee's prose spoke to the ages: "wounds and death, with some partial resistance followed; and many of our soldiers fell under

27 Lee, *Memoirs*, 79.
28 Ibid.
29 Lee, *Memoirs*, 78n, 79n.

the British sabre requesting quarters."[30] Here, at last, lay the problem. The public believed Tarleton and his cavalry killed and wounded hundreds of American soldiers after they had surrendered. The public might forgive Tarleton the slaughter of men in line of battle. The Americans could never accept the slaughter of soldiers who had surrendered. While the British authors labored to minimize the problem, no American in the Revolutionary generation would forgive, or forget, "Bloody Ban" Tarleton at the Waxhaws.

Lee's impassioned cry found strong support in Buford's official report, where he insisted many of his men were killed "after they had lain down their arms."[31] The shadow of the Waxhaws would loom over every event that followed in the southern campaign. Lee went far to express the feelings of the nation. The slaughter of surrendered men at the Waxhaws "placed it first in the records of torture and death in the west."[32]

Lee's turgid language helps modern readers understand the emotions generated by the engagement at the Waxhaws. Always sanguine, Lee saw an odd glimmer of silver lining in the overwhelming despair surrounding Buford. The Waxhaws "produced the unanimous decision among the troops to revenge their murdered comrades whenever the blood-stained corps should give an opportunity."[33]

Lee made it clear that the opportunity would soon arise at Cowpens. Lee wrote with the full light of hindsight. He knew the fickle gods of war had tossed another coin for Tarleton, and this one came up vastly different from its predecessor. At Cowpens, revenge was in the air, the water, the soil itself. Revenge for the disaster at Charleston, for the disaster at Camden, but most of all, for the atrocity at Waxhaws. At Cowpens, Cornwallis again cried "Havoc!" and let slip his preferred dog of war. Given a chance, the Americans would be merciless in return.

---

30 Lee, *Memoirs*, 79.
31 Abraham Buford to Virginia Assembly, 2 June 1780, in Jim Piecuch, *The Blood Be Upon Your Head: Tarleton and the Myth of Buford's Massacre* (Lugoff, SC: Southern Campaign of the American Revolution Press, 2010), 63.
32 Lee, *Memoirs*, 80.
33 Ibid.

Chapter 1: The Commanders

The opposing commanders, with their unique abilities, deficiencies, and quirks, formed the essential substructure to the Battle of Cowpens. As with all military encounters, the commanders determined the course of the battle. Understanding the individualities of the commanders on both sides is necessary to understanding the mechanism of the engagement.

The Americans

The fighting at Cowpens took place on 17 January 1781. The date stood at a crossroads in the trail of successive commanders on both sides of the conflict. Major General Horatio Gates was the outgoing commander of the American southern army.

Horatio Gates (1727–1806) attracted great controversy throughout much of his military experience. Born in England, he began his career as a British officer in the War of the Austrian Succession, which he followed with service in America during the conflict known to the British as the Seven Years' War, to modern Americans as the French and Indian War. Under either name, the war ended with British victory in 1763. Gates, at this point a major, returned to England.

Gates had neither money nor influential friends, a deadly combination for an officer looking to rise in the British service. He acknowledged his fate, and left the army for a plantation near present-day Shepherdstown, West Virginia. When war returned in 1775, Gates returned to active service, this time as the Adjutant General of the Continental Army.

Ambition was a constant feature of Gates's military endeavors. Although a competent adjutant general, staff work never satisfied him, and he lobbied for the excitement and rewards of field command. He believed he merited the position of commander-in-chief, a view shared by several influential political figures. Held in check by George Washington and his supporters, Gates maneuvered for command in the northern department of the army. He finally achieved command of the northern department following Philip Schuyler's downfall after the defeat at Fort Ticonderoga.

Gates's career reached its apex with the Battle of Saratoga. Gates's command of the northern department of the army gave him responsibility for the American forces fighting in the turning point of the war. The American victory at Saratoga did not diminish the depth of controversy surrounding Gates. Bolstered by success at Saratoga, Gates and his supporters did not cease their agitation for replacing Washington as commander-in-chief. At the same time, there were rumblings from the northern department of the army that Gates's leadership had little to do with the tremendous victory at Saratoga. Since then, history has bestowed the laurels of victory at Saratoga to Gates's many talented subordinates, notably Daniel Morgan and Benedict Arnold.

After the American disaster at Charleston, Congress sent Gates, still the hero of Saratoga to the public, south to command the southern department of the army. He took command on 25 July 1780. He issued a series of ill-considered orders, leaving no doubt he had no idea how or why the Americans had won at Saratoga. His plan of action culminated in an engagement with British forces under Cornwallis at Camden, South Carolina, on 16 August 1780.

Camden was an epic defeat rarely matched in the history of American arms. It recalled the monumental loss at Charleston the previous May, and foreshadowed the performance of Confederate General Braxton Bragg's forces at Missionary Ridge in

November 1863. Although numerically superior to the British, 275 were killed and wounded, and an astounding one thousand captured. The American effort at Camden ended with a mass rout, capped by Gates's personal retreat of three days' duration, 170 miles to Hillsborough, North Carolina.

Gates never again held command. His supporters retained sufficient strength to quell a movement for a board of inquiry into Gates's conduct at Camden. Gates was provided a place on Washington's staff, where he remained for the duration of the war.

Although Gates had been rusticated to a staff position in the north by January 1781, his legacy remained vibrant and alive in the south. Camden was more than a defeat; it was a complete humiliation. Those inclined to view life imitating art saw the hand of Hubris at work, in the form of Gates's ambition and aggression, too powerful for his abilities.

Gates's downfall resonated deeply with the officers in the south. The lesson was unmistakable: too much aggression may prove fatal. In a curious dance of foil characters, the lesson of Camden followed directly on the heels of the lesson of Charleston. Benjamin Lincoln, mild-mannered and deferential, conceded decision-making to civilian authority. Lincoln allowed his army to become blockaded inside Charleston, resulting in disaster. The lesson was equally unmistakable: too much timidity may prove fatal. After these two object lessons, southern commanders walked a tightrope between the two.

Nathanael Greene (1742–1786) felt the lessons of Charleston and Camden especially deeply. A major general in the autumn of 1780, Congress allowed him the onerous, and dangerous, position as the third commander of the southern army in six months.

Greene started life in a Rhode Island Quaker family. Early in life, he developed an interest in military matters. He read military treatises voraciously. Before Lexington and Concord, he helped organize a Rhode Island militia unit, but a visible limp disqualified him from service as an officer.[34] In an odd turn of

---

34 Terry Golway, *Washington's General: Nathanael Greene and the Triumph of the American*

fate, after hostilities commenced, Congress raised him to brigadier general in the Continental Army. He was thirty-four years old. He served three years as a commander of regular troops, establishing a record lacking distinction, but more importantly, lacking scandal or disaster. In March 1778, he received an appointment to Washington's staff as quartermaster general. He served as a brilliant staff officer for two years. In the complicated politics of the Congress and the army, Greene's faithful support of Washington was constant and unremitting. Washington invested great confidence in Greene. After Gates's catastrophe at Camden, Washington strongly urged Greene as his replacement.

Greene took over direction of the southern army upon his arrival in Charlotte on 3 December 1780. Greene confronted several obstacles. He could not avoid the twin, conflicting legacies of Lincoln and Gates. He did not have a major victory in his background, as did, for example, his subordinate Daniel Morgan. After service as a staff officer for two years, he was unused to command, even to the idea of command. Greene's abilities and quirks played roles in the southern war after he arrived. One quirk stood out: Greene expressed intense disregard for the militia. His experience in the field had been with regular troops, and Greene never developed an understanding of these temporary soldiers who took time out from farming to fight the British. Greene held fast to his belief system even in the presence of massive evidence contradicting it. For example, on 24 January 1781, the day after he learned of Morgan's coup at Cowpens, in which the militia had fought well, Greene wrote to a correspondent: "it is the greatest folly in the world, to trust the liberties of a people" to the vagaries and irresponsibility of the militia.[35]

Greene commanded the southern army in one of the most successful campaigns fought in North America. Cornwallis, the British commander opposing Greene in the southern theater,

---

Revolution (New York: Henry Holt and Company, LLC, 2005), 44–45. Greene's first biographer disagreed, writing that his Quaker background disqualified him, Johnson, *Life*, 1:21.

35 Greene to James M. Varnum, 24 January 1781, in Showman et al., *Greene*, 7:188.

ultimately was required to surrender his army and British hopes at Yorktown in October 1781. Beneath this canopy of success lay a dark paradox: Greene lost every battle in the campaign. Historians have struggled to explain Greene's unique combination of victory and utter failure. Greene left a poignant summary of his experiences: "We fight, get beat, rise and fight again."[36]

A detailed exposition of Nathanael Greene as commander exceeds the scope of this book, which is, after all, about Cowpens, where Greene never stood. There was, however, one aspect of his abilities as a commander that played a significant role at Cowpens. This facet of his personality related closely to his thoughts on the militia. James Bartholomees was an incisive thinker and military historian. He completed a doctoral thesis on the distinctly different performances of the North Carolina militia at Cowpens and later at Guilford Courthouse, which remains the seminal discussion on the subject.[37] He went on to a distinguished career as a historian at the U.S. Army War College.[38] Bartholomees concluded Greene handled Continentals well. But, these regular soldiers had internalized discipline, esprit de corps, and military norms absent in militia formations. Bartholomees concluded it required a "strong and rather magnetic personality" to weld militia into an effective fighting force.[39] Greene's talents lay elsewhere.

History has awarded Greene the highest laurels in the realms of strategy and logistics. The accolades in these areas are unquestioned. Less universal are high marks as a battlefield commander. British military historian Jeremy Black spoke for many when he gave Greene credit as "one of the most effec-

---

36 Greene to the Chevalier de la Luzerne, 28 April 1781, in Dennis M. Conrad, Roger N. Parks, Martha J. King, and Richard K. Showman, eds., *The Papers of General Nathanael Greene, vol. 8: 30 March–10 July 1781* (Chapel Hill: University of North Carolina Press, 1995), 168.

37 James Boone Bartholomees, Jr., "Fight or Flee: The Combat Performance of the North Carolina Militia in the Cowpens-Guilford Courthouse Campaign, January to March 1781," PhD dissertation, Duke University, 1978.

38 The War College sits at the apex of the Army's educational institutions. Students are limited to the most promising colonels and lieutenant colonels, and upon graduation are awarded a master's degree in strategic studies

39 Bartholomees, "Fight or Flee," 209.

tive American generals."⁴⁰ He remarked that Greene stood as "an effective administrator and good strategist." Missing from Black's praise was any notion of Greene as leader.

Concern over Greene's abilities as a field commander has a long tradition. Brigadier General William R. Davie was an officer on Greene's staff and a genuine admirer. Davie was a blunt speaker who declined to temper his sharp tongue when speaking of others. He praised Greene's bravery on the field at Guilford Courthouse, writing that "nothing was more conspicuous this day than the personal courage of General Greene." His admiration did not cloud his judgment on Greene's abilities in other respects. In the chess game of the Race to the Dan that preceded Guilford Courthouse, "General Greene evinced his superiority upon every movement." The final confrontation on the battlefield shone a bright light on Greene's deficiencies. Davie lamented that once the fighting started, "the ascendancy of the British general was apparent."⁴¹

Cowpens stood out as a glorious American victory. Greene's individuality played a key role in this development. Part of Greene's deficiency as a commander manifested as a willingness to delegate complete, unrestricted authority to subordinates. In advance of Cowpens, Greene detached Morgan from the main army, with orders to move west. Greene left Morgan entirely to his own devices, a plan of action consistent with his usual preferences. As a result, Cowpens, from first to last, was entirely the product of Morgan's tactical thinking. Greene had no hand in it. Accordingly, the Americans basked in the benefits brought by Morgan, victorious at Saratoga, rather than the less generous gifts of Greene, on the losing side at Guilford Courthouse, Hobkirk's Hill, and Ninety-Six.

Brigadier General Daniel Morgan (1736–1802) was the American commander on the ground at Cowpens. Originally from New Jersey, he settled as a very young man in the Shenandoah Valley in Virginia. He served as a teamster for the British during the French and Indian War, an experience which led to

---
40 Jeremy Black, *Warfare in the Eighteenth Century* (London: Cassell, 1999), 123.
41 Robinson P. Blackwell, ed., *Revolutionary War Sketches of William R. Davie* (Raleigh: North Carolina Department of Cultural Resources, 1976), 32.

his nickname, "The Old Wagoner." While serving with the British, he got into an altercation with a British officer, for which he was sentenced to 500 lashes, a punishment usually fatal. He fortunately survived. He told the story for the rest of his life, attributing his survival to the fact the British miscounted, and only gave him 499 lashes.

While still in the British service in the French and Indian War, Morgan joined a provincial group of Virginia rangers. He took a severe wound in his mouth, the scars of which were visible the rest of his life. When the Revolutionary War broke out, he raised a company of riflemen that became a unit of the Continental Army. In 1775, he joined Benedict Arnold's ill-fated invasion of Canada, and although he survived, he was kept prisoner by the British until exchanged in early 1777. He was promoted to colonel while a prisoner, as a reward for his remarkable bravery in Quebec. Upon return from captivity, he was made commander of a rifle regiment, a position in which he distinguished himself. He was particularly valuable in organizing the stunning American victory at Saratoga.

After Saratoga, he conducted raids on British formations and supply lines in New Jersey. He became increasingly frustrated with the politics of the army and the colonial government. He lacked important political connections, and officers with less ability and experience obtained promotion over him. In addition, he suffered health problems, and finally left the army in mid-1779. George Washington recalled him temporarily to fight in the Sullivan Expedition later the same year. In 1780, Gates urged him to return to active service with him in the southern department, which he declined. The loss at Camden persuaded him to change his mind, and he elected to return. Gates, still in command, saw Morgan promoted to brigadier general on 13 October 1780.

Morgan continued to experience health problems. After his triumph at Cowpens, he suffered such chronic pain that he left the army again, on 10 February 1781. A general of his ability nevertheless continued to draw attention, and he was recalled to active service briefly in July 1781, and again in 1794 to serve in the forces opposing the Whiskey Rebellion, when he received promotion to major general.

Morgan had a grasp of tactics and strategy met by few of his contemporaries. Perhaps most of all, Morgan had a rare ability to understand and lead the American soldier. As much as Washington, Morgan knew how to obtain the maximum benefit from the militiamen. The accounts of Cowpens are replete with his many encouragements to his soldiers on the battle line; this was leadership distilled into its pure form. It is not an exaggeration to state that Morgan's presence on the battlefield was the single most important factor in the overwhelming American victory at Cowpens.

William Washington (1752–1810) was born into wealth in Stafford County, Virginia. He was a distant relative of George Washington.[42] Washington established a county militia in 1775, which the government incorporated into the Continental Army as part of the 3rd Virginia Regiment. James Monroe, later to serve as the fifth President of the United States, was his deputy. In early 1777, Washington received promotion to major and reassignment to the 4th Continental Light Dragoons. The following year, the army again reassigned him, this time to the 3rd Continental Light Dragoons, ultimately a fateful move. The British devastated the unit in the Baylor Massacre of 1778, a loss that included capture of the commander. Washington received promotion to lieutenant colonel and command of the unit. After a year of refitting, the unit moved to the southern army on 19 November 1779. Tarleton mauled the unit again in April 1780, and as a result, its remnants were integrated into the 1st Continental Light Dragoons. Lieutenant Colonel Anthony White, the commander of the 1st, had seniority over Washington and commanded the combined unit. White departed after the fighting in Charleston, leaving Washington in overall command.

Washington was an aggressive and innovative cavalry commander. His agility and courage under fire were instrumental at Cowpens, as they were to prove later at Guilford Courthouse. In September 1781, he was captured at the Battle of Eutaw

---

[42] Modern scholarship has determined they were second cousins, once removed.

Springs, and spent the rest of the war under house arrest in Charleston.

Andrew Pickens (1739–1817) was a celebrated South Carolina militia commander. Although originally from Pennsylvania, his family moved to the Waxhaws, a region bordering North Carolina, when he was 13. As a young man, he moved to Abbeville County on the Georgia border, in the South Carolina backcountry.

Pickens began his militia career in the Anglo-Cherokee war of 1760–1761. When the Revolutionary War broke out, he was made a captain of militia, ultimately rising to brigadier general. In May 1780, Pickens served as a colonel in command of a small fort. After the British victory at Charleston, Pickens surrendered the post and accepted British terms of parole. A band of Tories, energized by the new British preeminence, ransacked his property and terrorized his family. He grew famous for his response: Pickens informed the British they had breached their parole agreement, to which he no longer felt bound, and resumed his active role in the rebellion.

At Cowpens, Pickens distinguished himself as commander of the militia forces. Afterward, he continued to serve as a remarkable militia commander.

John Eager Howard (1752–1827), a Continental officer from Maryland, was a lieutenant colonel at the Battle of Cowpens. Commissioned a captain at the opening of hostilities, he ultimately rose to colonel in the Continental Army. He had extensive battlefield experience in the northern campaign. In April 1780, the Marylanders were assigned to the southern department, in time to participate in the Battle of Camden. Although the battle ended in disaster for the Americans, Howard was one of several American officers who distinguished themselves in the fighting. At Cowpens, Howard had command of the forces on the main line of battle, most notably Continental light infantry from Maryland and Delaware. Howard's conduct was unsurpassed, to the extent the Continental Congress awarded him a special silver medal for his distinguished service at Cowpens. After the war, Howard went on to serve three terms as Governor of Maryland.

Robert A. Ford

The British

The Battle of Cowpens took place at a time of change on the British side as well as the American. General Henry Clinton (1730–1795) was the commander-in-chief of the British forces in America at the time of the siege of Charleston, which he commanded personally. After the victory at Charleston, Clinton returned to New York in June, leaving Lieutenant General Charles Cornwallis in charge of British forces in the southern colonies. Originally friends, their relationship deteriorated over the ensuing months as the southern campaign failed to meet the government's expectations. After the war, Clinton received a great deal of blame for the loss of the American colonies. He was replaced as commander-in-chief in 1782, and returned to England, but his military career was effectively at an end.

Charles Cornwallis (1738–1805) at the time of these events was a lieutenant general, newly in command of all British forces in the southern colonies. The British government awarded him a lengthy set of aristocratic titles in recognition of his distinguished service: 1st Marquess Cornwallis, 2nd Earl Cornwallis, Viscount Brome, and Baron Cornwallis of Eye. A professional soldier, he served as well in such important posts as Governor-General of India and Lord Lieutenant of Ireland. As a commander, he could be duly cautious as well as appropriately aggressive.

Cornwallis's record as the commander in the southern theater presented another in the series of paradoxes that marked the war in the south. Cornwallis always conducted himself properly. He insisted on civilized deportment, even from his opponent. He never shied from writing a dispatch chastising Greene for the actions of an American officer he found objectionable. At the same time, he never hesitated to release such men as Tarleton, James Wemyss, and Patrick Ferguson on the Americans, knowing the deeds of which they were capable.

Cornwallis's personality has similarly resisted explanation. One school of thought portrayed the British commander as cold and distant. For example, his report to the government after Cowpens referred to the disaster only as "the unfortunate affair of the 17th of January."[43] A second school endorsed a more driven, emotional commander. Adherents to this school reveled in a tale of Cornwallis, overcome by news of Cowpens, breaking his sword in two while swearing vengeance on Morgan.[44]

Banastre Tarleton (1754–1833) has been introduced. At the time of the Battle of Cowpens, he was a lieutenant colonel in command of the British Legion, a unit the size of a regiment containing both cavalry and infantry. Founded in 1778 in New York, the British Legion was British only in spirit; its soldiery consisted entirely of American Loyalists. Americans knew the unit as Tarleton's Legion, in recognition its notorious commander. To the Patriots, Tarleton was famously the most hated officer in America. His nickname, "Bloody Ban," spoke volumes about his reputation.

Some historians have proposed revisions to Tarleton's black legend. Canadian historian Thomas H. Raddall fired a salvo in the 1940s. He criticized American scholarship, noting that the "well-proved maxim" that the victors write the history applied "especially" to the American Revolution. He lamented that Americans trumpeted their victory "with scant regard for the truth where the truth diminished in any way the glory of their achievement."[45]

Raddall reserved his strongest criticism for American renditions of Tarleton's actions. To Raddall, Tarleton was an honored predecessor and a hero. Raddall acknowledged the failure of British arms in the Revolution, but asserted Cornwallis's army performed heroically, against the grain of the rest of the British effort. Within Cornwallis's army, Tarleton's star shined brightest of all.

Raddall's version of the engagement at the Waxhaws highlighted his views on Tarleton generally. In enumerating a listing

[43] Cornwallis to George Germain, 17 March 1781, in Charles Ross, ed., *Correspondence of Charles, First Marquis Cornwallis*, 3 vols. (London, 1849), 1:503.

[44] Frankin Wickwire and Mary Wickwire, *Cornwallis: The American Adventure* (Boston: Houghton Mifflin Co., 1970), 269.

[45] Thomas H. Raddall, "Tarleton's Legion," *Collections of the Nova Scotia Historical Society* 28 (1949). (Halifax, Nova Scotia: Nova Scotia Historical Society, 1949, Mersey Heritage Society, 2001), www.mersey.ca/tarletonslegion.html.

of Tarleton's achievements, he included, "the smart action at Waxhaw ... where Tarleton's Legion after a march of 105 miles in 54 hours fell upon and destroyed a Virginian force under Buford which considerably outnumbered themselves."

Historians following Raddall have taken up the challenge presented in his work. One example must suffice: in 2010, Jim Piecuch, a professor of history in Georgia, published a point-by-point challenge of the American narrative of Tarleton at the Waxhaws.[46]

Alexander Leslie (1731–1794) was a major general at the time of Cowpens. He had fought in the northern theater since the beginning of hostilities in 1775. Leslie was a competent general. Leslie served on the periphery of Cowpens. Well before the battle, Cornwallis knew that Leslie was on his way to reinforce his dwindling army. Knowing Leslie was *en route* strongly affected Cornwallis's strategy. However, Leslie was delayed, and arrived the day after the battle. He went on to command Cornwallis's right flank at Guilford Courthouse.

The Historians

Having discussed the commanders on the field, another aspect of the battle requires attention. In addition to the shooting war, there was another war in progress. This war, much longer lasting, was the war of words. Many of the officers in this story left memoirs. Others left records of another sort: letters, orders, any manner of writing. Others find their voices only in secondary source materials. In whatever source, the materials are the substance of the war of words that followed behind the war on the battlefield. This book has already touched on the conflict that

---

46 Piecuch, *The Blood Be Upon Your Head*, 27–44. This book is not the forum to reconcile conflicting views on Tarleton's legacy. Raddall and Piecuch have space in this book to forestall confusion. Reading modern sources, one may believe that the dark story of Tarleton at the Waxhaws was exaggerated. Although inaccurate, the point is that this was a position advanced by modern-day historians. In the eighteenth century, the Whigs accepted the traditional narrative in its entirety, without question. For the pieces of the Battle of Cowpens to fall into place, one must accept that Tarleton earned every facet of his bloody reputation.

arose between the writings of Lee and Morgan over the tactics on the field at Cowpens, as well as the controversy in the written sources over the events at the Waxhaws. This book will focus on the sources, on the war of words, in an effort to define what actually took place, and separate this body of knowledge from the legends and frank misinformation that has grown up around the battle. The authors, as much as the commanders, influenced what people understand, or believe, about Cowpens.

Chapter 2: Prelude to Conflict

Nathanael Greene took command of the southern army from Horatio Gates late in 1780.[47] He arrived at the southern army's headquarters in Charlotte, North Carolina, on 3 December.[48] Washington had great faith in Greene. The war in the north stalemated after the Battle of Monmouth Courthouse in 1778. The British shifted their focus to the south, signaled by their attack on Savannah late in 1778. The American disaster at Charleston in 1780 was a direct product of the revision in British strategic thinking. Washington, responding to the initiative in the south, sent his favorite general to Charlotte to deal with the new British offensive.

Greene arrived to find only the dregs of an army. The southern army had suffered defeats across the deep south. It had lost Georgia and South Carolina to the British. It was weak in both men and stores. While Greene might eventually count on reinforcements from farther north, his immediate problem was supply. Charlotte, then the location of his headquarters, was exhausted.[49]

In a pattern that will repeat with devastating consequences later in the war, Greene blamed the militia for the bulk of his problems. Greene's experience in command at the start of the

---
47 Stedman, *History*, 2:317.
48 Greene to Catherine Greene, 7 December 1780, in Richard K. Showman, Dennis M. Conrad, Roger N. Parks, Elizabeth C. Stevens, eds., *The Papers of General Nathanael Greene, vol. 6: 1 June 1780–25 December 1780* (Chapel Hill: University of North Carolina Press, 1991) 6:542.
49 Stedman, *History*, 2:318.

war had been with Continental regulars. More recently, he had made his reputation serving two years as a staff officer. He had no experience commanding militiamen. He was candid in his utter contempt for these citizen-soldiers, asserting that their existence, by itself, mandated the ruin of the nation:

> The great Bodies of Militia that have been kept on Foot, from the manner of their coming out all on Horse back, has laid Waste the whole Country. The Expense and Destruction that follows this Policy must ruin any nation on Earth, and the very mode of the Defence must terminate in the Ruin of the People. [50]

Greene's position was ambitiously self-destructive in an officer whose theater of war included hundreds of regulars and thousands of militiamen. Greene often expressed his sentiments to confidants, emphasizing that formations of regular soldiers were the only possible bulwark against the British.[51] Greene's contempt for the militia will have dire consequences later in the campaign. For now, he blamed them for stripping the country around Charlotte, requiring him to move in order to feed his army. The other major commanders in the war did not share Greene's views. Tarleton's Legion contained no British regular soldiers. Morgan achieved tremendous success with a largely militia force at Cowpens. While Morgan entertained no illusions that the training and discipline of militiamen equaled that of the regulars,[52] he had the skills and experience to employ them advantageously. George Washington, a skilled commander of both regulars and militiamen, stated that when led properly, the militia were "the finest fellows in the world."[53]

Greene decided to divide his forces. He created two divisions, one under his direct command in the east, one to move west

---

50 Greene to Henry Knox, 7 December 1780, in Showman et al., *Greene*, 6:547.
51 E.g., Greene to Knox, 7 December 1780, in Showman et al., *Greene*, 6:547.
52 Daniel Morgan to Greene, 20 February 1781, in Showman et al., *Greene*, 7:324.
53 "Notes on Conversations with John Beckley and George Washington, 7 June 1793," *3. Volumes Bound in Marbled Paper.* The Papers of Thomas Jefferson, www.jefferson3volumes.org/?q=content/notes-conversations-john-beckley-and-george-washington-7-june-1793.

independently. Greene's decision reflected no tactical planning; it was a concession to the practicalities of feeding an army. Greene was a student of military history, and was well aware of the classic warning against dividing one's forces in the presence of the enemy.[54] Unfortunately, necessity prevailed. A prominent modern history lamented that "later historians have challenged Greene's decision, based on the principles of war."[55] Rightfully so; it was a complete violation of the principles of war. Stedman, viewing the decision from the British point of view, insisted that Greene wanted to expand his presence in South Carolina, in order to revitalize the flagging spirits of local Whigs.[56] In actuality, this was a collateral benefit: food was the goal. If the Patriots found solace in Greene's presence, so much the better.

Stedman unwittingly started a debate that continues to the present. One recent volume praised Greene's decision on strategic grounds, noting that by dividing his force in the face of Cornwallis, he multiplied the ground the British would need to occupy and defend. These historians sided with Stedman: "In effect, Greene created rallying points for the backcountry partisan bands."[57]

Praising the strategy in Greene's division of his forces within the shadow of the British Army misguides the admiration due to Greene. He was a master logistician, proving his capabilities in two years as Washington's quartermaster general. His decision was a bold move, at one stroke acknowledging his painfully inadequate service of supply and defying the established principles of war. Greene intended no strategic advantage in what he knew was a tactical error made necessary by circumstance. Major Todd J. Johnson, in a report published by the U.S. Army's School of Advanced Military Studies, stated the professional officer's position on Greene's decision:

---

54 While this maxim has been credited to figures as diverse as Clausewitz and Napoleon, it actually dates to Sun Tzu, *The Art of War*, trans. Lionel Giles (1910; Project Gutenberg, 2005), www.utoledo.edu/rotc/pdfs/the_art_of_war.pdf, chap. 6, maxims 13–14.

55 Lawrence E. Babits and Joshua B. Howard, *Long, Obstinate, and Bloody: The Battle of Guilford Courthouse* (Chapel Hill: University of North Carolina Press, 2009), 9.

56 Stedman, *History*, 2:318.

57 Babits and Howard, *Long, Obstinate, and Bloody*, 10.

One of the first command decisions that Greene made was the decision to split his small force on 16 December 1780. His Continental regulars and militia augmentees were running short of food and so Greene decided to divide his army even though he was outmanned by Lord Cornwallis's troops.[58]

Major Johnson's report emphasized the point: Greene's division of his forces was logistical, not strategic. It was a necessary decision mandated entirely by the need to feed the army.

Lee, writing years after the war, remembered the events differently, and in doing so added a third voice to the conversation. Lee was an enthusiastic supporter of Greene, and remained so when writing long years after Greene's death. While he acknowledged Greene's supply problems, he saw these as a mere *bagatelle*. As Lee described matters, tactical questions and supply deficits equally provided fodder for Greene's intellect:

> Such means and resources badly comported with the grand design of arresting the progress of the conqueror, and restoring the two lost states to the Union. Capable of doing much with little, Greene was not discouraged by this unfavourable prospect. His vivid plastic genius soon operated on the latent elements of martial capacity in his army, invigorated its weakness, turned its confusion into order and its despondency into ardour. A wide sphere of intellectual resource enabled him to inspire confidence, to rekindle courage, to decide hesitation, and infuse a spirit of exalted patriotism in the citizens of the state.[59]

Lee fought under Greene's command for years, infusing his views on Greene with credibility. Even with this leniency in hand, Lee lacked access to two qualities available presently: insight driven by two centuries of analysis, and an atmosphere devoid of the overheated emotion following a successful war. The truth is, Greene simply got lucky. After Morgan's departure, he described the main portion of the army camped with him near Cheraw in grim and depressing terms:

---

58 Todd J. Johnson, "Nathanael Greene's Implementation of Compound Warfare During the Southern Campaign of the American Revolution" (Fort Leavenworth, Kansas: School of Advanced Military Studies, United States Army Command and General Staff College, 2007), 23.
59 Lee, *Memoirs*, 126.

> The small force that I have remaining with me are so naked & destitute of every thing, that the greater part is rendered unfit for any kind of duty. The Officers have reported them as incapable of attending the parade for discipline, the want of which was never greater in any Army.[60]

The rump of Greene's army, dressed in rags and mocking discipline, was in no position to resist the British. Greene never contended his force represented any menace to Cornwallis. Any praise of Greene for thinking strategically here is entirely misplaced. There is an unfortunate tendency in some writers, ancient and modern, to credit our national predecessors with almost superhuman levels of genius, courage, and intuition. While we must respect Lee's admiration for Greene, we must tone down the enthusiasm that imbued Greene's every decision with a universal genius. The simple fact was that there was nothing standing in the way of Cornwallis wiping Greene off the map, turning west, and doing the same with Morgan. Cornwallis, normally aggressive, never explained why he elected not to do so. Stedman, usually the best resource for the British viewpoint, declined to speculate on his commander's reasoning. Given what Greene wrote about his own force, it seems apparent that Cornwallis, correctly, realized Greene was no threat.

Greene violated long-standing principles of war so his troops could eat. In doing so, he converted one easily defeated medium-sized force into two more easily defeated smaller forces. At bottom, this was a gift to Cornwallis, which the latter, for reasons still unclear, declined. To suggest this gift made Cornwallis's job more difficult rather than less is to misconstrue the basic, fundamental importance of the size of military units. Providence, we are told, always favors the big battalions.[61] Greene solved this problem for Cornwallis by creating small ones.

Greene delegated Brigadier General Daniel Morgan with the western division of his army. The exact count of soldiers in

---

60 Greene to Samuel Huntington, 28 December 1780, in Showman et al., *Greene*, 7:8.
61 Although attributed to Napoleon, this maxim actually originated in the seventeenth century, with several candidates nominated as its originator. See Shannon Selin, "10 Things Napoleon Never Said," *Imagining the Bounds of History*, www.shannonselin.com/2014/07/10-things-napoleon-never-said/; *The Oxford Reference*, www.oxfordreference.com/display/10.1093/oi/authority.20110803100351363.

Morgan's force varies between sources. This is not an exercise in arcana, in that his numbers will gain significance once the fighting starts. Stedman, with a reputation for rigorous equanimity, provided an apt starting point. Stedman asserted that Greene gave Morgan three hundred light infantry under Lieutenant Colonel John Eager Howard, 170 riflemen under Major Francis Triplett and seventy light dragoons under Lieutenant Colonel William Washington.[62] These numbers totaled 540 soldiers, mostly Continental regulars. Lee allotted numbers very close to those enumerated by Stedman.[63] Lee wrote that Howard led four hundred Continental infantry, to which were added two companies of Virginia militia under Captains Triplett and Taite. Washington, he insisted, had one hundred regular cavalry; all in all, a total of approximately 550 soldiers, given the customary size of a Virginia militia company.[64]

Given that both Stedman and Lee were estimating, they were remarkably close. Moreover, the combination of two influential writers established a mild consensus. For example, James Graham, in his 1859 biography of Daniel Morgan, endorsed a figure of 580 soldiers.[65] One prominent dissenter was Lieutenant Colonel Howard, who wrote that his line contained 350 soldiers, which included his light infantry and both Virginia militia companies.[66] On this point, Howard, brilliant in command, was, at times, less so in writing, and he was almost certainly wrong in these numbers. The essential problem with Howard was that he wrote no memoir, and historians have drawn his information in small increments from letters he wrote to friends. The number under discussion here is from an undated letter, so there is no way to determine how much time passed between the event and

---

[62] Stedman, *History*, 2:318.

[63] Lee, *Memoirs*, 127.

[64] Lawrence E. Babits, *A Devil of a Whipping: The Battle of Cowpens* (Chapel Hill: University of North Carolina Press, 1998), 31–32. Babits asserted that militia companies usually numbered between 20 and 30, and a militia captain rarely commanded as many as 40 soldiers.

[65] James Graham, *The Life of General Daniel Morgan, of the Virginia Line of the Army of the United States, With Portions of His Correspondence, Compiled from Authentic Sources.* (New York, 1859), 260.

[66] Showman et al., *Greene*, 7:157n4.

the writing. As a letter to a friend rather than an official report, there is no way to assess the level of effort he invested in its accuracy. His force, including both the Continental light infantry and the Virginia former Continentals, well exceeded 350 men. An additional two hundred men, a force within the consensus established by Stedman and Lee, has a great deal more credibility.

The constituency of the Virginia companies, once settled, has recently attracted controversy. Lee, an officer in the southern army, and William Johnson, writing in 1822, both asserted that the Virginians were former Continentals, discharged from the army and reentered into active service as militiamen.[67] Morgan used them as Continentals, putting them on the same line as Howard's regulars.[68] While Lee and Johnson wrote authoritatively, the fact that Morgan put them on the line with the Continentals spoke volumes about his faith in them, contrasting sharply with his lack of confidence in militia units generally. Morgan, although a skilled commander of militia, was realistic in assessing their abilities. As one example among many, a letter he wrote stated his position: "The Militia who have already Joined will desert us, and it is not improbable, but a Regard to their own safety will induce them to Join the Enemy."[69] Greene may have thought them poor soldiers, but Morgan feared many were potential traitors. With respect to the Virginia units in his army, Morgan's demonstration of faith in them closed the case: these were units of former Continentals. Morgan's conduct formed the basis of a consensus that lasted two hundred years.[70]

The recent controversy started in 1998, with the publication of *A Devil of a Whipping: The Battle of Cowpens* by Lawrence E. Babits, an influential history that challenged this long-standing consensus. Babits asserted that the Virginians were not Continental veterans, and for that matter, were barely veterans at all. Babits's point was that the pension applications for these Virginia soldiers did not mention their service as Continentals.[71]

---

67 Lee, *Memoirs*, 131; Johnson, *Life*, 1:374–375; Graham, *Morgan*, 290.
68 Morgan to Greene, 19 January 1781, in Showman et al., *Greene*, 7:153.
69 Morgan to Greene, 4 January 1781, in Showman et al., *Greene*, 7:51.
70 E.g., Graham, *Morgan*, 290.
71 Babits, *Devil*, 34.

On this basis, he downgraded them from Continental equivalents to ordinary militiamen, a hefty fall from grace in Morgan's army. The use of pension applications has a more detailed examination below. At this point, Morgan's confidence in these Virginia soldiers, in light of his poor opinion of the militia generally, confirmed their status as former Continentals and ended any debate before it started.

On the other side of South Carolina, Greene's division kept a low profile. It was a sad commentary on the state of the southern army that the force Greene gave to Morgan, as much as he could spare, was about the size of the force lost by Buford, at the time a straggling band unworthy of Cornwallis's personal attention. Greene's portion was larger numerically. As always, the count varied by source. Lee insisted Greene had no more than two thousand effectives altogether, the vast majority of which were militia.[72] Tarleton gave Greene 1400 regulars, plus an uncounted number of militia.[73] These approximations will have to substitute for an elusive precision.

Greene gave Morgan orders to head for the western fringes of South Carolina, seek cover in the mountains, and harass the British as much as possible. In particular, the British strong point at Ninety-Six was a tempting target, well within range for Morgan.[74] Greene took the rest of the army east to the area around Cheraw. Circumstances limited Greene's activity. He wrote several strong letters to the governors of Virginia and North Carolina, alternately requesting troops and materiel, and chiding them for their poor provision of both.[75] Militarily, he engaged in no contact with the British, in fact, avoiding any notion of provocation. In a candid moment, Greene acknowledged he had established a "camp of repose."[76]

In summary, authors proposed three drives motivating

---

72 Lee, *Memoirs*, 124.
73 Tarleton, *Campaigns*, 213.
74 Stedman, *History*, 2:318.
75 E.g., Greene to Abner Nash, 9 February 1781, in Showman et al., *Greene*, 7:263; Greene to Thomas Jefferson, 10 February 1781, in Showman et al., *Greene*, 7:271.
76 Greene to unidentified recipient, 1–23 January 1781, in Showman et al., *Greene*, 7:175.

Greene's decision to divide his forces: strategy, forage, and support to the local Whigs. Dealing with the first two is simple: there was no strategy, and his army foraged relentlessly in order to eat. The third was more subtle: What did he do to encourage Patriotism in a discouraged land? As with so many facets of the Cowpens story, the answer depends on one's sources.

Stedman, entirely consistent with his studied equanimity, wrote that the British victory at Charleston created a short-term boost in Toryism. He noted with regret:

> But too soon the sky became overcast; and it was perceived in the southern as it had been already experienced in some of the northern colonies, that the inhabitants, after their submission, and even whilst the British troops remained amongst them, did not perform the duties of their allegiance without reluctance, and when left to themselves, quickly reverted to their old courses, and joined the standard of revolt.[77]

Tarleton saw things differently. Stedman was unwilling to give Tarleton any credit arising out of the atrocities at the Waxhaws. Any benefit Stedman saw derived exclusively from the victory at Charleston. Tarleton, in trouble for the Waxhaws, was determined to defend himself. In describing Clinton's departure for New York in June 1780, he wrote that Clinton "before he sailed, had the agreeable intelligence of the defeat of the Americans at Waxhaws; a circumstance that evinced the total extirpation of the continental troops within the provinces of Georgia and South Carolina." Tarleton, however, could not leave it there. He had to prove that the Waxhaws produced a real and positive good for the British:

> This event tended to increase the satisfaction he had before experienced, on account of the favourable reports from Augusta and Ninety-Six; where the inhabitants had manifested their peaceable intentions, and some thousands of militia men had flocked to the royal standard.[78]

---

77 Stedman, *History*, 2:317.
78 Tarleton, *Campaigns*, 33–34.

This seemingly minor dispute between two British officers provides a perfect microcosm of the literature on Cowpens. Imagine: two completely conflicting views of the same subject, written at about the same time, by two eyewitnesses. Who was right?

Once more, to resolve the question of credibility, the only recourse is to the agendas of the authors. Tarleton was in trouble the rest of his life over the Waxhaws, and he never stopped defending what had happened. Even allowing some leeway for self-justification, Tarleton's views were hopelessly overblown. The events at the Waxhaws did not impel Toryism on the scale driven by the British victories at Augusta and Charleston. Stedman, in stark contrast, had no recriminations to answer. Disregarding Tarleton entirely on this point, as one must, the record disclosed an initial bump in Toryism, after which the South Carolinians returned to rebellion.

This discussion commenced with an examination of Greene's actions to support the Whigs while rusticated to his camp of repose near Cheraw. Greene's correspondence gave an unexpected answer: he did nothing to bolster rebellion among the people. Greene was committed to solving the logistical problems tormenting his forces, and this task occupied him fully. At the same time, Greene could read the *zeitgeist* as well as anyone. He did not need to do anything to encourage the local Whigs. The initial surge in Loyalism after the British military victories waned. The population reverted to the Whig side, even in areas dominated by the British Army. It did not need the poor, depleted American army to encourage Whig sentiment. The people were perfectly able to dislike the British all by themselves.

This piece of information was not secret. Stedman was not the only British officer who realized the Whigs were strong throughout the south.[79] Nevertheless, a recurring theme in British governmental thinking insisted the southern colonies harbored vast stores of Tories, hidden from view, just waiting for

---

[79] Brigadier General Charles O'Hara was another famous advocate of pessimism. His letters to the Duke of Grafton remain a classic exposition of the position, "Letters of Charles O'Hara to the Duke of Grafton," *The South Carolina Historical Magazine* 65, no. 3 (Jul. 1964) 158–180.

the arrival of the British Army to blossom into open support for the government. North Carolina, for reasons not entirely clear, was especially favored in British planning. Tarleton wrote that Loyalists "were computed to be the greater proportion of the inhabitants" of North Carolina,[80] although the methodology supporting the government's calculation was lost in the Stygian darkness only a truly dense bureaucracy could create. While Greene was in repose near Cheraw, Cornwallis was preparing for the major action: the thrust into North Carolina, to empower the thousands of Tories waiting to join the royal colors.

In preparation for the mission into the promised land of North Carolina, the British dispatched to Cornwallis 1530 troops from Virginia, commanded by Major General Alexander Leslie. Leslie was an experienced commander with a good war record.[81] Cornwallis started off on his march northward on 8 January 1781, with plans to meet Leslie on the way. He and Leslie successfully joined forces, but too far from Cowpens, and too late, to prevent the disaster.

The genesis of the disaster lay in the offensive move into North Carolina. The attack was the priority. Everything else was a distraction, to the point Cornwallis was prepared to leave Greene in his rear area, unmolested and unguarded, in order to expedite the move northward. Cornwallis was not immune to the contagious delusion that legions of Loyalists were simply standing by, waiting for his promised arrival to reinforce royalism. He would liberate them from what their British overlords saw as the frightening prospect of self-government.[82]

Moving northward, Cornwallis left much unsettled in South Carolina. Although Greene remained static on the banks of the Pee Dee, Morgan was hard at work, bedeviling the British farther west. Two actions, in particular, riled Cornwallis. On 29 December, immediately after arriving in the west, Morgan learned of a group of Georgia Tories active in the Fair Forest Creek area of South Carolina.[83] He sent William Washington

---

80 Tarleton, *Campaigns*, 215.
81 Tarleton, *Campaigns*, 216.
82 Tarleton, *Campaigns*, 236, 263.
83 Bartholomees, "Fight or Flee," 107.

with a force of 280 cavalry and mounted infantry to confront the Loyalists at a place called Hammond's Store. After a short fight, the Tories gave way, suffering 150 killed and wounded and another forty captured. Washington's force was untouched. On the way back to Morgan's encampment, Washington detached a small force to harass Fort Williams, a small post manned by 150 Loyalists. The Tories abandoned the fort, which Washington burned.[84] These actions, taken together, convinced Cornwallis that Morgan was a problem that needed solving.[85]

Late in December, Cornwallis learned Morgan had crossed the Catawba and Broad Rivers, moving westward. Cornwallis was especially protective of the British fort at Ninety-Six. Morgan's position west of the Broad River positioned him to threaten the British stronghold.[86] In this region, both the Catawba and the Broad flow north to south. The Catawba transits through Charlotte, while the Broad lies twenty-five miles farther west. Depending on which river crossing is used, it is no more than sixty-five miles from the Broad to Ninety-Six. With Morgan across the Broad, he was three or four days from Ninety-Six. On 1 January,[87] Cornwallis assembled a force under Tarleton with orders to stop Morgan.[88]

Cornwallis used Tarleton's unit, the British Legion—Tarleton's Legion—for the core of the detachment assembled to fight Morgan. He added the 1st Battalion of the 71st Regiment, known as Fraser's Highlanders, as well as units of light infantry, additional cavalry, and two artillery pieces with their crews. Stedman estimated Tarleton's total strength as about one thousand, of which 350 were cavalry.[89] Other estimates regarding

---

84 Morgan to Greene, 4 January 1781, in Showman et al., *Greene*, 7:50–51.
85 Bartholomees, "Fight or Flee," 108; Cornwallis to Germain, 17 March 1781, 1:503.
86 Bartholomees, "Fight or Flee," 109; Stedman, *History*, 2:318.
87 Tarleton, *Campaigns*, 217.
88 Stedman, *History*, 2:318.
89 Stedman, *History*, 2:318. Stedman conflated certain events. In his initial tally of Tarleton's forces, he included the 7th Regiment, known as the Royal Fusiliers. It is true that the 7th Regiment fought with Tarleton at Cowpens, but they arrived after 1 January, as discussed below. Some additional cavalry arrived with the 7th Regiment, and Stedman's figure of about 1,000 men included these late arrivals.

Tarleton's strength abounded. As one example among many, British historian Ian Saberton estimated it at 1,150.[90] At the other end of the spectrum, Roger Lamb, a British foot soldier turned famous diarist,[91] insisted Tarleton had only a skeleton force of six hundred soldiers. A bounty of interim positions populated the landscape between these two extremes. A more precise tabulation of Tarleton's strength awaits below. At this point, Stedman's position ably estimated the number sufficient for a discussion: "about 1,000 men."

The artillery component within Tarleton's force consisted of two three-pound cannons commonly known as "grasshoppers." Lightweight and maneuverable, grasshoppers jumped noticeably when fired.[92] The literature of Cowpens burst with discussions of Tarleton's deployment of the two cannons. The witnesses and historians indulged no further comment on the artillery. Paradoxically, these two pieces had no impact on the course of the fighting. The Americans had no artillery, and Tarleton's two pieces should have given him a measurable advantage. They did not. Cowpens stood out for many reasons, and the utility, or lack of it, of the British artillery was one more facet of its uniqueness. After discussion the artillery placement at the outset, the next mention of the artillery appeared at the end of the battle, as several different Americans contested for the honor of capturing the British cannons. In the Revolutionary War, artillery pieces were prized as war trophies by both sides. Capturing an enemy cannon served as a marker for success on the battlefield. In one of the oddities of the conflict, Tarleton's two cannons' highest use was service as war trophies for his enemies.

Morgan departed from Greene with a force between five hundred and six hundred soldiers. Most were Continentals.

---

90 Ian Saberton, "Cornwallis and the Winter Campaign, January to April 1781," *Journal of the American Revolution*, April 28, 2020,
www.allthingsliberty.com/2020/04/cornwallis-and-the-winter-campaign-january-to-april-1781.
91 R. Lamb, *An Original and Authentic Journal of Occurrences During the Late American War, from its Commencement to the Year 1783* (Dublin, 1809), 342.
92 Lee, *Memoirs*, 132.

In addition to the regular infantrymen, Greene gave Morgan a more important gift, their commander, Lieutenant Colonel John Eager Howard, one of the most able commanders in the war. Events would show this was quite a gift, in that Howard and his unit performed with unique heroism and ability at Cowpens. Greene also gave Morgan another amazing gift, his sole remaining cavalry unit, the remnants of the 1st and 3rd Continental Regiments of Dragoons under Lieutenant Colonel William Washington.[93] These soldiers, as well as Washington himself, would also distinguish themselves at Cowpens. When added to the two companies of Virginia militia,[94] it was all quite a present. Morgan, seemingly by action of magnetism, acquired militia as he moved west. Stedman urged the reader to accept that Morgan picked up four hundred or five hundred militia early in his march, and another two hundred once he got closer to Ninety-Six.[95] As with so much in this story, consulting a different source will yield different numbers. Lee, for example, asserted the number was less than five hundred militiamen in total.[96] There seems little point in dissecting the many others; all these numbers were simply estimates. Stedman summarized it best: the two sides were now very close in numbers, although the British regulars with Tarleton far outweighed in quality the militiamen following Morgan, a solid point both sides learned through hard experience.[97]

The militia strength in Morgan's army focused light on a recurring theme in eighteenth-century military history. Repeatedly, highly educated and insightful scholars have looked at the same sources and drawn contrasting conclusions. An example: James Bartholomees became a distinguished military historian

---

[93] Lee asserted he arrived in South Carolina "soon after" Greene took up his position near Cheraw, confirming Washington commanded Greene's sole cavalry at the division of forces. At the time, Greene knew Lee was on the way, Lee, *Memoirs*, 128.

[94] Stedman did not revel in detail when it came to enumerating units. He simply stated Morgan had 170 riflemen under Major Triplett. As riflemen, there was no question they were militiamen. The subdivision of the Virginia forces was the work of other authors, Stedman, *History*, 2:318.

[95] Stedman, *History*, 2:319.

[96] Lee, *Memoirs*, 127.

[97] Stedman, *History*, 2:319.

at the U.S. Army War College. As a graduate student, he wrote a dissertation examining the North Carolina militia in extreme detail during the period of time encompassing Cowpens. Bartholomees insisted that the militia, without question, did not flock to Morgan on his march west out of Greene's army, to the point that Morgan abandoned plans to harass the British and focused entirely on foraging.[98] On this point, Bartholomees was simply wrong. The eighteenth-century sources, vague and contradictory in many ways, reached near consensus on Morgan's magnetic attraction to militiamen. Further, Bartholomees noted that Morgan conducted operations against the British, and posed a genuine threat to the British at Ninety-Six, direct contradictions to his assertion that Morgan limited his activities to foraging. As the story of Cowpens works its way through plot, climax, and *dénouement*, the warring conclusions of historians will arise again and again.

In reducing the militia forces to simple numerics, Stedman overlooked a key point supplied by Lee.[99] With the group of several hundred militia added to Morgan's force, part of the militia package, perhaps the most important part, was Colonel Andrew Pickens. Pickens was an experienced South Carolina militia commander, one guaranteed to extract the very best performance from the militiamen. Through accretions, Morgan's team had improved steadily and dramatically. The gods of war made Pickens their final gift to Morgan; he arrived on the evening of 16 January.[100]

Greene, as well, benefited from newcomers. Lee, moving south from Virginia, joined Greene's army near Cheraw. Lee's command arrived "in excellent condition," a providential gift to a recipient sorely in need of one.[101] Lee immediately started harassing the British in his area. Lee's arrival had no direct impact on the Battle of Cowpens. He stayed east with Greene, and was not involved in the action. Nevertheless, his arrival illustrated the degree to which the states further north were willing,

---

98 Bartholomees, "Fight or Flee," 104, 107.
99 Lee, *Memoirs*, 127.
100 Lee, *Memoirs*, 127; Bartholomees, "Fight or Flee," 117.
101 Lee, *Memoirs*, 128.

and able, to reinforce Greene in the south. The reinforcements to Greene stacked on top of the hundreds of militiamen flocking to Morgan. From the British perspective, American soldiers were coming out of the woodwork. This was not the result the British had anticipated. Once subdued, the British expected South Carolina to stay subdued. Experience quickly demonstrated the folly in the government's expectations. Cornwallis, a professional soldier with a poor grasp of colonial politics, sought a purely military solution: beat the Americans on the battlefield and the rest would follow. Ultimately, the roots of the problem were social and political. Americans wanted the British gone, in sufficient numbers to muster huge military forces despite punishing losses. Throughout the southern campaign, Cornwallis never grasped the social and political forces at work against him. As one modern historian emphasized, "the primary weakness of the British efforts in the south was the inability of their leadership to understand the true nature of the conflict in the south."[102]

In the journey thus far, Morgan has crossed the Broad River, moving west, putting himself in a position to threaten Ninety-Six, a strong point in the British frontier defenses of South Carolina, about to become a strong point in Cornwallis's rear as he moved northward into North Carolina. Cornwallis, in no mood to be trifled with, reinforced Tarleton, and turned him loose on Morgan. He would leave Greene alone but would not accept the loss of Ninety-Six to Morgan.

Cornwallis moved north in the gap between the Broad and Catawba Rivers.[103] This route offered him some advantages. It included favorable approaches to fords over both rivers. More importantly, and this was the meat of it, if Morgan escaped Tarleton by retreat, the main British Army could cut him off, then crush him. Stedman offered the additional possibility that Cornwallis used this route to separate Greene from further reinforcements. Although hard to believe, Stedman was correct;

---

[102] Johnson, "Compound Warfare," 8.
[103] Stedman, *History*, 2:319; Cornwallis to Germain, 17 March 1781, in Ross, *Cornwallis*, 1:503.

Cornwallis believed that by using this route of march, he could interdict supplies coming to Greene from Virginia. Whether this was a true *folie à deux* or a simply an admirable act of loyalty by Stedman, a glimpse at a map of North Carolina will reveal it as pure fantasy.[104]

Once turned loose by Cornwallis, Tarleton moved with his characteristic ardor toward Morgan.[105] Morgan retreated over the Pacolet River. The Pacolet runs generally east to west, then turns just west of Cowpens to run north to south. The turn in the river's course lies approximately eighteen miles west of the Broad River. As Stedman told the story, Morgan fortified the fords on the Pacolet, but Tarleton found a way around Morgan's defenses. On 6 January, Tarleton approached so close that Morgan had to retreat speedily, leaving his camp with breakfast half-cooked.

Tarleton continued his energetic pursuit of Morgan. On 17 January, he captured two American pickets and learned from them the Americans were forming for battle at the Cowpens.[106] Tarleton's capture of the American pickets marked first contact with the enemy. Active combat must follow. Before dealing with the fighting, a foundational matter requires attention. Stedman and Tarleton are two irreplaceable sources on the British actions before the battle. At the same time, Tarleton was a key actor, as was Stedman, vicariously at least, as Cornwallis's staff officer. The ways in which they portrayed each other gained great significance as the separate threads of the plot weaved into the tapestry of the battle. Their depictions of each other rested on a curious footing: contempt. Stedman despised Tarleton.[107] Here is a sampling of the outrage he spewed in Tarleton's direction:

> During the whole period of the war no other action reflected so much dishonour on the British arms ... The British were superior in numbers. ... Every disaster that befell lord Cornwallis, after Tarleton's most shameful

---

104 See Stedman, *History*, 2:319; Cornwallis to Germain, 17 March 1781, in Ross, *Cornwallis*, 1:503.
105 Stedman, *History*, 2:320.
106 Ibid.
107 Stedman, *History*, 2:324; 2:354n.

defeat at the Cowpens, may most justly be attributed to the imprudence and unsoldierly conduct of that officer in the action... Is it possible for the mind to form any other conclusion, than that there was a radical defect, and a lack of military knowledge on the part of colonel Tarleton?[108]

One can imagine the blistering language Stedman would use to describe Tarleton's "radical defect." He blamed Tarleton for the loss at Cowpens, and this was only the barest beginning. Cowpens, he decided, cost Cornwallis hundreds of soldiers the British could not replace. Their absence was the source of the heavy ambiguity in Cornwallis's victory at Guilford Courthouse. Stedman blamed Cowpens for the British loss in the south, believing it led in a direct line to Yorktown.[109] Stedman obviously intended a great deal of blame to fall on Tarleton's shoulders. At the same time, Stedman gave Tarleton credit for nothing. Even Lee, who fought him regularly for months, spewed less venom at Tarleton.

The Stedman-Tarleton relationship was history on a very human level. The study of history often mires itself in abstractions and facts, forgetting that it was made by people. In this case, real people with real faults. Stedman earned his reputation as a historian with a devotion to even-handedness. He was always careful to explain the war from a rational, unemotional perspective, evenly and dispassionately. His demeanor changed when his narrative encountered Tarleton. The mask slipped, and one saw a glimpse of the inner Stedman. Stedman was an American Loyalist who obtained a British Army commission; he backed the wrong horse. As a result, his life was upended, and he blamed Tarleton for his misfortunes. The inner Stedman never forgave Tarleton, and he had no shyness in discussing his thoughts in detail. Tarleton, for his part, disdained to mention Stedman. Five hundred thirty pages of history, and Stedman's name never appeared. An absence of this magnitude transcends

---

108 Stedman, *History*, 2:324.
109 Stedman, *History*, 2:324–325, 2:332. Stedman's view on the significance of Cowpens has gained a consensus. UK historian Ian Saberton echoed Stedman: "Cowpens was a turning point in the war," Ian Saberton, ed., *The Cornwallis Papers: The Campaigns of 1780 and 1781 in the Southern Theatre*, 6 vols. (Uckfield, Sussex: Naval & Military Press, 2010), 3:12.

accident or oversight. Stedman and Tarleton remind us that real people, not abstractions, make history.

The Stedman-Tarleton relationship impinged on the story of Cowpens in a very direct way. Stedman's predilection highlighted an issue common throughout the literature of Cowpens: bias. Another example may illustrate the problem. Leslie brought reinforcements from Virginia. Cornwallis planned to meet Leslie on the way into North Carolina. In documenting the event, Stedman, normally precise, was uncharacteristically vague on details. Specifically, details on dates.[110] He wrote that Cornwallis and Leslie met on the road, mentioning nothing about when and where. Superficially a minor point, the matter raised another dimension of bias.

Stedman, even long after the war, retained his loyalty to Cornwallis. He would never have suggested that Cornwallis erred in moving too far north too fast while paying insufficient attention to Morgan in his rear. However, he was only too glad to create the impression that Tarleton had moved precipitously and incautiously against Morgan. When Cornwallis and Leslie joined forces, they created an awesome military machine of 2400 British regulars and Provincials.[111] Stedman asserted that when Tarleton caught up with Morgan, he "resolved, without loss of time, to make an attack upon the Americans."[112] This assertion was part and parcel of Stedman's picture of Tarleton as the unthinking, overaggressive commander. Stedman allowed the reader to believe a more prudent commander with better skills would have held Morgan in place, or moved him gradually north, to crush him like a stale walnut in a nutcracker against the

---

110 Stedman, *History*, 2:320.

111 This number is a subtraction of Tarleton's detachment from the total for the second invasion of North Carolina, for which estimates among modern historians vary. They run from 2,400 by Thomas E. Baker in *Another Such Victory: The Story of the American Defeat at Guilford Courthouse that Helped Win the War for Independence* (New York: Eastern Acorn Press, 1981), 23, to 2,915 by Ian Saberton in his "Winter Campaign" article. I advocate the figure of 2,700, derived from the battlefield return from Guilford Courthouse of 1,924 soldiers of all ranks, backing in the baggage detail of 300 to 400 men, and adding back 400 casualties from all causes in the time preceding the battle. Any more detailed discussion of the troop counts will get this book too far afield of its topic.

112 Stedman, *History*, 2:321.

huge force amassed by Cornwallis and Leslie. Stedman made this belief possible by eliding any mention of dates in his discussion of Leslie and Cornwallis. The plain fact was that Leslie did not arrive until 18 January, after Tarleton's defeat at Cowpens. Leslie's arrival date was fluid until he was actually on hand, and Cornwallis had no means to work hypothetical reinforcements into his battle planning. While Stedman's tacit suggestion may have been possible, it would have required a complete reworking of everything that actually took place on the ground.

Stedman was the author who acquired the reputation for calm equanimity. These examples using Tarleton and Leslie emphasize that even the most even-handed authors can fall prey to bias.

The tale of Tarleton interrupting Morgan's breakfast invested the reader emotionally with its human touch. For Stedman, it served as further proof that Tarleton was a victim of his own impetuosity. When Stedman began the narrative of the Battle of Cowpens, he again was uncharacteristically vague. He was clear the tale of Morgan's breakfast took place on 6 January.[113] He segued immediately into the story of Cowpens, allowing the reader to believe the events were sequential. Stedman returned to his tacit suggestion: If Tarleton was so close he could grab Morgan, what was the hurry? Why not use the main army to crush him in the nutcracker?

In actuality, Tarleton chased Morgan another eleven days before finally catching him at Cowpens on 17 January. At this time, before the union with Leslie, was Cornwallis's depleted army strong enough to crush Morgan? Arguably, but the uncertainty was Stedman's point. Tarleton never considered it. To Stedman, this should have been Cornwallis's decision, not Tarleton's. Like a bull seeing the matador's cape, Tarleton charged as soon as he caught Morgan, immediately and with no regard for consequences, which in this case were extreme. Once again, Stedman deferred subtlety in letting the reader believe a better commander would have dealt with Morgan differently, and more successfully.

---

113 Stedman, *History*, 2:320.

Relying on Stedman's work necessarily involved dealing with Stedman's strongly held beliefs regarding Tarleton. Stedman on Tarleton was one-sided. Tarleton on Tarleton was equally one-sided, but in ways that balanced Stedman. We must hear from Tarleton in order to flesh out an understanding of the events leading up to the battle. After all, Cowpens presented a tale of disaster in British arms such as happened perhaps once in a century. The first Afghan War in 1842 and the fall of Singapore in 1942 were more catastrophic in size, but there were few total tactical failures that rivaled Cowpens. Tarleton, under fire the rest of his life for Cowpens as much as the Waxhaws, again used his memoirs as a forum to rebut criticism.

Tarleton started with a critique of the government's strategy overall, that is, the idea of liberating expectant bodies of Loyalists in North Carolina.[114] The government believed the Tories "would make indefatigable exertions to render themselves independent of Congress" upon Cornwallis's arrival.[115] By the time he wrote his memoirs, he knew better, and he dared pose three burning questions: "whether the scheme itself was visionary, or the plan to complete it injudicious, or whether the force employed was inadequate to the purpose."[116]

Tarleton allowed the questions to hang in the air, but to his enthusiastic, partisan readers, the answer to all three was an unequivocal "yes;" *yes*, the scheme was visionary, *yes*, the plan injudicious, and *yes*, the forces were inadequate. One might forgive Tarleton for trying to shift the blame back to the government. The entire burden of Cowpens was onerous, even for Tarleton's massive ego. While the questions were entirely appropriate in a macrocosm, they failed to exonerate their author. The resolution bore down to relevance. The overall forces committed to the endeavor may or may not have been adequate; this question had no bearing on Tarleton, who had plenty of strength within the microcosm of Cowpens.

Tarleton agreed that if the British intended to invade North

---

114 Tarleton, *Campaigns*, 215.
115 Ibid.
116 Tarleton, *Campaigns*, 215–216.

Carolina, the time was right. With Leslie on the way, the British forces would be massive. The only problem was Morgan in the rear, able to threaten Ninety-Six from his position west of the Broad River.[117] With respect to solving the Morgan problem, Tarleton acknowledged Cornwallis's orders in a general way. He asserted that on 1 January, Cornwallis reinforced him and sent him after Morgan, but with limited orders. Tarleton was only to compel Morgan back across the Broad River.[118] Once safely east of the Broad River, he was in no position to threaten Ninety-Six, and Cornwallis could move northward in complete security.

At this point, Tarleton was clutching at straws. Buford, who had caused no trouble, caused Cornwallis to unleash Tarleton without restrictions, and no real orders other than to get rid of him. Morgan, on the other hand, was a thorn in Cornwallis's side, and to the British on the ground a real menace to Ninety-Six. Tarleton's assertion was nonsense. Sending Tarleton against Buford was, at most, mopping up. Sending Tarleton against Morgan was dealing with a genuine threat. Moving Morgan eastward a few miles would not reduce the threat, especially once Tarleton joined the northward march. After Tarleton joined the main army in North Carolina, Morgan could walk into Ninety-Six at his convenience.

Tarleton was trying to craft a narrative in which Cornwallis failed to perceive either the magnitude of the threat or the wonder of the prize represented by Morgan's army. At this early stage, he depicted a Cornwallis unable to understand that Morgan needed more than just a push out of the way.

Tarleton continued to develop his narrative.[119] Very soon, he decided that Ninety-Six was better defended than Cornwallis had believed, and, more importantly, that Morgan was too far from it to pose a credible threat. This was more creative writing on Tarleton's part. Cornwallis was diligent to a fault and knew exactly the strengths at Ninety-Six. Moreover, once Morgan was

---

117 Tarleton, *Campaigns*, 216.
118 Tarleton, *Campaigns*, 217.
119 Ibid.

across the Broad River, which he was, he was no more than three or four days from Ninety-Six.

Tarleton wrote that his new information caused him to pause his mission, and pass it on to Cornwallis for his decision.[120] Tarleton added a twist to his narrative. Cornwallis, unable to perceive the risk or the benefits, was still in charge, and despite his shortcomings needed to give the orders. Tarleton breathed life into Stedman's view. Here was Cornwallis, not Tarleton, planning the campaign. Sadly for the British, this was another exaggeration on Tarleton's part. Tarleton wrote that he detailed to Cornwallis a long list of items: Morgan's force and likely plans; the plan of operation needed to defeat him; the exact "mode of proceedings to be employed" against Morgan; and the geographical point Cornwallis's army should reach. Once reached, "it should be [Tarleton's] endeavour to push the enemy into that quarter." This was exactly the plan Stedman had wanted. Tarleton, too aggressive by half, would be limited to pushing Morgan into Cornwallis's main army. Tarleton assured his readers that Cornwallis approved the suggested operations.[121]

Unfortunately for the British, the items on Tarleton's list were fictions. Tarleton appended original documents to his memoir throughout its length. In this instance, the documents showed nothing of the detail suggested in the narrative. A typical letter between Cornwallis and Tarleton was the former's of 2 January 1781: "If Morgan is still at Williams', or any where within your reach, I should wish you to push him to the utmost."[122] Absolutely: push him to the utmost. Sound strategy, but lacking any sign of campaign planning by Cornwallis. The closest they reached was Tarleton's letter of 4 January, in which he asserted, "When I advance, I must either destroy Morgan's corps, or push it before me over Broad river, towards King's Mountain."[123] Again sound strategy, and again markedly lacking Cornwallis's imprimatur. The generalities that passed between the two offi-

---

120 Tarleton, *Campaigns*, 218.
121 Tarleton, *Campaigns*, 218.
122 Tarleton, *Campaigns*, 250–251. Fort Williams was an outpost 15 miles from Ninety-Six, Bartholomees, "Fight or Flee," 108.
123 Tarleton, *Campaigns*, 252.

cers lay far from the kind of step-by-step planning that might have saved the day for the British. Cornwallis approved the barest outline: crush Morgan or move him. Despite his protests, Tarleton never came close to getting Cornwallis's approval of his specific plans for dealing with Morgan once he caught him.

On 15 January, Tarleton approached Morgan.[124] Tarleton needed to cross the Pacolet River. Morgan had established formidable guard posts at all the river fords.

Tarleton, normally a blunt instrument, received credit for clever resourcefulness in dealing with Morgan and his guards. Bartholomees wrote that Tarleton, knowing the river guards were watching him, followed the river upstream for a few miles, then settled down as if to camp for the night. After time passed, the militia guards stopped watching and went to sleep, assuming Tarleton had done the same. He had not. Tarleton roused his troops and crossed the crossed the Pacolet without incident.[125] Bartholomees, normally a stickler for form, did not disclose the provenance of this anecdote. Therefore, the record shows only the unusual instance in which Tarleton exchanged his bludgeon for a rapier. In any event, regardless of how he managed it, Tarleton was across the Pacolet and within a short reach of Morgan.

Tarleton located a series of log houses between his position and Morgan. He moved quickly to seize the area. According to Tarleton, it was at this point, on 16 January, that his soldiers found the Americans had left so quickly they had abandoned a half-cooked breakfast.[126] Stedman, dating it to 6 January, used the story of the half-cooked breakfast to suggest Tarleton had Morgan where he wanted him, and could afford to take his time. Tarleton's message, dated to 16 January, was exactly the opposite. To Tarleton, the half-cooked breakfast was the red cape to an enraged bull. Morgan was almost in his grasp, so it was time to pour on the speed.

Tarleton put out patrols, and learned Morgan was again on the move. He decided to keep close to Morgan's rear, to prevent

---

124 Tarleton, *Campaigns*, 219.
125 Bartholomees, "Fight or Flee," 113–114.
126 Tarleton, *Campaigns*, 220.

further reinforcements by the ongoing inward trickle of militia, as well as to prevent his recrossing the Broad River unseen. Tarleton made a point that he could "call in the assistance of the main army if necessity required."[127]

His mention of calling on the main army warrants explanation. Throughout the war, Tarleton in the presence of the enemy was a shark smelling blood in the water. Everyone knew that once he caught Morgan, he would attack. Absent a direct order from Cornwallis, there was no force on Earth that would stop him. He had been looking for Morgan for over two weeks. Now that he had him, it beggared credibility to believe he would wait the three or four days necessary to get a courier to Cornwallis, ask for help, and wait for the main army to arrive. Nevertheless, Tarleton insisted he would "watch the enemy closely." This could mean only that Tarleton would watch Morgan long enough to line up in attack formation. He never expressed any of these matters to Cornwallis. Although, in all fairness to Tarleton, in turning him loose on Morgan, Cornwallis knew what he was getting. More to the point, he knew what the Americans were getting.

In summary, two primary British sources painted vastly different pictures of the events leading to the battle. Stedman described an unreasoning and aggressive Tarleton, an officer driven by restless ambition to abandon both caution and the protection of the main army to pursue Morgan in ways the readers knew would end in disaster. To Stedman, Cornwallis was the rock on which Tarleton, in his arrogance, refused to rely.

Tarleton on Tarleton portrayed a completely different animal. In his memoir, Tarleton was the one officer who understood any aspect of the campaign: the futility of the government's mission, the danger manifested by Morgan's army, and the actual strength of Ninety-Six, to name only a few. Cornwallis, benign and mildly clueless, by virtue of rank and position was an obstacle to be tolerated.

The concept of two competing visions will repeat many times in the story of Cowpens. At this early juncture, resolution

---

127 Ibid.

of the conflict rests with the agendas of the two writers. Stedman assigned Tarleton the full measure of blame for the disaster at Cowpens. Further, he saw Cowpens at the top of a slippery slope ending at Yorktown. Tarleton's agenda burned as brightly. Under attack for the result at Cowpens, he used his memoirs to describe himself as the one competent actor in the drama.

While history has been generous to Stedman in his judgments generally, it has been less so with his insistence that simple arrogance drove Tarleton to avoid recourse to the strength of the main army. Cornwallis dispatched Tarleton against Morgan much as he had released him against Buford. He relied on Tarleton's aggression, and did not anticipate he would hover in the shadow of the main army. Stedman, ever loyal, was unable to state that Cornwallis erred in allowing Tarleton too much discretion.[128]

History has been unkind to Tarleton's views on himself as portrayed in his memoir. While he was not the unthinking and unskilled devotee of arrogance in Stedman's work, his record demonstrated high levels of aggression and ambition.

The resolution of these conflicting visions of events lay in the common ground between the two extremes. Stedman was correct that Tarleton brandished aggression. He was incorrect in his assertion that arrogance alone kept him from seeking support from the main army. Tarleton was right that he was more thoughtful than Stedman allowed. He was wrong in his assertion that he was the only officer with insight into the strategic and tactical situation facing the British.

Tarleton pursued Morgan relentlessly on 16 January. Early on 17 January, he caught him. The events which followed were, once again, the objects of competing visions. Stedman and Tarleton once more stood out prominently in the debate. Tarleton

---

[128] The criticism, when it arose, came from Tarleton: "it is necessary for the commander in chief to keep as near as possible to his detachments… A steady adherence to that line of conduct would prevent the misfortunes detachments are liable to," Tarleton, *Campaigns*, 226. General Clinton agreed, writing, "I was ever against detachments and penetrating the country in small parties," Clinton to Duke of Newcastle, 17 March 1781, in William B. Willcox, *Portrait of a General: Sir Henry Clinton in the War of Independence* (New York: Alfred A. Knopf, 1964), 371n4.

encountered Morgan's pickets around 8:00 a.m. From them, he learned that the American general was forming in line of battle at Cowpens. Stedman returned to his theme: Tarleton "resolved, without loss of time, to make an attack upon the Americans."[129] In a painful twist of the knife into Tarleton, Stedman wrote that he was "impatient of delay, and too confident of success," and personally led the first line into the attack "even before it was fully formed." Screaming silently from the page was Stedman's refutation of Tarleton's suggestion of waiting patiently for several days to consult with Cornwallis.

Tarleton described an army, well-disciplined and confident, forming for battle, briskly but not in haste. Tarleton "did not hesitate to undertake those measures which the instructions of his commanding officer imposed," adding his "own judgment … equally recommended" them. The troops, not hurried, showed "animation" and "alacrity" which "afforded the most promising assurances of success."[130]

Controversies of this nature have made Cowpens a fertile ground of study. They are, ultimately, what has given Cowpens its hook, its hold on the imagination of the reader. The stories of Cowpens in all their disagreement arose for a reason, just as they have retained popularity for a reason. It is history's task to explain why a story has proven durable. In doing so, one question is paramount: What is there about a story that has made it attractive? At bottom, a truly durable story, one that has stood the passage of time, has attractions that draw in the reader, that make people want to believe it.

By every American account, Morgan was an exceptional field commander. The British were silent on opinions of Morgan as commander. Had the British encountered *faux pas* by this troublesome Patriot, they would have gladly papered the record with them. The Americans, on the other hand, extolled Morgan as the ideal commander for the situation. Not just in fighting Tarleton, but in doing so with a huge contingent of militia out of the North and South Carolina backcountry.

---

129 Stedman, *History*, 2:321.
130 Tarleton, *Campaigns*, 221–222.

Morgan understood the backwoodsmen. He took steps to lead these amateur soldiers, as well as his Continental professionals, in such a way as to get the best performance from every soldier in his army.[131] The militiamen drawn into Morgan's army were enthusiastic, but as one prominent historian wryly noted, "enthusiasm does not necessarily correlate directly with effective performance."[132] Morgan, realizing this fact, channeled the enthusiasm into work. Not mere busy work, but tasks such as preparing food and ammunition, things necessary for the upcoming battle. Short on cavalry, he selected forty-five volunteers to serve as mounted militia under Major McCall. Morgan issued them cavalry sabers and instructed them personally in their use. This kind of action on Morgan's part left his imprint on the soldiers.

Morgan realized the importance of personal contact in creating effective leadership. The backcountry militiamen, having none of the discipline and very little of the belief system of the Continental regulars, needed the commander's personal touch to feel integrated into the unit, a necessary part of any military enterprise.[133] With this point in mind, once he drew up his battle plan, he moved among his soldiers, of all ranks, to explain it to them. Businesspeople call this process "buy-in," that is, getting the rank and file to endorse a plan, and by doing so feel a part of it. Once the troops bought in to the battle plan, Morgan knew he had a much greater chance of getting them to put it into action.

An important part of Morgan's skill was his ability to mingle with the soldiers. As he moved among them to explain the battle plan, he joked with them, and gave them encouraging messages about fighting the British. In the same breath, he would remind them of Tarleton's cruelty, and predict the welcome they would receive as heroes when they returned home.[134] Thomas Young

---

131 Bartholomees, "Fight or Flee," 118.
132 Bartholomees, "Fight or Flee," 117.
133 Bartholomees, "Fight or Flee," 118.
134 Bartholomees, "Fight or Flee," 118. Joseph Johnson, *Traditions and Reminiscences, Chiefly of the American Revolution in the South: Including Biographical Sketches, Incidents, and Anecdotes, Few of Which Have Been Published, Particularly of Residents in the Upper Country* (Charleston, 1851), 449–450.

fought at Cowpens as a teenage recruit, and later rose to become a militia officer. As an old soldier, long years away from military service, he related his recollections in 1843:

> The evening previous to the battle he went among the volunteers, helped them fix their swords, joked with them about their sweethearts, and told them to keep in good spirits, and the day would be ours. Long after I laid down, he was going about among the soldiers, encouraging them, and telling them that the "Old Wagoner" would crack his whip over Ben [Tarleton] in the morning, as sure as he lived... And then, when you return to your homes, how the old folks will bless you, and the girls kiss you, for your gallant conduct.[135]

The battle plan that Morgan explained to his troops represented an improvement of several orders of magnitude over its predecessors. It solved the central problem in every previous battle plan on the American side. The problem was simple to express, difficult to solve: what to do with the militia? They lacked discipline. They received minimal training. To fix bayonets and charge was a basic British military maneuver, and the militia were never expected to withstand it. Lee famously asserted it was "murder" to deploy militia in the path of British bayonets.[136] The militia would break and run; this much was commonly understood.

Commanders typically tasked the Continental regulars with the heavy lifting against their British professional counterparts. Continentals were always in short supply. Morgan's army was no exception. By the morning of 17 January, through acquisition of militiamen he had increased his force to approximately 975 soldiers. He commanded 290 Continental infantry, eighty Continental cavalry, forty-five militia cavalry, and 560 militia infantry. These numbers were established over two hundred years ago by William Johnson, a South Carolina jurist, in the first biography of Nathanael Greene.[137] These numbers retained a

---

135 Johnson, *Traditions and Reminiscences*, 449–450.
136 David Schenck, *North Carolina. 1780–'81. Being a History of the Invasion of the Carolinas by the British Army Under Lord Cornwallis in 1780–'81* (Raleigh, 1889), 342; Lee, *Memoirs*, 200n.
137 William Johnson, *Sketches of the Life and Correspondence of Nathanael Greene, Major*

high level of acceptance for many years.[138] Recently, however, they have become the subject of controversy.[139] The controversy must await discussion below; at this point, the focus is on the fact that most of Morgan's soldiers were militiamen.

Beneath the militia numbers lay the problem of militia capabilities, and in this question one finds the point in spending time and effort distinguishing the numbers of regulars from the numbers of militiamen. The militia, undisciplined and untrained, were part-time soldiers. Depending on state and circumstances, they enlisted for periods as short as six weeks or three months. The Continentals, on the other hand, enlisted for long periods, years, or, at times, for the duration of the war. Each Continental represented a body of institutional knowledge unavailable in the militia forces. The Continental commanders imposed a code of silence on themselves in dealing with the cruel and unforgiving mathematics of militia deployment. A commander could lose uncounted numbers of militiamen, but a killed or wounded Continental meant the loss of years of training and experience. Morgan, in his role as the hero of Cowpens, brushed against the *omertà* in a later letter to Greene, advising the latter on his upcoming fight with Cornwallis at Guilford Courthouse. He warned Greene on problems with the militia: "if they fight, you'll beat Cornwallis if not, he will beat you and perhaps cut your regulars to pieces, which will be losing all our hopes." He went on to emphasize another dimension of the cruelty in using militiamen: he advised Greene to post riflemen behind the militia lines, to shoot those trying to run away.[140]

Years after the war, the first cracks appeared in the code of silence. Joseph Graham was a North Carolina militia officer, a captain during the Revolutionary War, a general in the War of 1812. Although intensely proud of his militia service, he held few illusions of the military expertise of militiamen generally. In the 1820s, he wrote a series of letters setting out his wartime

---

General in the Armies of the United States in the War of the Revolution, 2 vols. (Charleston, 1822), 1:374, 1:377–378.
138 E.g., Bartholomees, "Fight or Flee," 122.
139 Babits, *Devil*, 150.
140 Morgan to Greene, 20 February 1781, in Showman et al., *Greene*, 7:324.

experiences, some of which saw publication in a magazine in the 1850s, the totality which were published in book form in 1904.[141] Graham observed in defense of the Continental officers that at times "it became necessary to sacrifice one part of the command to save the rest," and under these circumstances, "the loss to the cause of three or four militiamen whose term of service would expire in a week or two was not as great as the loss of one regular."[142] Coming from Graham, a distinguished militia general, these assertions carried great credibility.

As Americans, we have placed our Revolutionary War ancestors on pedestals. This tradition is admirable as fuel for our national pride. For example, Nathanael Greene as a national hero makes sense, and forms an important foundation of patriotism. At the same time, the literature is short on critical analyses of Greene as a commander. Greene manifested good points and bad points within his skill set, and it does not diminish him as a hero to suggest he had flaws as a field commander. There are few Pattons, just as there are few Custers. Our adoration is not limited to individual heroes. The militia is part of our historical DNA. It is responsible for the national myth of the minuteman, the citizen-soldier who plowed his fields between campaigns. The myth is out of focus in a nation whose superior armed forces are based on professionalism and advanced technology. As with Greene in microcosm, we do not diminish the luster of the militia's legend by suggesting the individual soldiers were not the equals of trained professionals.

Morgan's innovation was a battle plan that solved both aspects of the militia question. He employed the militia in new ways that emphasized their skills while acknowledging their limitations. Before discussing Morgan's deployments, the story turns to the question of the number of soldiers he deployed. Once again, the sources conflict.

Tarleton was an eyewitness to Morgan's army. Even with this advantage, Tarleton's views were skewed. Eighteenth-century troop counts were ephemeral in everyone's hands. Tarleton had

[141] William A. Graham, *General Joseph Graham and His Papers on North Carolina Revolutionary History* (Raleigh: Edwards & Broughton, 1904).
[142] Graham, *Graham*, 346.

additional, powerful incentives to magnify the size of Morgan's army in order to minimize the scale of his personal disaster. He reported up the chain of command that he faced a front line of one thousand militia, a second line of five hundred Continental infantry and three hundred "backwoodsmen," and a reserve of 120 Continental cavalry.[143] This amounted to a total of 1920 Americans. It is unlikely anyone believed Tarleton at the time; there is no question no one has believed him since.[144] William Johnson, in his biography of Greene, penned a sarcastic reply to Tarleton that spoke for the ages:

> Colonel Tarleton, with characteristic candour, seems to have been resolved to exempt his adversary from the reproach of having engaged with a great disparity of force, for he asserts upon "accurate knowledge," that Morgan's force amounted to 1300 militia, 500 regulars, and 120 cavalry, —exactly double of what it did consist of. Colonel Tarleton may have consoled his mortified feelings with believing this "accurate account."[145]

Morgan, for his part, reported to Greene that his total force consisted of 800 soldiers.[146] Like Tarleton, Morgan had incentives to adjust the number of American soldiers present for duty, in this case, in the other direction in order to magnify the size of his victory. James Graham, an early historian of the battle and an admirer of Morgan, phrased the issue tactfully:

> Besides that furnished in the letters of Morgan himself, there is abundant evidence to show, that the whole number of his forces engaged did not much exceed eight hundred. It is true, his entire command, including all the militia that arrived previous to the battle, would appear to be about nine hundred and eighty men, if army returns and muster rolls were alone consulted. But every one acquainted with military affairs knows that such evidences of strength always exceed the reality.[147]

---

143 Tarleton, *Campaigns*, 222.
144 With a caveat: Babits, in *A Devil of a Whipping*, advocated a similar total, although not drawn from Tarleton.
145 Johnson, *Life*, 1:374.
146 Morgan to Greene, 19 January 1781, in Showman et al., *Greene*, 7:155.
147 Graham, *Morgan*, 295.

He went on to note that some units had been detached for baggage or prisoner duty, plus some of the militia ran away. Graham believed none of these should detract from Morgan's achievement. He finally decided that the total number "did not exceed 850 men." Graham's analysis raised a serious point: Morgan told Greene he had eight hundred men on the battlefield, while the present-for-duty rosters showed almost two hundred more. Graham tried hard to reconcile the numbers, but there were important differences between the eight hundred reported to Greene, the 850 Graham believed present, and the 980 on the books and records of Morgan's army.

Other writers have arrived at different numbers. Stedman began a consensus by asserting Morgan had just under one thousand men.[148] Stedman was meticulous in his details, giving his number great weight. William Johnson, in his biography of Greene, generally agreed with Stedman. He added specificity. Morgan had 975 soldiers: 290 Continental infantry, eighty Continental cavalry, forty-five militia cavalry, and 560 militia infantry.[149] Numbers in this range achieved a consistent respect for a very long time. For example, Bartholomees, writing his dissertation 150 years later, counted 975 present for duty.[150] All these authors, writing across centuries, reached numbers in a range consistent with the numbers in Morgan's "army returns and muster rolls," these documents constituting the reliable gold standard for troop counts in the fluid reporting of the eighteenth century.

Absent truly compelling evidence, there is no basis to disregard contemporary, written records. This axiom returns the story to Lawrence Babits's *A Devil of a Whipping*. This book challenged the working consensus on the American strength. In it, Babits asserted Morgan mustered between eighteen and twenty-four hundred soldiers on the battlefield.[151] If Babits was correct, then Morgan either was terrible at arithmetic, or lied shamelessly to

---

148 Stedman, *History*, 2:319.
149 Johnson, *Life*, 1:374.
150 Bartholomees, "Fight or Flee," 118.
151 Babits, *Devil*, 150. Buchanan, in discussing Tarleton's similar count of 1,900 Americans, asserted the figure was "nonsense," Buchanan, *Guilford Courthouse*, 319.

Greene. Before ascribing either quality to Morgan, one should first examine Babits's methodology.

Babits made extensive use of a resource that had remained largely untapped for years: the applications by war veterans for pensions. These were generally filed with the states based on pension laws passed in 1818 and 1832.[152] Babits did not invent reliance on pension applications, but he gave them significance in ways not seen in previous works. One example is the *Cowpens Staff Ride and Battlefield Tour*, a monograph published in 1996 by the Combat Studies Institute of the U.S. Army Command and General Staff College. The author, Lieutenant Colonel John Moncure, explained the "staff ride" was a technique inherited from the Prussian general staff, in which officers would tour a battlefield site and give it a detailed examination, in an effort to learn as much as possible from the engagement. The value of the staff ride depended on the amount of available information as well as its accuracy. Moncure made extensive use of pension applications, but only after he cautioned the reader:

> The American sources are ... from the mouths of American veterans trying to justify pensions—and perhaps embellish their personal exploits—after a popular war... I trust careful readers will be able to weigh this shortcoming as they evaluate the evidence.[153]

The specter of embellishment was only the beginning. Because the pension enabling laws dated to 1818 and 1832, many of the accounts in the applications were forty years old when given. The age of the stories, although problematic, was not the central question. Methodology was the issue. If one discounts Morgan's count of eight hundred soldiers to Greene as puffery, one is left with his army returns and muster rolls on the day of the battle showing 980 soldiers. What justifies doubling this number using pension applications submitted forty years after the battle?

Babits selected ten companies, a sample consisting of both

---

[152] Babits and Howard, *Long, Obstinate, and Bloody*, xiii.
[153] Moncure, *Staff Ride*, ix–x.

Continental and militia units.[154] Babits started with counts of the companies' total membership. For example, the South Carolina company commanded by Samuel Sexton had a complement of twenty-four men. Of these, one filed a pension application, for a ratio of one application per twenty-four soldiers. Other units had different ratios. Virginia's Rockbridge Rifles had forty-four members and six applications, making a ratio of one application per 7.3 soldiers. Of the ten companies examined, the ratios covered a range from one to two, to one to twenty-four. From these data, Babits inferred there were three men for every pension application for the army as a whole. For the militia, the numbers were fewer, with a ratio of about one application for every four militiamen.[155]

An initial question concerned the five Continental companies, each composed of exactly sixty soldiers. At the beginning of the war, a Continental army company at full strength consisted of ninety officers and men.[156] A company early in the war might shrink through battle losses, illness, desertion, or any number of causes, but it was unlikely that five companies in unison contracted by exactly thirty soldiers.

The numbers of men per company changed over time. The Continental Congress legislated several major revisions to the Continental Army. For this discussion, the most significant revisions took place in May 1778 and January 1781.[157] The U.S. Army's official history noted that the latter revision changed the strength of each company from fifty-six to sixty-eight men.[158] Therefore, at the time of the Battle of Cowpens, a Continental infantry company at full strength contained either fifty-six or sixty-eight men, never sixty. The army revisions made the question more pointed: how did these five companies all achieve

---

154 Babits, *Devil*, 32.
155 Babits, *Devil*, 32–33.
156 Robert K. Wright, Jr., *The Continental Army* (Washington, DC: United States Army Center of Military History, 2006), 47; Moncure, *Staff Ride*, 7; "List of American Regiments in the Revolutionary War," *American Revolutionary War Continental Regiments*, www.revolutionarywar.us/continental-army.
157 Wright, *Continental Army*, 153–157.
158 Wright, *Continental Army*, 158.

sixty soldiers, whether by growth or attrition, at exactly the same time? Five concurrent headcounts of sixty men would represent a huge statistical anomaly. It seems much more likely to be an estimate within a field of calculated numbers.

Babits acknowledged the Continentals were not counted. Babits noted that by January 1781, Continental companies usually numbered sixty.[159] This proposition did not take into account that three of the Continental companies in the sample were from Maryland. Cowpens occurred as seven Maryland regiments, decimated by combat losses and disease, were combined into a single regiment. Losses of this magnitude and a dramatic reorganization described a situation removed from the usual.

If the devil is in the details, the discipline of statistics is rife with demons. One lies in the problem of sample size. Babits drew his conclusions using a numerator of 452 and a denominator centered on 2100. He acknowledged this was "an admittedly small sample."[160] If his numbers were accurate, he based his conclusions on a sample of less than 20 percent of the total.

A second devil in statistics is the matter of examples. Babits used ten companies, with no proof, and no means of proof, they were exemplary of the rest. The units sampled might equally have been the most or the least aggressive in filing pension applications.

A third pitfall in statistics is drawing conclusions using an insufficient foundation, and this issue reached the nub of the problem. The book calculated a total of eighteen to twenty-four hundred Americans on the field at Cowpens; the numbers center on 2,100 men, a figure which warrants examination.

Numbering the militia present on the field presents the problem in microcosm. Babits advocated a multiplier of four men for each militia pension application. This was a purely subjective evaluation, in that the ratios from the militia units were higher, most of them markedly so. In the five militia companies analyzed, the actual ratios were 1:7.3, 1:5 through 1:7.5, 1:24, 1:15,

---

159 Babits, *Devil*, 27.
160 Babits, *Devil*, 32.

and 1:8.[161] None yielded the ratio of 1:4 stated in the text. In actuality, all stayed unbridgeably distant.

The total of eighteen to twenty-four hundred Americans at Cowpens was simply a calculation, one derived from estimates. Of the numbers of soldiers in the ten companies in the statistical sample, five were estimates. Calculating the army size as a function of the numbers of pension applications filed raised other problems. Because the total numbers in five of the ten units were estimates, there was no way to know the actual ratio of pension applications per soldier. Since this was the case, as the book acknowledged, the adopted ratio was simply one more estimate.

The difficulty lay not in the fact of the estimation, but in using an estimate not supported by the evidence. Six hundred men filed pension applications claiming service at Cowpens.[162] Using the stated range of one pension application per three or four men, the calculations generated totals on the field of eighteen hundred (three men per application) to 2,400 (four men per application). Setting aside any questions of the size of the Continental units or the validity of the sampling, the data revealed the scope of the problem. Even assuming validity of the sampling and the sample size, the data did not support the conclusions. The ratios of pension application per soldier within the Continentals were 1:6, 1:4, 1:6.5, 1:2, and 1:8.5, and within the militia were 1:7.3, 1:5–1:7.5, 1:24, 1:15, and 1:8. The actual data calculated to average ratios far removed from the 1:3 or 1:4 proposed in the text. The mathematical average of the Continental units in the sample was 1:5.4. Calculating the total Americans on the field using this ratio, Morgan's army totaled 3240 men, a number skewed beyond recognition. The average from the militia units was in a range of 1:11.6 to 1:12.3. Using these ratios, Morgan commanded about 7200 men, a figure beyond credibility.

At bottom, calculating soldiers on the field as a function of later applications for pensions proved unworkable. Eschewing

---

161 Ibid.
162 Babits, *Devil*, 150.

subjectivity and following the data where they led gave way to impossible numbers. The effort to use pension applications to double the count of American forces from Morgan's army returns and muster rolls reinforced the foundational axiom: Absent truly compelling evidence, there is no basis to disregard contemporary, written records. Pension applications were not the evidence justifying such a move.

Even with this difficulty in hand, there was a deeper problem lurking within the applications themselves. Lieutenant Colonel Moncure's caution on the risk of embellishment intimated the problem: credibility. The pension program represented a huge amount of government largesse at a time when such things were rare. Forty years after the war, it was child's play to fabricate a war record and qualify for a pension. Here is one example, taken from *A Devil of a Whipping*. In discussing a militia company with men drawn from counties in north-central North Carolina, the book stated that "so many Guilford County men claimed service under Rowan County's Captain William Watson that it is possible he led this 'Northern Company' at Cowpens."[163] It was equally likely that these Guilford County men worked their farms miles from the shooting, heard the veterans' stories after the war, and filed applications forty years later using the name Watson they had heard so often, in order to gain credibility on their applications.

The sad fact is that people lie for money. It is the single point that explains the existence of the Internal Revenue Service. It is the salient factor underscoring the bulk of the legal system. The remainder is based on the more tragic fact that people will kill for it, so lying for it seems mundane by comparison. It beggars common sense to assume that thousands of pension applications were free of misstatements and misrepresentations when there was so much government money at issue. Other than a naive belief in a universally benign humanity, there is no compelling reason to accept *en masse* the contents of the pension applications.

Babits commented on the discrepancies between the pension

---

163 Babits, *Devil*, 35.

applications and the memoirs left by other witnesses: "Participants' details often seem to be in conflict with other contemporary and later accounts."[164] Conflict, indeed; the pension applications proposed a body of information in diametric opposition to the other accounts. Babits explained this gap as a matter of perspective, that a private in the mud would have a different view from a colonel on horseback. Such an explanation is entirely too superficial. Seymour, an enlisted man on the ground, would have no different perspective than Babits' hypothetical private in the mud, yet his memoir was as reliable as anything by Howard or Lee. Lamb, a British foot soldier well acquainted with the mud in America, wrote a memoir that has been a reliable resource for over two hundred years. The problem with the pension applications was not perspective. It was, at bottom, simple credibility, or better said, the shortage of it.

A final consideration: Misrepresentation was the order of the day. Morgan, in reporting his victory, shaved his force to eight hundred, a number no one believes. At the same time, Tarleton augmented the Americans to 1920, a number in equally grave doubt. Cornwallis, normally the picture of propriety, in the face of over eight hundred British casualties, reported the British losses at Cowpens "did not fall short of 600 men."[165] No one is suggesting these instances made these commanders liars. A little slanting of the numbers apparently seemed harmless to them. *A Devil of a Whipping* has maintained that Morgan did more than slant. In this book, Morgan was off by 60 percent, a serious charge against a commander as competent as Morgan. If we are to accept these commanders slanted matters, or worse, simply to look better, it is not a leap to suggest a number of ordinary citizens slanted things for a great deal of money. Human nature being what it is, money can be a powerful incentive for misconduct and misrepresentation.

---

164 Babits, *Devil*, xv.
165 Cornwallis to Germain, 17 March 1781, in Ross, *Cornwallis*, 1:503. The modern scholarship on Cowpens casualties is dealt with below. However, it is interesting that Cornwallis's imaginary figure of 600 still appears in some British sources, including, oddly, the *Encyclopedia Britannica*, "Battle of Cowpens," *Encyclopedia Britannica*, www.britannica.com/event/Battle-of-Cowpens.

The lack of credibility inherent in the pension applications prevents their use as the compelling evidence needed to overturn contemporary, written records. There was a consensus for two hundred years on the size of Morgan's force at Cowpens, a record supported by the army returns and muster rolls. An examination of pension applications has refreshed the merit of the consensus. Morgan fielded a number consistently expressed by many, for example, by Stedman as just under a thousand men, in the army records as 980, and by Johnson and Bartholomees as 975 men.

With the American forces in place, refining the size of the British Army requires attention. Earlier, the discussion paused with Stedman's estimate of Tarleton's force on 1 January.[166] There was no suggestion of any attrition by casualties or disease in the two weeks leading up to the battle, leaving this estimate as Tarleton's strength at the time of the battle, about a thousand British soldiers. Stedman's number has stood the test of time. Johnson, in the early nineteenth century, and Bartholomees, in the late twentieth, both used 150 British soldiers.[167] Babits and contemporary British historian Ian Saberton both advocated 1,150 British soldiers, a number not radically different from the historical consensus..[168] With respect to this mild disagreement between Stedman and the later writers, Stedman had the stronger position. He witnessed Tarleton's force. As an officer on Cornwallis's staff, he could access the British fit-for-duty reports. No reason cries out to modify his original assessment.

The terrain featured prominently in the preparations for the battle. The terrain at Cowpens was distinctive in its pronounced disfavor for the Americans. More notable was the fact Morgan had selected it.[169] At least, had selected it under duress. Cred-

---

166 Stedman, *History*, 2:318.
167 Bartholomees, "Fight or Flee," 127; Johnson, *Life*, 1:374. Johnson added 50 Loyalist militia, an erroneous assertion lacking foundation, properly ignored by historians following in his wake.
168 Saberton, "Winter Campaign;" Babits, *Devil*, 42–47. Babits did not include a total. To remedy this oversight, a radical proposal: try Wikipedia. The author of the article on Cowpens had the patience to total Babits's figures, www.en.wikipedia.org/wiki/Battle_of_Cowpens.
169 Stedman, *History*, 2:320–321; Bartholomees, "Fight or Flee," 114; Johnson, *Life*, 1:375–376.

iting Tarleton begrudgingly, Stedman asserted that he pressed Morgan relentlessly, to the point the latter could retreat no further. Morgan "resolved to hazard an action rather than be overtaken in the ford of the river."[170] Morgan had spent the night of 16 January at Hannah's Cowpens, a space local farmers used to round up cattle before driving the herds to market.[171] Resolving to run no further, Morgan deployed his troops in line of battle to wait for Tarleton. Hannah's Cowpens, or Cowpens as it has been known since, was very well suited for corralling cattle, less so for fighting the British. Bartholomees wrote it was "not an ideal, and not even a good, location for the Americans to offer battle."[172] William Johnson, 150 years earlier, had offered the same opinion: "the subject on which Morgan has been most severely censured, was the choice of ground."[173] Lee, although envying Morgan the chance at Tarleton presented at Cowpens, thought the choice of locations "erroneous."[174]

A road bisected the battlefield. The road provided the British axis of advance and served to mark the center of the battlefield for both sides. Changes to the landscape over time have drastically changed the appearance of the road, both in the battleground and outside of it. Confusingly, it is known by more than one name. One school of thought prefers Mill Gap Road,[175] while another prefers Green River Road.[176] Babits, in a tradition all should follow, used both.[177]

The battlefield at Cowpens presented open ground, low in the front, rising gently for about three hundred yards to the crest of a small ridge. Behind the ridge, the land dropped to a grassy field eighty yards long, then rose again to a second ridge,

---

170 Stedman, *History*, 2:320–321.
171 Bartholomees, "Fight or Flee," 114. Johnson remarked that the name came from the site serving "as the grazing establishment of a man of the name of Hannah," Johnson, *Life*, 1:377.
172 Bartholomees, "Fight or Flee," 114.
173 Johnson, *Life*, 1:375.
174 Lee, *Memoirs*, 131.
175 Moncure, *Staff Ride*, 48.
176 Green River Road is the name appearing on National Park Service maps of the battlefield.
177 See Babits, *Devil*, 64.

parallel to the first. From this ridge, the land dropped gently to the Broad River in the rear.[178] Many authors have criticized the ground selected by Morgan.[179] Three factors figured in the critiques: first, the open terrain was favorable for cavalry, which the British had in numbers about 3:1 over the Americans;[180] second, the fact there were no natural barriers of consequence on the sides, leaving the American flanks dangling in the air;[181] and third, the presence of the Broad River about five or six miles to the rear, which would cut off any retreat and make escape impossible.[182]

With respect to the first criticism, a preponderance of flat ground favoring the British edge in cavalry, the best reply was a repetition of the truism, "it is what it is." Morgan, under duress, selected his best option. It offered some advantages, but the flat ground proved it was not universally advantageous. Morgan had no choice but to rely on his skills as a tactician to devise a battle plan that compensated for this disadvantage in the terrain.

Much of the second criticism, regarding flank protection, has been resolved through the passage of time. The terrain has changed over time, and many of the criticisms were based on the terrain as it appeared at the time criticism arose, and not its appearance in 1781. When Morgan prepared his after-action report in 1781, he mentioned no watercourses on his flanks.[183] The combination of flat ground and no streams meant Morgan had no natural protections for his flanks. As time passed, authors became more and more convinced that there were tactically significant watercourses bordering Morgan's position. A visitor in the 1830s insisted, "the American Army ... encamped between the head waters of Suck & a branch of Buck Creek," a distance of two hundred or three hundred yards.[184] Babits asserted the best insights into flank coverage came from an 1898 visitor, who

---

178 Bartholomees, "Fight or Flee," 114–115.
179 Lee, *Memoirs*, 130; Stedman, *History*, 321; Johnson, *Life*, 1:375.
180 Bartholomees, "Fight or Flee," 115; Lee, *Memoirs*, 130.
181 Johnson, *Life*, 1:375; Lee, *Memoirs*, 131.
182 Bartholomees, "Fight or Flee," 115; Lee, *Memoirs*, 131; Johnson, *Life*, 1:375.
183 Morgan to Greene, 19 January 1781, in Showman et al., *Greene*, 7:152–155.
184 Babits, *Devil*, 62.

asserted that springs on the battlefield made "a flank movement of cavalry or artillery difficult, if not impossible."[185] Almost one hundred years after this visitor, Bartholomees saw two small creeks on either side of the battlefield, enough to protect against "wide turning movements," but emphasized the terrain would not prevent smaller, tactical adjustments in the lines.[186] Headwaters–springs–creeks; there seems little doubt that the landscape on Morgan's flanks has changed as time passed.

With this in mind, the criticisms of his flanking protection are best left unacknowledged. Morgan was a skilled tactician and experienced commander. In 1781, he believed there were no tactically significant bodies of water in his sector. Regardless of any water features on Morgan's flanks, then or now, there is no evidence sufficient to overturn Morgan's original assessment of their insignificance. This means, of course, that his flanks lacked natural barriers. His army would have the flank protection it could provide with fire and maneuver. Morgan knew this point well, and asserted, "as to covering my wings, I knew my adversary, and was perfectly sure I should have nothing but downright fighting."[187] As with the concerns over the flat terrain, the lack of natural flank protection spurred Morgan to master the field with a superior battle plan.

Closely related to the issue of flank protection was the question of the amount of lateral space Morgan needed to cover. Less a criticism than a debate, it, too, was the product of temporal changes in the landscape. One group of historians, writing in 1994 but citing an earlier study, asserted that the American side of the battlefield was three hundred yards wide at its widest point.[188] Bartholomees, in his 1978 work, wrote that the field was five hundred yards deep and almost as wide.[189] Forested land comes and goes over time, and the best one can say today

---

185 Babits, *Devil*, 65.

186 Bartholomees, "Fight or Flee," 115.

187 Johnson, *Life*, 1:376.

188 The historians were Richard K. Showman, Dennis M. Conrad, Roger N. Parks, and Elizabeth C. Stevens, the editors of Greene's correspondence. They based their conclusion on an earlier, unpublished paper by Anthony Walker, Showman, et al., *Greene*, 7:158n6.

189 Bartholomees, "Fight or Flee," 114–115.

is that Morgan's lines needed to cover several hundred yards of cleared terrain. Whether this was three hundred or five hundred, we have no assurances.

The third criticism took issue with Morgan's decision to deploy his army in front of a river. Morgan was keenly aware of this problem, as well, and saw the situation as an advantage. In his hands, it was. A general with no illusions about his militia, he asserted that the river in the back cut off the militia from escaping,[190] and was "better than placing my own men in the rear to shoot down those who broke from the ranks."[191]

With respect to the terrain generally, and all the criticisms of his selection, he acknowledged the problems, and reminded the public that tactics and leadership would carry the day regardless of the advantages to one side or the other in the landscape. At the same time, he reminded the world that the ghost of the Waxhaws still haunted the Americans:

> When men are forced to fight, they will sell their lives dearly; and I knew that the dread of Tarleton's cavalry would give due weight to the protection of my bayonets, and keep my troops from breaking as Buford's regiment did.[192]

---

190 Although Morgan was an innovator, he was also a shrewd adapter. This idea premiered two months earlier at Blackstock's Farm, when Thomas Sumter and his militiamen formed with their backs to the Tyger River to confront Tarleton successfully.
191 Johnson, *Life*, 1:376. His comments about Cowpens echoed in a later letter to Greene in advance of Guilford Courthouse, advising his commander to post riflemen behind the militiamen to discourage deserters and shoot those making the attempt, Morgan to Greene, 20 February 1781, in Showman et al., *Greene*, 7:324.
192 Johnson, *Life*, 1:376.

Chapter 3: Plan of Battle

Tradition has endowed a neat three-line battle plan that modeled eighteenth-century tactical ideals. Mathematical orderliness was the rule of the day. Battles, admirable ones at least, needed to mimic the rigidity and precision of the chessboard. Cowpens proved incapable of escaping this imposition of unreality onto facts on the ground. After all, the reality of battles, even with neat, precise plans, was filthy and gritty. Cowpens was as messy as any. It had the additional burden of a battle plan that defied eighteenth-century ideals of orderliness. The clash of traditional ideals with the reality of Morgan's achievement defined the story of Cowpens for two hundred years.

Introduction: The Problem

The narrative in this book has traced through many debates in the larger story of Cowpens. Much about Cowpens depends on sources. In actuality, much of what one knows about Cowpens depends on one's sources.

The battle plan triggered the most intense of the controversies populating the Cowpens narrative. The basic source of the battle plan should have been Morgan himself. He submitted a detailed after-action report to Greene, in which he laid out in clear terms his disposition of soldiers in expectation of Tarleton's advance.[193] Morgan's report discussed his mastery of fire

---

193 Morgan to Greene, 19 January 1781, in Showman et al., *Greene*, 7:152–155.

and maneuver in the face of the British attack. A distinguished veteran of the campaign, Samuel Hammond, a militia captain in the battle, later lieutenant colonel, later still to serve as Governor of the Missouri territory, wrote a brief memoir illustrated with two maps. It appeared as "Battle of the Cowpens," in a volume of memoirs published by Joseph Johnson in 1851.[194] The combined force of General Morgan and Lieutenant Colonel Hammond should have started and concluded the discussion of the battle plan. Tradition decided otherwise.

One problem, in part, was age. The memoirs of old soldiers have proven unevenly reliable. Lee was the most visible of this group. Lee wrote his memoirs thirty years after the war, and while much of what he wrote was uniquely detailed, his recollection was imperfect. For example, at Guilford Courthouse, his rendition of the third line fighting was unsurpassed, but he confused the names of the brigade commanders on the first line. His description of the battlefield terrain never found acceptance.

Hammond did not record the date he wrote down his recollections. He left clues it was long years after the war: the memoir was "not meant as a correct report of the order, but as nearly so as the memory, influenced by such events, could be expected to retain."[195] Even with the lapse of time, Hammond, as much as Lee, was entitled to the deference due a participant to the events he witnessed. However, as matters developed, Hammond, as much as Morgan, was lost with the passage of time.

Benson J. Lossing published a widely read history of the war in 1852.[196] Lossing may have done more than anyone else in the period to bring the Revolutionary War into the popular consciousness. Part of the attraction of Lossing's book was his extensive use of illustrations. Lossing, however, balked at Hammond. He did not use Hammond's recitation of the battle, and declined to republish his maps. To justify his decision, Lossing

---

[194] Joseph Johnson, *Traditions and Reminiscences, Chiefly of the American Revolution in the South: Including Biographical Sketches, Incidents, and Anecdotes, Few of Which Have Been Published, Particularly of Residents in the Upper Country* (Charleston, 1851).

[195] Johnson, *Traditions and Reminiscences*, 528–529. Hammond's memoirs were found by his son after his death in 1842, a few days shy of his 85th birthday.

[196] Benson J. Lossing, *Pictorial Field-Book of the Revolution*, 2 vols. (New York, 1852).

asserted that "no accurate plan of the arrangement of the troops on this occasion has ever been made. Captain Hammond made a sketch many years afterward from memory ... As it does not fully agree with official reports, I forbear copying it."[197] Lossing did not identify which reports he meant. Morgan provided the only official report. Lossing could have meant any number of collateral sources, and if this was his intent, none were official.

Lossing's work exemplified the problem. No one followed Morgan's version. It was as if no one believed it. The problem with Morgan's report was not credibility, in fact, the real problem did not seem like a problem at all.

The crux of the matter was the power and attractiveness of Lee's prose. Lee's version—gripping, fascinating, riveting—grabbed attention, and Morgan's version, possessing none of these qualities, did not. Lee's version has dominated history books for two hundred years. Historians as diverse as William Johnson in 1822,[198] Lossing in 1852,[199] Schenck in 1889,[200] Bartholomees in 1978,[201] and John Buchanan in 1997[202] all relied on Lee's version of the events, and disregarded Morgan's report to Greene. These books contain no mention of anything other than a three-line defense in depth, with the British marching into increasingly deadly circumstances. Morgan's simpler, and less poetic,[203] two lines fell into obscurity. While three lines versus two was in itself not fatal, the real tragedy was these authors' admiration, misdirected to a defense in depth, thrust aside Morgan's true innovation, the use of massed rifle fire.

Failing to accredit Morgan's idea deferred a true assessment of his tactical skills. The matter had further repercussions. The

---

197 Lossing, *Field-Book*, 2:639n1.
198 Johnson, *Life*, 1:377.
199 Lossing, *Field-Book*, 2:639.
200 Schenck, *Invasion*, 207.
201 Bartholomees, "Flight or Flee," 120–121.
202 John Buchanan, *The Road to Guilford Courthouse* (New York: John Wiley & Sons, 1997), 120.
203 The idea of three increasingly hazardous challenges resonates deeply with readers. It has a long tradition, going back at least to the New Testament. When Satan tempted Jesus in the desert, he did so with three challenges of increasing difficulty, Matt. 4:1–11.

study of Cowpens, an emblematic engagement in itself, reached its apotheosis in the analysis of its successor engagement, the Battle of Guilford Courthouse, where Greene and Cornwallis clashed with their entire armies. It is an article of faith among historians of Guilford Courthouse that Cowpens established the pattern for Greene. One example among many must suffice. Thomas E. Baker published *Another Such Victory* in 1981,[204] and for decades it stood as the standard popular work on Guilford Courthouse. Baker accepted the conventional view of the relationship between the two battles: Greene "seemed to draw more direct inspiration from the example Morgan had set at Cowpens... Keeping the advantages of [his] terrain and the example of Daniel Morgan in mind, Greene decided to divide his army into three lines."[205] Once again, a neat, three-line battle plan, conforming to eighteenth-century ideas of orderliness. Tradition held that Greene drew his neat three-line battle plan directly from Morgan at Cowpens. The power in this tradition has made understanding the actual tactics at Cowpens the predicate to a grasp of Greene's thinking at Guilford Courthouse.

The essential inquiry is to determine the reason the Lee version dominated the official version related by Morgan. Once committed to paper, the two versions contested for the popular imagination. Lee won, and Morgan lost. Determining the reason for Lee's victory is the next step in the winding narrative of Cowpens.

Lee's Version vs. Morgan's Version: A Comparison

Lee was not present at Cowpens. He was miles away, encamped with Greene near Cheraw. Lee was a born *raconteur* who loved stories. He loved battle equally, and his tale of Cowpens reflected his admiration for both. Sadly, it also reflected the fact he wrote it thirty years after the fact. Morgan, on the other hand, was

---

[204] Thomas E. Baker, *Another Such Victory: The Story of the American Defeat at Guilford Courthouse that Helped Win the War for Independence* (New York: Eastern Acorn Press, 1981).
[205] Baker, *Another Such Victory*, 43–44.

present at the battle and wrote his report to Greene two days later.[206] The indicia of credibility all pointed in favor of Morgan. What made Lee's version so popular?

The force and energy of Lee's prose drove his *Memoirs* into the forefront of contemporary histories. It remains a preferred starting point for military historians of the period. Lee's mind wielded an attention to detail that proved phenomenal many times. On the other hand, writing thirty years after the war and shortly before his death, his impressive memory failed him at the worst possible times.

Relying on Lee, usually fruitful, at times proved perilous. His narrative from Guilford Courthouse was long, and provided a rich ore of examples, more accessible than those from his much shorter tale of Cowpens. At Guilford Courthouse, he was the only memoirist who recalled such diverse facts as the temperature of the weather and the name of the commander of the rearward American artillery battery. At the same time, he confused the identities of the North Carolina militia commanders on Greene's first line, and switched the identification of the Guards battalions in the second and third line fighting. His version of the intense fighting on Greene's third line has enjoyed great credibility, but no one has accepted his description of the battlefield terrain. In one memorable example, he prepared an exciting memoir of the fighting around the New Garden Friends meeting house which preceded the main battle. However, he erroneously insisted the fighting was not at the New Garden meeting house, but at an entirely different institution. He added a long footnote decrying the contrary literature, which, of course, was right while he was wrong.[207] Good news, bad news; Lee unwittingly incorporated both into his narrative.

Lee offered ample advantages in his narratives. Lee's version of Cowpens formed part of his memoirs, a popular history intended to cater to the interests of the reading public. Aesthetically, Lee's version demonstrated the neatness and orderliness in vogue in battle plans of the day. Rigid lines of soldiers

---

206 Morgan to Greene, 19 January 1781, in Showman et al., *Greene*, 7:152.
207 Lee, *Memoirs*, 170–171, 172–174, 177.

dressed shoulder-to-shoulder impressed readers as well as generals. Substantively, Lee's version was easy to understand. As Lee told the story, each of the three lines was uniquely composed and charged with a distinct mission. It could not have been less complicated. In contrast, Morgan's narrative, a dry memorandum written for government files, lacked the literary panache Lee injected into his narrative. Morgan's content was much more complicated, and Hammond's map almost required an interpreter.

Lee's first line, the line closest to the British, consisted of skirmishers, advanced 150 yards in front of the second line.[208] The skirmishers were North Carolina and Georgia militia, grouped by state. The skirmishers deployed in a line, but were able to deviate to take cover behind trees or other objects of opportunity as they presented.[209] The North Carolina troops were on the right, commanded by Major Joseph McDowell,[210] while the Georgia militiamen, on the left, were commanded by Major John Cunningham.[211] The second line consisted of the main body of militia, South Carolina on the left, North Carolina on the right. Colonel Andrew Pickens commanded this main militia force.[212] The third line, commanded by Lieutenant Colonel Howard, provided the main fighting force. It held Morgan's Continental infantry and the two companies of Virginia militia, commanded by Captains Triplett and Taite.[213] These soldiers occupied the crest of the first small ridge line, about 150 yards behind the second militia line. The cavalry, under Lieutenant Colonel Washington, stationed itself as a reserve, behind a second small ridge.[214]

An interesting dissent to the latter point came from Lieu-

---

208 Lee, *Memoirs*, 131; Bartholomees, "Fight or Flee," 121.
209 Lee, *Memoirs*, 131; Bartholomees, "Fight or Flee," 121.
210 McDowell is the accepted spelling. A conflicting view was expressed by Samuel Hammond, who spelled it "McDowal." Johnson, *Traditions and Reminiscences*, 528–529.
211 Lee, *Memoirs*, 131; Morgan to Greene, 19 January 1781, in Showman et al., *Greene*, 7:153.
212 Lee, *Memoirs*, 131; Graham, *Morgan*, 297.
213 Lee, *Memoirs*, 131.
214 Lee, *Memoirs*, 131. The second ridge did not come from Lee, but from authors following in his wake, i.e., Johnson, *Life*, 1:377; Bartholomees, "Fight or Flee," 121.

tenant Colonel Howard. In a letter long years after the war, he wrote, "I do not think there was such an eminence; there was a slight rise in the ground; nor was Washington's horse posted behind it, but on the summit; for I had a full view of him."[215] So, as always at Cowpens, nothing is certain.

Nothing, except, that Lee's version had the advantage of believability. It was concise, innovative, brilliant. Everyone knew Cowpens had been a triumph for the Americans; here was an easy-to-grasp explanation. Skirmishers, then militia, then Continentals. Three neat lines of increasing deadliness. As the British moved forward, they mired deeper. People flocked to Lee's rendition and held it close to their breasts for two hundred years.

Cherished, certainly, but was it true? If one accepts Morgan as reporter as readily as Morgan as commander, then, no, it was fiction. Lest one idolize too quickly, this was the Morgan who, in this report, told his commander he had only eight hundred soldiers on the field.[216] So, with some measure of skepticism, the story turns to Morgan's report to Greene, to investigate what the Old Wagoner said about his battle plan, and compare it to Lee's version.

Morgan did not break his description down into three neat lines, so a comparison with the Lee version will not be problem-free. Morgan started with his major force: the Continentals under Howard. These, together with the Virginia militia under Major Triplett, formed on the forward ridge line, as described by Lee.[217] Morgan, however, added an important detail, one that can bedevil the unwary. He noted that this formation, the third line in Lee's account, was actually two lines: the Continentals and Virginians lined up in a double rank.

This kind of thing can prove controversial and problematic. Professional armies following the European fashion lined up in

---

[215] H. Lee, *Campaign of 1781 in the Carolinas with Remarks Historical and Critical on Johnson's Life of Greene* (Philadelphia, 1824), 97. This author, Light-Horse Harry Lee's son, wrote that he received Howard's letter shortly before publication in 1824. In his assertion, Howard was almost certainly wrong. Hammond joined the large numbers placing a second hill behind the first, Johnson, *Traditions and Reminiscences*, 527.
[216] Morgan to Greene, 19 January 1781, in Showman et al., *Greene*, 7:155.
[217] Morgan to Greene, 19 January 1781, in Showman et al., *Greene*, 7:153.

multiple ranks, of which three was the most common number.[218] The militia would not be expected to form in masses of multiple ranks. No one considered them the peers of the professional soldiers, and they lined up shoulder-to-shoulder, in a single line one man deep. The Continentals were different; they were a match for any professional European army. They used similar tactics. The problem for historians in later years was just that: they used customary tactics, so there was no need to describe their deployment. To cite one prominent example, at Guilford Courthouse, of the huge numbers of first-hand accounts of the fighting by the Continentals—Lee, Tarleton, Howard, Stedman, Greene, Cornwallis, and hundreds of memoirists, letter-writers, and pension-seekers—no one mentioned whether the Continentals lined up one deep, two deep, or any number deep. Everyone at the time knew how they deployed. People are less certain today. At Guilford Courthouse, given the number of soldiers on the line and the length of the line, the Continentals must have formed in a single line containing three close ranks. A line three men deep was the Continentals' preferred formation.[219] Its use would be expected, and not worth mentioning.

In contrast to Guilford Courthouse, Cowpens stood out as a battle in which someone commented on the Continentals' formation for battle. Morgan reported to Greene the Continentals and their Virginia associates deployed two ranks deep. Morgan's point was that his Continental line was stretched thin. The Continentals did not deploy in their typical formation of a single line of three close ranks. Two deep was unusual and worth mentioning. Simple geometry was the reason; there was too much lateral space to cover. Had they formed three men deep, the line would have been much too short.

Morgan stated that Washington and the cavalry were in the rear, positioned out of danger of musket fire, but close enough to the action to respond to emergencies.[220] Lee and his followers placed Washington behind the second ridge line. While Lee

---

218 Wright, *Continental Army*, 4; Jeremy Black, *Warfare in the Eighteenth Century* (London: Cassell, 1999), 158.
219 Wright, *Continental Army*, 4.
220 Morgan to Greene, 19 January 1781, in Showman et al., *Greene*, 7: 153.

made sense, Morgan's rendition had a different emphasis. He asserted that the reserve was in the rear of the Continentals "at such a Distance ... as not to be subjected to the Line of Fire directed at them."[221] In contrast with those historians in the Lee school who wrote that the cavalry was out of danger because they hid behind the ridge line, Morgan said it was simply a question of distance. Howard, in his critique of the Lee version, agreed, allowing at most for a slight rise in the ground, with Washington posted atop, not behind.[222]

To summarize, Lee said three lines: skirmishers, militia, Continentals. Thus far, Morgan has put a single line on the ground. The single line, with soldiers massed in double ranks, consisted of the Continentals and the Virginia militia units of former Continental soldiers serving in the capacity of regulars. Going forward, the comparisons will get more complicated.

The lack of any natural flank protection formed the basis of much of the criticism of Morgan's selection of Cowpens. Lee and those following behind him never really solved this problem, other than to suggest Morgan's genius compensated for the deficiency. The problem was more serious and merited more attention. An unprotected flank cost Hooker the Battle of Chancellorsville, and lost Pope the Battle of Second Bull Run. Morgan adopted a solution requiring more than his tactical skill. Morgan wrote that Colonel Andrew Pickens, "brave and valuable," commanded militia of North Carolina, Georgia, and South Carolina.[223]

Morgan posted Pickens "situated to guard the flanks."[224] This development presented a sea change from the three unique lines proposed by Lee. Pickens, no longer in the second line by himself, shrank to the flanks of the Continentals. A fall from grace for Pickens, but more importantly, a major change in the troop dispositions. Morgan's description of Pickens on the flanks of

---

221 Ibid.
222 H. Lee, *Campaign of 1781*, 97.
223 Including South Carolina was one more point of disagreement between Morgan and Lee. Lee had mentioned only North Carolina and Georgia, on reflection an obvious mistake given the location of the battle.
224 Morgan to Greene, 19 January 1781, in Showman et al., *Greene* 7:153.

the Continentals obviated any discussion of Lee's second, main line of militia: in Morgan's version, it did not exist.

Lee and Morgan diverged further as they depicted the front line. Lee described a very simple first line composed of skirmishers: North Carolinians under McDowell and Georgians under Cunningham. Later historians in the Lee school, working to mediate Lee and Morgan, added the details of McDowell on the right and Cunningham on the left. Morgan wrote that 150 yards in front of the Continentals, on the right, he posted Major Joseph McDowell of the North Carolina militia. On the left, he positioned Major John Cunningham of the Georgia militia.[225] Thus far, on the front line, Lee and Morgan were distinct, but not divergent. Morgan immediately disturbed the equilibrium. He posted a unit of South Carolina militia on McDowell's right, and another on Cunningham's left. This was a major disagreement with Lee's version. Not two, but four corps on this line, the one in front of the Continentals.

Was this, at last, the dedicated militia line, the equivalent of Lee's second line? No, not at all. These were riflemen.[226] Riflemen fought as skirmishers in irregular formations, not in conventional straight lines. Lee allowed only for "two light parties of militia" as skirmishers. Morgan described a massive force of four corps on his front line.[227] The two cannot be reconciled.

Several motivators propelled Lee's version into the forefront. He described a simple, obvious, and winning battle plan. Morgan lacked Lee's deftness with the pen, and left behind a memoir with no punch, no sense of the action, and, sadly, a measure of unclarity.

Morgan lacked Lee's literary acuity. One example may illustrate the differences. On selecting Cowpens as a battle site, Lee wrote of Morgan: "Confiding in his long tried fortune, conscious of his personal superiority in soldiership, and relying on the skill and courage of his troops, he adhered to his resolution." Lee's enthusiasm screamed from the written page. Morgan, on the

---

225 Ibid.
226 Hammond made this point clear, Johnson, *Traditions and Reminiscences*, 529.
227 Lee, *Memoirs*, 131; Morgan to Greene, 19 January 1781, in Showman et al., *Greene*, 7:154.

same point, wrote, "My Situation at the Cowpens enabled me to improve any Advantages I might gain, and to provide better for my own Security, should I be fortunate."[228] Morgan's dry recitation could not form a greater contrast with Lee's dynamic prose.

Clarity, or its lack, was a central distinction between the two. Lee was always sure of himself, forever precise to a fault. Even when Lee was wrong, he was certain. Lee insisted that all the militia on the field at Cowpens used rifles, not muskets.[229] Lee was mistaken. He had heard, or read, that Morgan used massed rifle fire, but either Lee or his sources, schooled in conventional tactics, were strangers to Morgan's innovation. Lee, failing to grasp the concept, guessed wrong when he put pen to paper.

Morgan's writing steered in the opposite direction. Even when he was right, he could be unclear. He posted Pickens "to guard the flanks" of the single main line. Right, left, or both? He placed a different unit on the right, so, by default, this put Pickens on the left. Lee would never have left something this important unspecified. For people who looked for a reason to disregard Morgan, this kind of unclarity was grist for their mill of criticism.

Two lines or three? The number of lines serves as a convenient shorthand for a deeper question. Was Morgan's new idea a defense in depth, or a creative use of the rifle? The analysis must look beyond Lee's skills as a storyteller, as well as his command of literary clarity. On any objective basis, there was every reason to believe Morgan, and no reason to doubt him. He was at Cowpens; Lee was not. He drew up the battle plan and put it into operation. Lee had no connection with the engagement other than to admire it after the fact. Lee, an extraordinary officer, detracted from his memoirs by writing them years after the war. Morgan wrote his report two days after the battle. Lee's adept prose did not clarify Morgan. All Lee managed to do was generate confusion that has lasted two hundred years.

The British, not in thrall to Lee's credentials either as com-

---

228 Lee, *Memoirs*, 131; Morgan to Greene, 19 January 1781, in Showman et al., *Greene*, 7:153.
229 Lee, *Memoirs*, 132n.

mander or *raconteur*, never joined in the latter's school of Cowpens history. The British sources rigidly held to the concept of two lines of Americans, not three. Tarleton and Stedman have been noted already; both asserted there were two lines of Americans. These two, and two more, must stand for the uncountable weight of British scholars. The first new one is Roderick Mackenzie, a British officer who served under Tarleton and took exception with the latter's self-justifying memoir.[230] Mackenzie, who was present at Cowpens, emphasized the Americans formed in two lines, militia in the front, regulars in the back, as described by Morgan.[231] The second new addition is British military historian John W. Fortescue, who prepared the official regimental history of one of the British units that fought at Cowpens.[232] Fortescue made it clear that there were two American lines at Cowpens, one militia, one regulars. Tarleton, Stedman, Mackenzie, and Fortescue represent the British scholarship on the American lines at Cowpens, and sharply contrast with the American literature in the Lee tradition.

A final point needs emphasis. There is no way to reconcile the Morgan and Lee versions. Many historians have tried to find some way to mediate the bodies of opposing concepts represented by two versus three lines. It cannot be done. As exemplified by his misidentification of the first line commanders at Guilford Courthouse, at times Lee was simply wrong. In this vein, Babits wrote that the battle plans reflected in Morgan's report and in Hammond's writings demonstrated that Morgan altered his planning from what he might do if attacked, to what he would do when attacked.[233]

Babits asserted that early in the evening of 16 January, Morgan planned to meet Tarleton's expected charge with a double envelopment. As more reinforcements arrived, Morgan changed the plan to a defense in depth, with Tarleton to con-

---

230 Roderick Mackenzie, *Strictures on Lt. Col. Tarleton's History of the Campaigns of 1780 and 1781 in the Southern Provinces of North America* (London, 1787).
231 Mackenzie, *Strictures*, 92, 97–98.
232 John W. Fortescue, *A History of the 17th Lancers* (1895; Project Gutenberg, 2022), 57, www.gutenberg.org/cache/epub/68270/pg68270-images.html.
233 Babits, *Devil*, 70.

front increasingly strong infantry lines as he moved forward through skirmishers and the main militia line to the Continental line.[234] Ultimately, this was the plan depicted after the fact in Lee's *Memoirs*.

Babits acknowledged, rightfully, that his thesis confirmed no part of Morgan, Hammond, or any of the three known contemporary maps of the battle.[235] In an effort to bridge this gap in the evidence, Babits postulated that Morgan "was very busy during the night" of 16 January.[236] Certainly, but this effort could not explain how Morgan's report, written after the battle concluded, would reflect preliminary planning he had abandoned days before. Further, Morgan's level of activity would never explain Hammond's map, prepared years later, by someone other than Morgan.

In the question of Lee versus Morgan, Morgan was the clear victor. Lee's version simply did not stand up to scrutiny, a point the British accepted from the beginning and Americans have been slow to recognize.

Babits's comments raised the matter of the three battlefield maps. The maps are known as the Hammond map, the Clove map, and the Pigree map. Of these, the Hammond map is the best known and easiest accessed. The text will focus on the Hammond map, but they are similar enough that to bring up one is to raise them all. While the three maps do not agree on all details, such as the identities of some commanders, all three confirm Morgan's version and disavow Lee and a defense in depth.

Morgan's Version in Detail

Morgan reported that on the evening of 16 January, Tarleton was twelve miles away.[237] The following morning, at an hour before daybreak, scouts told him that the British were five miles

---

234 Babits, *Devil*, 71.
235 Babits, *Devil*, 74.
236 Ibid.
237 Morgan to Greene, 19 January 1781, in Showman et al., *Greene*, 7:153.

distant. Morgan noted that once informed, "I hastened to form as good a Disposition as Circumstances would admit."[238]

Morgan and Hammond authored the most substantive original materials embodying the Morgan version of Cowpens. Many years after the battle, Hammond committed his recollection of Morgan's operations order of 16 January to paper. His memoir included two maps. The first map looked at troop dispositions before the battle; the second looked at actions during the fighting. Morgan prepared an after-action report to Greene, in which he discussed both his deployments as well as the course of the fighting. There were other sources, notably the many British witnesses and historians, but the British did not analyze the specifics of Morgan's troop dispositions. American authors were the best resources for information on the American forces. In looking to Americans after Morgan and Hammond, the reader will encounter authors in the Lee tradition, with the confusion engendered by some of the writers following Lee.

Hammond's memory was not flawless, and one needs to treat his materials with the same regard given to Lee and Howard: great Patriots and great soldiers, writing late in life, who may have had an occasional memory lapse. At times, Hammond's memory seemed to conflate the operations order of 16 January with the battle of 17 January. In such an instance, Hammond's material contrasted with Morgan's after-action report, which emphasized the battle. Hammond's map illustrated the operations order as well as it did the battle, which, although confusing, appears to have been his intention. Hammond drew "two armies formed for action" on the map, then suggested the map would also illustrate the action.[239]

Morgan started at the rear of the American formation. Never wordy, he noted tersely that Washington, commanding what he referred to as the 3rd Regiment of Dragoons, was in the rear and out of "the Line of Fire."[240] The British enjoyed a huge numerical advantage in cavalry. The point of leaving the

---
[238] Ibid.
[239] His words were, "the sketch annexed will give you a further illustration of the important event," Johnson, *Traditions and Reminiscences*, 529.
[240] Morgan to Greene, 19 January 1781, in Showman et al., *Greene*, 7:153.

American cavalry in the rear was to act as a reserve, to respond to incursions where needed, and to counterattack the British in the event an opportunity arose.[241] Hammond's writings, like Morgan's, suffered from a lack of clarity. Despite this shortcoming, they supplemented Morgan's lean prose. Hammond wrote that the cavalry would hold a position one or two hundred yards behind the Continental line. Hammond added a fact Morgan had omitted. In light of the American disadvantage in cavalry, Morgan augmented Washington's regular cavalry with forty-five mounted militiamen from South Carolina under Major McCall.[242] Hammond's map agreed with the descriptions of these troop dispositions.[243]

Moving forward from the rear, next in sequence was Morgan's main battle line. In the operations order, Morgan said he wanted Lieutenant Colonel Howard and the Maryland Continentals on his second line. He gave specific orders for flank protection. Howard would form an inclined line on his left, starting at his flank and going back 100 yards. On the right flank, he posted Triplett and his Virginia militia, and Captain Beaty commanding a South Carolina militia company, in an inclined line mirroring Howard's. Pickens, although mentioned in Hammond's memoir by name, received no task in the operations order. One may speculate on the reasons for an omission of this magnitude. The most likely was that Pickens's arrival occurred after Morgan issued the order.

Morgan infused changes into his battle plan as circumstances altered matters on the ground. He reflected these changes in his report. One change dealt with the regulars. He placed Howard, with the Continental infantry, on "rising ground," usually interpreted as the forward slope of the first elevation on the battle-

---

241 Ibid.
242 Johnson, *Traditions and Reminiscences*, 528, which referred to McCall as a colonel, a rank he would not hold until much later. Hammond did not specify a number of mounted militia; the number 45 comes from other sources, e.g., Johnson, *Life*, 1:375. Later authors contested the provenance of McCall and his soldiers, favoring Georgia for the former and North Carolina for the latter, e.g., Bartholomees, "Fight or Flee," 117.
243 Johnson, *Traditions and Reminiscences*, 529.

field.[244] Morgan incorporated Triplett and his Virginians into the Continental line, that is, he treated them as Continentals, and not as a militia company. A second major change, noted previously, was that he formed all these forces into a double rank. Hammond's map confirmed the change. It showed two ranks of Continentals in the line, the rear rank labeled as "The Continentals," and the forward rank as "Colonel Howard," leaving one to wonder what tricks his memory played. Whether the soldiers were denominated Continentals or Howard's, they were Maryland regular infantry, and formed the mainstay of Morgan's army. Standing with the Marylanders was a unit of Delaware regular infantry, discussed in more detail below. In much of the southern campaign, the Delawares fought alongside the Marylanders, often as part of the Marylanders.

The flanks of the Continental line received much attention in the writings from historians in the Lee tradition. On his flanks, Morgan implemented radical changes from the initial operations order. He posted the Augusta Rifles[245] under Captains Tate and Buchanan on Howard's right flank.[246] This modification left open his final dispositions for Howard's left flank. With Triplett integrated into Howard's line, events had overturned the flank protection portion of the operations order. Will Morgan leave Howard's left flank dangling in the air? That is: Will Morgan rely exclusively on his genius and improvisation, as Lee implied, or will he take concrete steps to defend the main line's left flank? Genius may take many forms.

Morgan wrote that Pickens, in command of militia units from North Carolina, South Carolina, and Georgia, was "situated to guard the flanks."[247] Having positioned Tate and Buchanan on Howard's right, did he intend Pickens to man both flanks, or just the left? Morgan was not clear. It defied logic to spread Pickens out and expect him to command soldiers on both sides of Howard's line, at least three hundred yards apart. Hammond's

---

[244] Morgan to Greene, 19 January 1781, in Showman et al., *Greene,* 7:153; Graham, *Morgan,* 295; Bartholomees, "Fight or Flee," 114, 120.
[245] Augusta, Virginia, not Augusta, Georgia.
[246] Morgan to Greene, 19 January 1781, in Showman et al., *Greene,* 7:154.
[247] Morgan to Greene, 19 January 1781, in Showman et al., *Greene,* 7:153.

map again supplemented Morgan's report. He showed Pickens on Howard's left flank, deployed in a single line three ranks deep.[248] Given the position of the Augusta Rifles on the right flank, this was the only configuration that made sense. Pickens and his formation of militia companies manned the main line's left flank. The fact they did so in depth made sense, as well. Morgan was a realist in his assessments of the capabilities of his militia soldiers. Much like Greene, he was skeptical of their ability to form in straight lines and match British professional soldiers in conventional warfare. Pickens's flanking force numbered approximately 200 men, meaning he had sufficient force to occupy his sector of the line in depth.[249] Morgan saw only futility and defeat in the traditional militia configuration of a single rank of men lined up shoulder-to-shoulder. Hence, three ranks of militia, a rare sight.

Hammond included Captain Beaty, from South Carolina, in the battle plan. Beaty was a militia commander tasked with protecting a sector of Howard's right flank. Beaty's name was absent from Morgan's narrative. Perhaps later sources can add clarification, or, at least, confirmation.

Sadly, only futility rewards those looking to later sources for help with Beaty. One good example is William Johnson, whose 1822 biography of Greene often proved valuable. In this instance, his writings proved otherwise. In Johnson's view, on Howard's right, Morgan posted two companies of Virginia militia, commanded by Triplett and Tate, with a company of Georgia militia under Captain Beatie. The latter was the same officer that Hammond had identified as Captain Beaty, from South Carolina. Seemingly, no source on Cowpens will completely agree with another. While Johnson may have confirmed Beaty's presence and mission, it opened the door to a much larger problem. Johnson provided for no flank protection on the left. Johnson relied on Lee's reconstruction of the battle. Triplett and Tate were names Johnson drew directly from Lee's memoir. In Morgan's scheme of the battle, left flank protection belonged

---

248 Johnson, *Traditions and Reminiscences*, 529.
249 Johnson, *Life*, 1:374, 1:377–378; cf. Lee, *Memoirs*, 127.

to Pickens. But Johnson, following Lee, could not agree. He had to put Pickens by himself in Lee's separate, second line of militia.[250] While Lee's story made for exciting reading, the plain fact was it made no sense. Johnson's work made it clear that if true, Lee's version allowed the left flank of Morgan's main line to dangle loosely in the wind, completely unprotected. As it developed, genius would take a smarter form.

James Graham's 1859 biography of Morgan provided a second good example of the perils inherent in later sources. Graham followed Morgan's version of the battle, but even with this refinement, found problems. Like all authors, he placed Howard on an eminence with the Continental infantry. In contrast to most, he placed Major Triplett, accompanied by a Captain Gilmore, on the left flank, with Captains Tate and Buchanan of the Augusta Rifles on the right.[251] Where did this leave Pickens? Graham never mentioned him. Placing Triplett on the left was a logical move. Morgan was clear that Tate and Buchanan were on the right. By default, Graham reasoned, Triplett must have been on the left. Ultimately, all these efforts at reconstructing a battle plan were guesses, a point proven in Graham's case by Pickens's startling absence. Historians will continue to provide guesses for years. At bottom, guesses are singularly unhelpful, and have obscured and confused what actually happened.

Morgan, supplemented by Hammond, and without the confusion of later writers, provided the bulk of the necessary information on American troop deployments. Washington, his regular cavalry, and the militia cavalry were in the rear as a reserve. Howard, with the Continental infantry, provided the main line in a double rank. William Seymour added that at least one Delaware company fought alongside the Marylanders in the main line.

Howard's flanks received layers of protection. There were two formations of Virginia militia: the Augusta Rifles, under Captains Tate and Buchanan, and a second formation, directly under Triplett. Triplett, senior by date of rank, was in com-

---

250 Johnson, *Life*, 1:378
251 Graham, *Morgan*, 295.

mand of the Virginians overall. Triplett's company, composed of Continental veterans, was integrated into Howard's line, not guarding the flanks. It made sense to put Triplett on the right. Tate and Buchanan, commanding the Augusta Rifles, stood on the right flank of Howard's line. Triplett, in overall command of the Virginians, stationed himself on the right to lead his company and oversee Tate and Buchanan at the same time. Pickens, commanding militia of three states, guarded Howard's left flank.

Hammond's map showed a plan very similar to the foregoing. There were some minor differences, and in these, Hammond erred. Hammond put Triplett on flank duty on the right, rather than as part of the main line. He added Captain Beaty on the right flank.

Hammond's comments return the discussion to Captain Beaty and his role in the battle for a final resolution. It was highly unlikely his unit occupied a sector on Howard's right flank. Morgan did not invest this kind of confidence in an ordinary militia unit. Only the August Rifles received an independent sector of the flank, but they were watched by Triplett and his company of former Continentals. As a South Carolina militia company, Beaty's unit would have been integrated into Pickens's command on the left flank, within a much larger number of militia from three states.

The main line consisted of Continentals and former Continentals, a picture consistent with Morgan's views on the relative utility of regular soldiers versus militiamen. Militia guarded both flanks of the main line. Pickens had nominal command of the militia on both flanks. As a practical matter, even a commander of Pickens's skill could not exercise command over two widely separated groups of men. To resolve this quandary, Morgan stationed Triplett on the right to command a unit in the line and oversee an adjoining militia formation on the right flank. Pickens maintained direct command of the large force of militia on the left flank.

At Cowpens, the armament of the soldiers played a role as significant as the staffing of the units. Morgan's presence put the infantry's weapons into a sharp focus not seen in other engagements. Morgan, a former rifleman and commander of a rifle regiment, understood the rifle and its usefulness, and in this he distinguished himself from his colleagues. Riflemen were special, often in their rarity. The musket was the standard military weapon of the age, as it was the standard civilian hunting weapon. The militiamen arrived for duty armed with whatever weapons they owned. There is no mention in the records of the weapons carried by the militia force on the left flank directly under Pickens, and this gap speaks volumes. Had they carried rifles, this development would have been noteworthy.[252] If they carried muskets, this information would have been well below the radar. The state of the record established that Pickens's forces carried what was expected of militia everywhere, the standard musket.[253]

Moving forward, matters became more complicated, especially in the wake of authors trying to explain Morgan's battle plan using Lee's narrative. Leaving Lee to one side, the story will focus on what the eyewitness accounts disclosed about the units, commanders, and weapons in front of the Continentals.

Hammond recalled the front line consisted of four units, all riflemen. These were led, from left to right, by Captain Donnolly,[254] of Georgia; Major McDowell, of North Carolina; Major Cunningham, of Georgia; and Hammond himself, from South Carolina, in command of the unit normally commanded by James McCall, who had been detailed to the cavalry.[255]

Morgan agreed, but expressed himself differently. He named

---

252 I.e., the Augusta Rifles.
253 Babits appears to be a dissenter, and seems to take the position that all of Pickens's militia were armed with rifles, Babits, *Devil*, 89–90, 92–93. In this, Babits is solidly in the Lee tradition. All agree the Continentals wielded muskets. Lee asserted that Morgan's militia, two-thirds of his infantry, were armed with rifles, Lee, *Memoirs*, 132n. Given the volume of fire produced by the militia, this mix of rifles and muskets would only be possible if, as Babits maintains, the rifle could be reloaded and fired in 15 seconds, *Devil*, 103. Babits is alone in this assertion, with other authors describing reloading and firing in the one-to-two-minute range, which would make a volume of fast, repeated rifle volleys impossible, Wright, "The Rifle in the American Revolution," 295.
254 Also spelled Donoly.
255 Johnson, *Traditions and Reminiscences*, 528, 529.

six officers in charge of units on his front line. McDowell and Cunningham he shared with Hammond. Morgan added four South Carolina colonels. At this stage in the war, a South Carolina militia unit with a full complement of officers had two colonels, one colonel in command, and one lieutenant colonel as his deputy.[256] Critical to understanding the front line was the fact that the units were composed entirely of riflemen.[257] As to the officers, Morgan, by naming four South Carolina militia colonels, meant he added two South Carolina units, that is, two colonels per unit. He stationed one unit each on the right and left of McDowell and Cunningham.[258]

Hammond and Morgan agreed on the strength of the first line. They also agreed very closely on the identities of the officers in command of the four front-line rifle units. Hammond stated, moving left to right: Donnolly, McDowell, Cunningham, and Hammond. Morgan held, again moving left to right: Hays and Hammond, Cunningham, McDowell, and Brandon and Thomas. In both cases, McCall was the actual commander of the end unit, but since Morgan had detailed him to the cavalry, Hammond, next in line, took command.

As with the main line, Morgan and Hammond disagreed in minor ways in the first line deployments. Perhaps the only matter of significance was Hammond's recollection that Morgan posted McDowell on the left and Cunningham on the right, while Morgan recorded the reverse. Babits asserted that Hammond had oriented his map incorrectly, as evidenced by the arrow in the middle. Misoriented, Hammond transposed left and right throughout his depictions of troop deployments.[259] Actually, entirely separate from the map, Hammond wrote in

---

[256] A. S. Salley, Jr., ed., *Col. William Hill's Memoirs of the Revolution* (Colombia, SC: The State Company, 1921), 6. Babits asserted that pension applications documented a rotating scheme by which some captains served under a major and lieutenant colonel one month, while the next month, the colonel and another major commanded the regiment. Babits, *Devil*, 29. It is not clear what advantages such a scheme, if it existed, might have produced.

[257] Manifest in Morgan's plan and execution, Hammond expressly stated the four units in the first line were riflemen, Johnson, *Traditions and Reminiscences*, 529.

[258] Morgan to Greene, 19 January 1781, in Showman et al., *Greene*, 7:153.

[259] Babits, *Devil*, 69.

his narrative that McDowell was on the left, Cunningham on the right.[260] Hammond, writing years after the battle, suffered a very minor lapse. The problem repeated in his treatment of Donnolly and Brandon, discussed below.

The differences between Hammond and Morgan in naming the first line commanders were part of a larger trend in Cowpens history, in which correctly identifying the commanders and units in the battle inevitably confounded the writer. Even with this uncertainty, Morgan and Hammond endowed a great deal of certainty. McDowell and Cunningham commanded rifle units in the first line. Cunningham was on the left, McDowell on the right, with the road separating the two. In light of McCall's delegation to the cavalry, his deputy, Hammond, commanded the rifle unit on the far left. For three of the four units on the first line, the eyewitnesses substantially agreed. The final unit remained controversial. It was either commanded by Donnolly from Georgia in the Hammond version, or by Brandon and Thomas from South Carolina in the Morgan version.

Donnolly or Brandon and Thomas? In disagreements between Morgan and Hammond, Morgan emerged as the most reliable source. Hammond's memory tended to conflate events. If Morgan had planned something in his operations order and events dictated a change in plans, Morgan proved the better resource on the change. Here, we take Morgan at his word. He originally planned four militia rifle units on the front line. He deployed all four. In order, they were commanded by Hays and Hammond, and Cunningham on the left; McDowell, and Brandon and Thomas, on the right. Donnolly was relegated to the flotsam and jetsam of history.

---

[260] Assuming the arrow represented Hammond's effort at orientation, it did not suggest any inclination to a seamless reversal of right and left. If, as Babits states, Green River Road was the British axis of advance, modern maps show historic Green River Road ran generally southeast to northwest. Accordingly, the arrow actually points generally south, but not due south; more like 190 degrees. There is nothing in 190 degrees to suggest a perfect transposition of right and left. Rather the opposite; 190 degrees is an awkward angle that suggests neither right nor left. The arrow, if it is directional, simply suggests Hammond, drawing from memory long years after the battle, had forgotten in which direction lay magnetic north, Johnson, *Traditions and Reminiscences*, 528.

Lossing dismissed Hammond's map as inconsistent with the official reports. In this assertion, Lossing was mistaken. Hammond's map agreed with Morgan in broad brush strokes: Continentals in the middle, riflemen out front, militia on the flanks, and cavalry in reserve. There were some very minor differences in the details. Ultimately, Hammond's map illustrated Morgan's battle plan and troop deployments well.

Other eyewitnesses left accounts of the battle. William Seymour prepared a brief, yet stirring memoir.[261] Seymour served as a sergeant major in the Delaware forces, one of the truly heroic units in the southern campaign. At one time a regiment, combat losses had shrunk the unit to two companies after the Battle of Camden.[262] Throughout a great deal of the campaign, the Delawares were attached to the Marylanders and, at times, fought as a unit of the Maryland forces. Seymour's narrative brought to bear the credibility of a soldier who served on the front line for most of the southern campaign.

Seymour's work was a journal, written contemporaneously with the events in the campaign. A soldier more than a wordsmith, his prose was clear enough to endorse what Morgan

---

261 William Seymour, *Journal of the Southern Expedition, 1780-1783* (Wilmington, DE, 1896).

262 The story of the Delaware Regiment could be a book in itself. The official U.S. Army history states the regiment was reduced to two companies after Camden, Wright, *Continental Army*, 273. Many sources state these were under the command of Captains Robert Kirkwood and Peter Jaquett, e.g., "American Delaware Regiments in the Continental Army," *Revolutionary War Continental Regiments*, www.revolutionarywar.us/continental-army/delaware. Lee, on the other hand, wrote there was only one Delaware company, commanded by "the brave captain Kirkwood," Lee, *Memoirs*, 96, 171. Seymour, the alpha and omega of all things Delaware, never mentioned any Captain Jaquett; e.g. Seymour, *Journal*, 8, 13, 18. A contrasting view was advanced by Major C. P. Bennett, a Delaware veteran and later Governor of Delaware, at "The Delaware Regiment in the Revolution," *The Pennsylvania Magazine of History and Biography* 9, no. 4 (Jan., 1886), 456. Major Bennett, who set down his memoir in 1836, asserted that after Camden, the former regiment was reduced to two companies, commanded by Kirkwood and Jaquett, Bennett, "Delaware," 459. However, Bennett noted only Kirkwood's presence at Cowpens. Despite Bennett's support, the name Jaquett seems to have disappeared from history, along with his company. However, the name Jaquett revived long enough for him to file a pension application in 1831, Pension Application of Peter Jaquett S46500, *Southern Campaign American Revolution Pension Statements and Rosters*. His application is *very* thin on wartime accomplishments, www.revwarapps.org/s46500.pdf.

wrote at the same time. Seymour noted a single line of militia in front of the line of Continentals, as related by Morgan, Hammond, and the British.

He stated that on 17 January 1781, "we were drawn up in order of battle."[263] As a Continental soldier, this meant his unit formed in the double line of Continentals that made up Morgan's main force. "The militia dismounted and were drawn up in front of the standing troops on the right and left flanks ... By this time the enemy advanced and attacked the militia in front, which they stood very well for some time until being overpowered by the superior number of the enemy."[264]

"The militia dismounted:" much of the militia infantry traveled by horse in between engagements. They would dismount to fall into battle formation. Seymour only mentioned one point that required explanation.[265] He reported the first line militia lined up on the flanks of the Continentals, 200 yards in front of the main battle line. He was not trying to say the first-line militia crowded into the sides of the battlefield and ignored the center. He made his point in his assertion that the enemy attacked the militia "in front," clarifying the militia line covered all the ground in advance of the Continentals.

Lieutenant Colonel Howard also left an eyewitness account, written years after the war. To reach Howard, a recapitulation of Morgan is necessary. Morgan reported "Capts Tate and Buchanan with Augusta Riflemen to support the right of the line."[266] Buchanan and Tate were Virginia militia officers in command of the Augusta Rifles. Morgan's sentence may have been awkward but his meaning was clear. Triplett, Tate, and Buchanan were part of the formation that included the Con-

---

263 Seymour, *Journal*, 13.
264 Ibid.
265 Additionally, he put the first line militia 200 yards in front of the Continentals. Morgan stated 150. Both numbers were estimates. Thomas Anderson was another Continental soldier leaving a memoir. Like Seymour, he recorded two lines of battle, Joseph Lee Boyle, "The Journal of Thomas Anderson, Delaware Regiment, Part 1, May 1780–March 1781," Journal of the American Revolution, July 25, 2023, www.allthingsliberty.com/2023/07/the-journal-of-thomas-anderson-delaware-regiment-part-1-may-1780-march-1781.
266 Morgan to Greene, 19 January 1781, in Showman et al., *Greene*, 7:154.

tinental infantry—"the line" as Morgan phrased it—and its flanking protection. Pickens deployed on the left flank of the Continentals. Triplett and his company were integrated into the main line, on the right. Tate and Buchanan, in command of the Augusta Rifles, guarded the right flank.

Hammond depicted Triplett guarding Howard's right, as well, and this conjunction of Morgan and Hammond brings the story to the fourth eyewitness, John Eager Howard. In a letter dating to years after the war, Howard disagreed with Morgan, and insisted that both Tate and Triplett were to the left of the Continentals.[267] With Tate and Triplett on the left, in Howard's view, Buchanan tacitly stood on the left with them. We will never reconcile these conflicting recollections. The witnesses' memories are too divergent to warrant an effort in trying. At bottom, Morgan, Howard, and Hammond performed better as commanders than as historians.

The quandary raised by Howard's memoir focused the story on a recurring theme. Should the narrative ignore the commander of the main battle line on a subject so basic as the composition of the line? *Yes.* One should overlook contemporary written records only when there is an overwhelming reason to do so. Morgan wrote his report contemporaneously with the events. Howard's letter dated from 40 years afterward. In this direct conflict, Morgan's report has the credibility of timing. Triplett was integrated into the main line on the right, and oversaw the actions of Tate and Buchanan on the right flank.[268]

Tarleton was an eyewitness to the events of the battle. Tarleton's report on the battle discussed an American troop deployment very close to that described by Morgan. Tarleton wrote that he faced a front line of militia, a main line of Continental infantry and what he termed "backwoodsmen," and a reserve

---

267 H. Lee, *Campaign of 1781*, 97.
268 Babits stationed Triplett on the left flank, and Tate on the right flank, Babits, *Devil*, 76–77. One problem with this solution is from Babits's book: he quoted a pension application of a militiaman who stated he was stationed in between McDowell and Triplett, *Devil*, 73. Babits accepted that McDowell was on the right, *Devil*, 74, 83, 85. If so, his militiaman could not have been between McDowell and Triplett if, as Babits asserted, Triplett was on the left.

of cavalry.[269] Setting aside the differences in numbers, the only distinction between Morgan and Tarleton was the single line of Continental infantry. Actually, this was not a disagreement. Tarleton knew the Continentals, like the British, lined up in multiple ranks when deployed for battle. He saw one formation of Continentals, but whether they were two or three ranks, or any number of ranks, was nothing meriting comment in his report to Cornwallis.[270]

British Forces

The estimates of British troop strength ranged from a low of six hundred to a high of 1150, with Stedman's "about 1,000" serving as an appropriate assessment. Who was in this thousand-man army? Stedman asserted Cornwallis added to Tarleton's Legion the 7th Regiment, the light infantry, the 1st battalion of the 71st Regiment, 350 cavalry, two artillery pieces, and a staff of artillerymen to go with them. Tarleton wrote that Cornwallis originally dispatched him with his Legion of cavalry and infantry, the first battalion of the 71st Regiment, and two artillery pieces. Later, he added the 7th Regiment and the 17th Light Dragoons. Although the two authors expressed themselves differently, they arrived at very similar totals. Tarleton wrote he had 950 men, exclusive of artillery, and, of course, this was almost identical with Stedman's accounting.[271]

The term "regiment" conjures a vision of a large formation of soldiers. While true in some cases, the idea is misleading here.[272] Tarleton received about two hundred members of

---

269 Tarleton, *Campaigns*, 222.
270 Tarleton's account is a good example of the British versions generally. They confirm Morgan's report, but are short on identification of the American units.
271 Stedman, *History*, 2:318; Tarleton, *Campaigns*, 217. On this point, Tarleton was more precise. As he asserted, after he was underway, he convinced Cornwallis to add the 7th Regiment and the 17th Light Dragoons. Ultimately, the two authors agreed on the composition of the force and its size.
272 There are many resources on the size of a British regiment, with some variance in numbers. A mild consensus puts the size of a full-strength British regiment at 477 officers and men divided into 10 companies, e.g., Edward S. Curtis, *Organization of*

the 7th Regiment and fifty dragoons from the 17th Regiment of Light Dragoons.[273] At the time, these men constituted these units' entire strength. An official history of the 7th Regiment noted that disease decimated the unit while fighting in South Carolina. Its entire complement was no more than nine officers and 167 enlisted men, mostly new recruits intended for garrison duty at Ninety-Six.[274] Tarleton's two complete regiments added fewer than 250 soldiers to his detachment. Although Tarleton's count of regiments may impress, the reality was more mundane. While these men were British regulars, the soldiers of the 7th were not seasoned professionals.

Stedman and Tarleton identified the British units in broad strokes. Refining the list of British units at Cowpens has proven surprisingly difficult. There are hundreds of sources across the spectrum of quality advocating an uncounted number of opinions. Rather than detail the myriad positions, one example must stand for all. Babits devoted much work in identifying the involved British units. He determined the light infantry of the 16th Regiment fought at Cowpens.[275] Opposing Babits stood a history published by the U.S. Army's Command and General Staff College. The author, Major Jesse T. Pearson, asserted that the 16th Regiment was not in Cornwallis's army. In January 1781, Cornwallis's only British infantry regiments were the 7th, 23rd, 33rd, 63rd, 64th, and 71st. Major Pearson's list included no part of the 16th Regiment. Either Babits or Pearson had erred. In this regard, the official history of the 16th Regiment noted it was stationed in Florida at the time, fighting heroically against a much larger Spanish force.[276]

Mackenzie numbered among those believing Tarleton's detachment included the light infantry of the 16th Regiment.[277]

---

the *British Army in the American Revolution* (New Haven: Yale University Press, 1926), 4.
273 Tarleton, *Campaigns*, 217.
274 J. P. Kelleher, "1781," *The 7th. Royal Fusiliers and Their Part in the American War of Independence 1775–1781 and New Orleans 1815* (n.d.), xvi, www.fusiliermuseumlondon.org/download?id=12390.
275 Babits, *Devil*, 45.
276 "A Brief History of the Regiment between 1688 and 2009, *The 16th Regiment of Foot*, www.bedfordregiment.org.uk/history/16thfoothistory.html.
277 Mackenzie, *Strictures*, 112.

Mackenzie was an eyewitness; the other sources, albeit secondary, included two unimpeachable official sources. Yet, someone was wrong.

When necessity obligates recourse to secondary authorities, official sources, where they exist, may suggest advantages over privately published ones. The National Park Service's website on Cowpens includes an enumeration of British units that formed a bridge between the lack of detail in the eighteenth-century sources and the granular approach seen in many modern histories. Thus, the official position of the Park Service: Tarleton led the 7th Regiment, the 17th Light Dragoons, the 1st Battalion of the 71st Regiment, and Tarleton's Legion. Cornwallis also assigned Tarleton two artillery pieces, staffed by 50 artillerymen.[278] As with Major Pearson, the Park Service mentioned nothing of the 16th Regiment.

Stedman included the light infantry in his broad brushstrokes at Tarleton's detachment. The term *light infantry* echoed repeatedly in the source materials. The basics were simple. Each British regiment contained two specialized units. These were a company each of grenadiers and light infantry, intended for special duties. The light infantry, designed to be especially mobile, was usually assigned front or flank duty. For example, once formed for battle, it was not unusual for an army commander to detach all the light infantry and grenadier companies from their regiments, and consolidate them to fight as two separate battalions, one on the right flank and one on the left.[279] In the case of Cowpens, the identities of the light infantry companies have become controversial. Stedman unwittingly started the problem: he wrote only that Cornwallis assigned Tarleton "the light and legion infantry."[280] Tarleton was less help, usually specifying only his own Legion infantry.[281]

Mackenzie enumerated the light infantry units he recalled in Tarleton's forces. He wrote that within the battalion of light

---

278 National Park Service, "British Units at the Cowpens," www.nps.gov/cowp/learn/historyculture/british-units-at-the-cowpens.htm.
279 Babits, *Devil*, 45.
280 Stedman, *History*, 2:318.
281 E.g., Tarleton, *Campaigns*, 217.

infantry under Tarleton, there were four companies: the light infantry companies of the 16th Regiment, the 1st Battalion of the 71st Regiment, the 2nd Battalion of the 71st Regiment, and the Royal Prince of Wales American Regiment.[282]

The 71st Regiment was organized differently from other British regiments. It was exactly twice the customary size. So, while the 63rd Regiment would normally have 10 companies, the 71st had 20, so each battalion of the 71st Regiment was the size of a conventional regiment.[283] As a double-strength unit, the 71st had two light infantry companies, confirming Mackenzie.

Mackenzie added clarity to the situation. In effect, Tarleton had two subsections of light infantry. First, he had the light infantry of the 1st Battalion of the 71st Regiment, a unit assigned to him in its entirety. Second, he had three other light infantry companies delegated by themselves, the light infantry of the 2nd Battalion of the 71st Regiment, the 16th Regiment, and the Prince of Wales Regiment. Tarleton deployed the light infantry into a single battalion. With the exception of one occasion by Tarleton himself, the sources spoke of the light infantry as a unified group, not divided into its organic components.

The best reading of Tarleton showed four light infantry companies in his detachment. In the single enumeration of his light infantry, he noted three companies forming his advanced guard while the 1st Battalion of the 71st Regiment marched separately. While there is ambiguity, the solution appears to be that at this point in events, the light infantry of the 1st Battalion of the 71st remained integrated with the rest of the regiment. Babits elicited four companies of light infantry from these materials, the light infantry companies of the Prince of Wales Regiment, the 1st battalion of the 71st Regiment, the 2nd battalion of the 71st Regiment, and the 16th Regiment.[284] Consistent with Mackenzie, Babits was correct, and Tarleton commanded four compa-

---

282 Mackenzie, *Strictures*, 112. Stedman indirectly confirmed the count of four light infantry companies, noting there were four at the Battle of Camden, *History*, 2:207.
283 Don N. Hagist, "Untangling British Army Ranks," *Journal of the American Revolution*, May 19, 2016, www.allthingsliberty.com/2016/05/untangling-british-army-ranks.
284 Tarleton, *Campaigns*, 221; Babits, *Devil*, 45.

nies of light infantry at Cowpens.

How does this solution resolve the problem of the 16th Regiment, at the time committed to war in Spanish Florida? The light infantry company of a regiment could be detached and redeployed. Tarleton received the light infantry of the Prince of Wales Regiment while the latter retained other duties. Similarly, the light infantry of a regiment in Florida could be detached and sent to South Carolina.

Stedman wrote of Cornwallis's difficulties after Cowpens, in which Tarleton lost all the light infantry assigned him. Stedman wrote as if Tarleton lost all of the light infantry in Cornwallis's army:

> The disappointment was galling ... But another consequence of the defeat was of a still more serious nature: The loss of the light troops, at all times necessary to any army, but on a march through a woody and thinly settled country, almost indispensable, was not to be repaired.[285]

One can read Stedman's passage to suggest that Cornwallis denuded the main army of light infantry, and gave it all to Tarleton. Another possibility was that of all the losses incurred by Tarleton at Cowpens, the loss of the light infantry cut the deepest. Either way, the loss of the light infantry, partial or complete, was one of the most important consequences of the Battle of Cowpens. Stedman was correct that Cornwallis felt its loss in the months that followed in North Carolina. Was the destruction partial or total?

The British Army in America underwent a reorganization early in the war. Many regiments were deprived of their specialized units, which were merged into permanent, exclusive formations of light infantry and grenadiers.[286] Viewed through this lens, Cornwallis's other regiments, such as the 63rd and 64th, would have had no light infantry at the time of Cowpens. Any discussion of the light infantry in Cornwallis's army after Cowpens was limited to the Guards, whose light troops joined

285 Stedman, *History*, 2:325.
286 Hugh H. B. Cook, *The North Staffordshire Regiment* (London: Lee Cooper Ltd., 1970), 10–11, 19, 22.

Cornwallis with Leslie after Cowpens.[287] Stedman was right. Cornwallis gave Tarleton all his light infantry. The loss of all the light troops at Cowpens was a severe blow, felt more deeply than the numbers suggested.

The question of the light infantry of the Prince of Wales American Regiment opened the subject of Loyalist forces in Tarleton's detachment, another area of controversy. Cornwallis made use of Loyalist forces throughout the campaign. William Johnson asserted Tarleton had fifty Tory militiamen in his army.[288] While Johnson was incorrect in this assertion, there was no question Tarleton had more Loyalists than those in his Legion.

The question of the Loyalist force was complicated, more so than with the Patriot militia. The nomenclature reflected the problem. Tarleton's Legion was a Loyalist force. They were "Provincials," and not "militia." The Tory militia was the military counterpart of the Patriot militia, enlisted for short terms of service and trained haphazardly. Provincials were the equals of British regulars, the products of diligent training and hard experience. Cornwallis deployed Tarleton's Legion as he would regulars, a treatment they had earned. With Cornwallis's blessing, a cadre of Provincial soldiers under Patrick Ferguson provided leadership for a significantly larger formation of Tory militia at King's Mountain.

The number of Loyalists on the field at Cowpens remains uncertain. Babits asserted that twenty-five to fifty men from the Royal Prince of Wales American Regiment were present.[289] Tarleton's Legion fielded about 530 men.[290]

---

287 E.g., Tarleton, *Campaigns*, 231; Cornwallis to Germain, 17 March 1781, in Ross, *Cornwallis*, 1:507; Colonel Mac Kinnon, *Origin and Services of the Coldstream Guards*, 2 vols. (London, 1833), 2:11.

288 Johnson, *Life*, 1:374. Johnson is one author who confused the matter by referring to Provincial units as regulars. Hence, his actual language was that Tarleton commanded 1,050 "regulars" and 50 "loyalists." Tarleton actually had many regulars and some Provincials. It is highly unlikely he fielded any militia.

289 Babits, *Devil*, 45.

290 Benjamin Franklin Stevens, *The Campaign in Virginia 1781. An Exact Reprint of Six Rare Manuscripts on the Clinton-Cornwallis Controversy with Numerous Very Important Unpublished Manuscript Notes by Sir Henry Clinton K.B. and the Omitted and Hitherto Unpublished Portions of the Letters in Their Appendices Added from the Original Manuscripts*, 2 vols. (Lon-

Tarleton grouped his light infantry into a single battalion for the battle. This fact meant the Loyalists fought side-by-side with the British regulars, the expected use of Provincial soldiers. After years of war, regulars and Provincials deployed interchangeably.

Seeing regulars and Provincials fighting side by side brings the story to the central question, the way in which Tarleton organized these men to fight Morgan, that is, the British order of battle. Tarleton marched toward the battle with the Legion infantry and three companies of light infantry in the vanguard; the 7th Regiment, the artillery, and the 1st battalion of the 71st Regiment in the main body; and the 17th Light Dragoons and Legion dragoons in the rear. He soon transferred two troops of dragoons into the vanguard.[291]

Once the British saw the main force of the Americans, Tarleton deployed his men in line of battle. He had the troops get rid of all their gear, excepting only weapons and ammunition; this was not an unusual step in preparing for fighting. He ordered the light infantry to file to the right until they were even with the American left flank. He sent the Legion infantry to form on the left of the light infantry. He began artillery shelling of the Americans, and ordered the line forward to a point within 300 yards of the Americans; this put his men at the edge of enemy rifle range. He moved the 7th Regiment to the left of the Legion infantry; this move put the 7th to the left of the road marking the center of the battlefield. He gave the 7th Regiment one of the two artillery pieces, stationed on the unit's right. Moving the 7th to the left of the Legion extended the British line well beyond the American right flank, a matter that will rapidly gain significance.

Tarleton assigned fifty dragoons to each flank of the British line, both to protect his flanks as well as threaten those of the Americans. He created a reserve of the 1st Battalion of the 71st

---

don, 1888), 1:376.

291 Tarleton, *Campaigns*, 221. Tarleton did not identify the source of the two troops moved to the front. He stated they were commanded by Captain Ogilvie, also spelled Ogilvy. Tarleton claimed Ogilvie as an officer of the Legion; Babits stated Ogilvie was an officer of the 17th detailed to the Legion, Babits, *Devil*, 47. Taken together, these positions suggest, but do not prove, the men led by Ogilvie were Legion dragoons.

Regiment, and posted it farther left, 150 yards to the rear of the line. He added two hundred cavalrymen to the reserve. Tarleton was ready to meet Morgan.[292]

Historians striving for precision have found gaps in Tarleton's dispositions. These gaps were literary, not military. He covered his ground very well. He failed to explain his moves completely.

One basic problem was the artillery. He assigned one grasshopper to the 7th Regiment, posted immediately left of the road. There was no obvious, logical emplacement for the second. Most commanders at the time posted artillery in the center, to be able to create damage across the entire opposing line. With one piece on the left, the traditional placement of the second would be in the road or immediately right of it.

A second problem was identifying the cavalry assigned to the three locations designated for mounted soldiers: right flank, left flank, and reserve. Tarleton commanded one large unit of Legion cavalry and one small unit of regulars. Where were they? Three reconstructions follow.

The American Battlefield Trust published a map of the battlefield, with details of the action.[293] The British order of battle at the opening of the fighting showed a line, going from left to right: the 7th Regiment, one artillery piece, Legion infantry, another artillery piece, light infantry, and the 17th Light Dragoons. The 71st was in reserve with the Legion cavalry. There was at least one omission. There was no unit of fifty dragoons on the British left. This error derives from trying to blend the Lee and Morgan narratives, and was the same mistake made 150 years earlier by William Johnson. The Trust opted for the 17th Light Dragoons to supply the dragoons on the right, with the Legion cavalry in reserve. One may reverse some piece of the mounted forces.

Babits hypothesized the British line as Legion Dragoons on the left flank; 7th Regiment, with a cannon in their midst; a second cannon directly in Green River Road, marking the middle of the line; Legion Infantry; Light Infantry; and the

---

292 Tarleton, *Campaigns*, 222.
293 "Cowpens Battle Map," *American Battlefield Trust*, www.battlefields.org/learn/maps/cowpens-january-17-1781.

17th Light Dragoons on the right flank.[294] He placed the 71st in reserve. While Babits discussed in his text the two hundred reserve cavalry, none of these horsemen appeared on either of his two maps depicting the opening order of battle, nor did he speculate on the identity of the cavalry unit held in reserve. As with the American Battlefield Trust reconstruction, the identities of the cavalry units may be shuffled.

A third guess was advanced by Lieutenant Colonel Moncure.[295] Moncure published a map which depicted the British line, in order, from left to right: Legion Cavalry on the left flank; 7th Regiment; one artillery piece; an unidentified infantry unit; a second artillery piece on Green River Road, directly marking the center; Legion infantry; light infantry; and the 17th Light Dragoons on the right flank. In reserve were the 71st and more Legion cavalry. What he said made sense, but the unidentified unit was a puzzle. He seemed to be saying that the Legion infantry started on the right side of the road and moved to the left side. The unit kept its position in line, but moved from the right of center to the left of center of the battlefield. With this understanding, Moncure's reconstruction covered the battlefield using information that tallied with the original sources. Where the sources left gaps, Moncure filled them in a manner consistent with eighteenth-century usages. As with the other two reconstructions, one may shuffle the mounted units.

The mounted troops have created the most controversy. Morgan left one ambiguous clue: "Lt Colonel Tarleton with his Cavalry was posted in the Rear of his Line."[296] Ambiguous, in that on 17 January, the 17th Light Dragoons were as much Tarleton's cavalry as the Legion. Will the evidence allow a resolution of this ambiguity?

Actually, the Moncure reconstruction pushed the evidence as far as it would go. The official history of the 17th Light Dragoons stated that "the loose expression legion-cavalry is so often used to cover the whole of the mounted force under Tarleton's

---

294 Babits, *Devil*, 84, 85, 91.
295 Moncure, *Staff Ride*, 49.
296 Morgan to Greene, 19 January 1781, in Showman et al., *Greene*, 7:154.

command, that it is frequently difficult to distinguish the detachment of the Seventeenth from the irregulars."[297] By irregulars, the author meant Tarleton's Legion. The author had a point: the identities of the mounted units were blank slates. He went on to describe the mounted units in the battle, and in doing so, never mentioned the 17th's role or its position in it:

> The 7th Foot and legion infantry formed [Tarleton's] first line, flanked on each side by a troop of cavalry; the 71st Foot and remainder of the cavalry were held in reserve. The Americans were drawn up in two lines, whereof the first was easily broken, but the second stood firm and fought hard. Seeing that his infantry attack was failing, Tarleton ordered the troop of cavalry on the right flank to charge, which it duly did under a very heavy fire, but being unsupported, was driven back by Morgan's cavalry with some loss.[298]

The official regimental history relied on the records and the institutional memory of the unit. If the regiment did not know which flank it was on, one may rest assured there was no way to determine which cavalry unit was where in Tarleton's order of battle.

Morgan's Strategy

Morgan was a terse writer. His report to Greene disclosed nothing of his strategy. He revealed his thinking only through the bare bones of his deployments. The literature contains much discussion of his battle plan, exclusively in secondary sources. Much of the lore of Cowpens, including much from Morgan, found preservation in the oral tradition. Two authors proved instrumental in their work with the oral tradition, James Graham[299] and Joseph Johnson.[300]

---

297 Fortescue, *17th Lancers*, 63.
298 Fortescue, *17th Lancers*, 57.
299 James Graham, *The Life of General Daniel Morgan, of the Virginia Line of the Army of the United States, With Portions of His Correspondence, Compiled from Authentic Sources*, New York, 1859.
300 Johnson, Joseph. *Traditions and Reminiscences, Chiefly of the American Revolution in the*

The rifle formed the centerpiece of Morgan's strategy. The militiamen on the first line carried rifles. This stratagem underscored the fact that Morgan comprehended the combat power of the rifle. The rifle had the advantage of much greater accuracy at longer ranges than the standard musket. In the hands of an experienced backwoodsman, it was deadly. The disadvantage was speed. A rifle could take one to two minutes for even a competent rifleman to reload. A musket could be reloaded three or four times a minute.[301] John Wright, a twentieth century expert in the field, explained the differences in reloading the two weapons:

> The rifle was much slower than the musket, about three to one. This was due to the laborious loading process. The bullet had to fit very tightly, to take the rifling, and so was forced in with an iron rod about six inches long and a wooden mallet, then driven home with the ramrod.[302]

There was one other difference of note. The musket could accommodate a bayonet, a rifle could not. American riflemen were useless in close combat against British soldiers with fixed bayonets.[303]

The accuracy of the American rifle at long distances was tantalizing, intoxicating. The rifle made it possible to eliminate the British command structure before the main body of British soldiers advanced close enough to use their muskets effectively. This practice, seemingly valuable, was oddly controversial. William Johnson noted that "a strange inconsistency of idea

---

South: Including Biographical Sketches, Incidents, and Anecdotes, Few of Which Have Been Published, Particularly of Residents in the Upper Country. Charleston, 1851.

301 John W. Wright, "The Rifle in the American Revolution," *The American Historical Review* 29 (no. 2, Jan. 1924), 295; Mark Maloy, "Small Arms of the Revolution," *American Battlefield Trust,* www.battlefields.org/learn/articles/small-arms-revolution. These figures contrast those provided by Babits, who asserted "experienced riflemen could fire one shot every fifteen seconds on a good day," Babits, *Devil,* 14. On this point, Babits misjudged. For the reasons Wright explained, reloading and firing the rifle was significantly slower than reloading and firing the musket, and not, as Babits asserted, twice as fast.

302 Wright, "The Rifle in the American Revolution," 295.

303 Wright, "The Rifle in the American Revolution," 295, 297.

prevails among military men on this subject. They justify the employment of marksmen, yet affect to execrate the direction of their skill to the use to which they know it will be applied."[304] Gentlemen, apparently, did not do this sort of thing. Morgan held no such internal conflict. He put the riflemen on the front line to do damage, and the most damage they could do was eliminate the enemy leadership.

How many rifles did Morgan mass on the front line? The traditional count of militia at Cowpens was 560 men. Of these, Morgan put four units of riflemen on the front line, and the Augusta Rifles on the right flank of the main battle line. Morgan and Hammond, even Lee, were reticent on the size of these units, including the basic point whether they were companies, battalions, or regiments.[305]

Whether they called themselves companies or regiments, in actuality they were company sized. They were hastily assembled and attached to Morgan on the march. They had no opportunity to achieve anything close to full strength. Babits's accounting of the size of the group of front-line militia units was about 150 riflemen.[306] This represented a huge contingent of rifles, with the capability to do significant damage to the British command structure. At the same time, it left about four hundred militiamen to divide between the Augusta Rifles on the right of the Continentals and Pickens's conventional militia armed with muskets on the left.[307]

What were Morgan's orders to the 150 men on the front line? For that matter, what were his orders to the militia generally?

---

304 Johnson, *Life*, 1:378.

305 Babits emphasized the problems inherent in discussing the size of militia units, given the leanness of many records. He hypothesized that a militia regiment numbered between 100 and 300 soldiers if at full strength, but, at the same time, even when a field grade officer commanded a unit, the unit rarely exceeded 200 soldiers, Babits, *Devil*, 31.

306 As with regiments, Babits discussed the difficulties in estimating sizes of militia companies. He concluded militia captains rarely commanded units larger than 40 men, and a company could easily number twenty or thirty soldiers, Babits, *Devil*, 31.

307 The Continentals carried muskets, as did Pickens's militia on the left flank, a total of approximately six hundred soldiers. The first line militiamen and the Augusta Rifles on the right flank, about 250 men, carried rifles. The total allocation of riflemen was about one-half of the militiamen, one-quarter of the total force.

These questions have generated intense controversy since the battle. As with the issue of two versus three lines, while important at Cowpens, they reached a climax in the study of Guilford Courthouse. The traditional view holds that Greene at Guilford Courthouse, just as he used Morgan's three-line battle plan, used Morgan's orders to the militia as a template.

Questions focus on two aspects of Morgan's orders. First, did Morgan order the riflemen to identify and shoot British officers? Second, and more importantly, how many shots did he want from the militia? Much ink has been spilled in debating these issues.

Adherents to the traditional view believe that Morgan asked for two volleys from the militia at Cowpens. Greene, following suit, did the same at Guilford Courthouse. As one example among many, historian Thomas Baker set out the accepted view:

> Morgan gave [the militia] a limited, attainable objective: Fire two rounds, then fall back, leaving the Continentals to finish off the redcoats... [Greene's] instructions to the militiamen, like those of Morgan at Cowpens, were pointedly simple: Fire two volleys at the advancing British, then fall back with their commander's blessings.[308]

Tradition has always insisted that Morgan wanted a limited number of firings from the militia. How limited is the question.

Thomas Young was a young militia recruit serving at Cowpens. His story is one of the oral histories preserved by Joseph Johnson. According to Young, Morgan told the militia: "Just hold up your heads, boys, give them three fires, and you will be free."[309] Lee was a prominent early advocate of the opposing view, insisting Morgan wanted only two volleys.[310] William Johnson, Greene's biographer, exemplified many authors who followed Lee, noting Morgan wanted two volleys. Johnson wrote in 1822. Proving the enduring force of the Lee tradition, John Buchanan, writing in 1997, said the same thing.[311]

308 Baker, *Another Such Victory*, 45–47.
309 Johnson, *Traditions and Reminiscences*, 449.
310 Lee, *Memoirs*, 131.
311 Buchanan, *Guilford Courthouse*, 320.

Bartholomees, a historian firmly in the Lee school, wrote in 1978. His work exemplified the problem with downstream consequences in dealing with the question of two versus three volleys. He wrote that there was a legitimate controversy in the question of two versus three volleys in Greene's orders.[312] But at Cowpens, he rigidly insisted Morgan wanted two.[313]

Thomas Young, an eyewitness, asserted the number was three. Starting with Lee, a number of non-eyewitnesses said it was two. Lee won the debate with Morgan on how history would view the battle plan, as exemplified in the question of two versus three lines of battle. The number of volleys was a second debate within the disagreements between Lee and Morgan. Again, it was a debate Lee won.

It was a debate Lee won regardless of merit. In the issue of two lines of battle versus three, Lee's position directly contradicted Morgan, the author of the battle plan and the general who put it into action. Lee's contrary position lacked substance and foundation. His position on two volleys stands in the same position. Lee was not present at Cowpens. He never disclosed his sources. He may have discussed the battle with veterans; he may as well have read contemporary histories and filled in the blanks with his own opinions. Either way, his position on two volleys reached the public wrapped in his exciting, literary narrative. The book's accessibility and attractiveness propelled it to popularity, and with it, the idea of two volleys.

The debate of two versus three volleys, critical at Guilford Courthouse, was much less so at Cowpens. One may understand the course of the battle perfectly using either number. The critical piece for Cowpens was the larger question whether Morgan limited the number of volleys. That is, did Morgan intentionally reduce the expectations he gave to the militia? The answer was

---

312 Bartholomees, "Fight or Flee," 177. Although beyond the scope of this book, the question of an order by Greene limiting the number of militia volleys at Guilford Courthouse rests on extremely thin evidence. The fountainhead of the tradition lay in a sycophantic work by Greene's grandson who awkwardly insisted his grandfather wanted three volleys, George Washington Greene, *The Life of Nathanael Greene, Major-General in the Army of the Revolution*, 3 vols. (Boston, 1867–1884).
313 Bartholomees, "Fight or Flee," 121.

yes, without question; the militia could fire a limited number of volleys and retire to the rear honorably.

The question actually was more nuanced than the simple arithmetic of two versus three. Did Morgan want a limited number of volleys from the riflemen on the front line, from the regular militiamen on the second line, or both? Morgan and Hammond said nothing. Morgan acknowledged giving orders to the militia, but never said what was in them.[314]

Graham, in his biography of Morgan, preserved an oral history that held Morgan gave explicit instructions to the riflemen on the front line:

> Riding up to the marksmen in the front line, he directed them to take the cover of the trees, and upon the advance of the enemy's line within good shooting distance, to show whether they were entitled to the reputation of brave men and good shots. They were directed to retire as the enemy advanced, seeking shelter from the trees, as opportunity might offer, loading and firing until they reached the main body of the militia, with whom they were then to act.[315]

Graham insisted Morgan wanted two firings from the regular militia.[316] Bartholomees took much the same position, writing that the riflemen were to shoot as many rounds as time permitted, then withdraw, but the regular militiamen were obligated to two volleys before withdrawal.[317]

Although in error on the question of two versus three firings, the position of Graham and Bartholomees had merit. The logic of necessity dictated treating the riflemen and musketmen differently. As discussed earlier, even an experienced rifleman could take two minutes to reload a rifle. On the other hand, assuming the regular militia lined up with their weapons loaded, they could fire, then reload and fire again, in much less than half a minute. Demanding three volleys from the musket-wielding militia presented no hardship. With respect to the riflemen, Morgan had no choice but to rely on their experience and skill

---

314 Morgan to Greene, 19 January 1781, in Showman et al., *Greene*, 7:154.
315 Graham, *Morgan*, 297.
316 Graham, *Morgan*, 297.
317 Bartholomees, "Fight or Flee," 121.

to discharge as many shots as time allowed before they moved rearward.

Morgan had specific targets in mind for the reduced number of firings. The reduction in the amount of fire spoke loudly about his plans. By reducing the volume of fire, he required more results from each shot. Morgan wanted the riflemen on the front line to target the British leadership. Bartholomees agreed, noting succinctly, "the foremost line of riflemen were to fire, aiming at officers and noncommissioned officers, and then withdraw."[318]

Some authors have disagreed, and done so in error. William Johnson felt compelled to defend Morgan's credentials as a gentleman. He wrote that the decision to take out officers arose spontaneously among the riflemen: "No particular orders were given to this corps to select objects."[319] This assertion lacked common sense. The militia soldiers, at best, followed orders. They never set tactical objectives.

Whether Morgan also wanted the conventional militia armed with muskets to target British officers raised a more complicated question. The confusion surrounding this issue stemmed from its origin in secondary source materials. Graham provided an excellent example of the problem: he asserted Morgan ordered the militia, not specifying rifle- or musket-wielding, to fire "well-aimed" shots, not specifying the target.[320] Writing a hundred years later, Dennis Conrad and Don Higginbotham insisted that Morgan ordered the conventional militia, not just the riflemen, to fire at British officers and noncommissioned officers.[321] This inference, imbued with logic, was correct. Morgan wanted all the militia to take aim at the opposing command structure. An analysis of his orders determining when to fire puts this stratagem into focus.

---

318 Ibid.
319 Johnson, *Life*, 1:378. "Objects" is a euphemism. Johnson, oddly delicate, almost refused to acknowledge that American soldiers would selectively target enemy officers.
320 Graham, *Morgan*, 297.
321 Showman, et al., *Greene*, 7:159n9; Don Higginbotham, *Daniel Morgan, Revolutionary Rifleman* (Chapel Hill, University of North Carolina Press, 1961), 133–134.

The traditional view of Morgan's orders holds that Morgan directed all the militia to fire when the British reached fifty yards' distance. Here, confusion has once more arisen from secondary source materials. In this instance, the secondary sources have failed to separate the different capabilities and infirmities inherent in the rifle and the musket, and therefore, failed to distinguish the differences in deploying soldiers armed with one or the other.[322]

Among his peers, Morgan demonstrated a superior understanding of the rifle and its capabilities, most importantly, the advantage of accuracy in long distances. A good marksman could hit a target the size of a man's head at two hundred yards, a target the size of a man at three hundred yards.[323] These distances were unthinkable with a musket.

Massed musket fire provided the organizing concept in conventional eighteenth-century combat. The limited range of the musket made aimed shots at a distance largely useless. Commanders used massed formations, and gained battlefield advantage through a volume of fire. This was the most important fact on the battlefield at the time.[324] The maximum range of a musket fired from the shoulder was 125 yards. A good marksman could hit a man-sized target 40 percent of the time at one hundred yards.[325] The "killing range" of a musket, the distance the military presently calls the effective range, was "about forty yards."[326]

In order for the musket to have any effect, the opposing sides needed to approach each other closely. As soon as the armies reached sufficient proximity, the officers ordered volleys to

---

[322] The erroneous view appears to command a majority of historians, e.g., Showman et al., *Greene*, 7:159n9; Babits, *Devil*, 81, 91; Graham, *Morgan*, 297; Bartholomees, "Fight or Flee," 121.
[323] Wright, "The Rifle in the American Revolution," 294.
[324] Wright, *Continental Army*, 4; Black, *Warfare*, 158.
[325] Wright, "The Rifle in the American Revolution," 294.
[326] The quote is from Babits and Howard, *Long, Obstinate, and Bloody*, 102, a work Babits coauthored with Joshua Howard. In his work on Cowpens, Babits insisted on a much longer effective range of the musket, 80 yards in lieu of 40, Babits, *Devil*, 13. Because the latter work predated the former by 11 years, the figure of 40 yards is presumed to represent a correction of the erroneous figure of 80 yards.

commence. Volleys might start with the two sides 150 apart, but the real work was done closer, starting at around a hundred yards of separation. At this distance, aiming provided little benefit, and armies could achieve results only through volume. The infantry closed the distance with the enemy while firing. Ultimately, massed volleys at fifty yards were common.[327] This was still beyond the musket's "killing range" of forty yards, and commanders at fifty yards were still relying on a volume of fire, rather than accuracy, for results.

Looking to Morgan's orders, it would have defied Morgan's command of the rifle for him to have limited the riflemen to a distance of fifty yards. The rifle was accurate at long ranges and took much time to reload. If Morgan limited the riflemen to firing first at fifty yards, he took away the one advantage, accuracy at distance, and multiplied the principal disadvantage, reloading time. At fifty yards, the riflemen could get off one shot, then they would have to leave; the advancing British would be on top of them before they could reload. He massed riflemen on the front line for a reason. He did not do so only to evade the advantages.

Looking to the conventional militia wielding muskets, the analysis changed. Since Morgan limited the number of volleys from this group, it follows that he did not want them wasted at 150 or one hundred yards. At fifty yards, the British were approaching musket range. Babits quoted a militiaman in a pension application: "General Morgan gave orders for the militia to fire on the enemy" at forty to fifty yards, or thirty to forty paces.[328] At this distance, accuracy arose as a factor in musketry. It made sense to acquire specific targets, and the most significant targets were enemy leaders. Morgan wanted three well-aimed shots from the conventional militiamen. He wanted these

---

327 Wright, *Continental Army*, 4, made the point: "the critical firefight took place at ranges of between fifty and one hundred yards."

328 Babits, *Devil*, 91. The statement in the pension application is in error, to the extent that Pickens commanded the militia in the battle, and it would have been up to him to give such orders, a point Babits corrected later in his book. He asserted that "Colonel Pickens directed the men under his command, to restrain their fire, until the British were within forty or fifty yards," Babits, *Devil*, 89.

directed at British leaders, fired within a range centered on forty yards' distance.

There is one more aspect of Morgan's orders to consider before turning to the conduct of the battle. Morgan made it clear that once the militiamen, riflemen and conventional militiamen, fulfilled their duty, they were to withdraw. The questions were where and how.

This is an area that has become encased in the debate between the Lee and Morgan schools over the number of lines Morgan fielded. To Lee and his followers, it was obvious: the first line was to retreat to the second line, and the second line, thus augmented, would fight until the British bayonets threatened, then seek shelter behind the third line. This scheme has been reflected repeatedly by historians following in the Lee tradition.[329] But, Lee, who was not at Cowpens, was wrong, and over-simplified Morgan's complex battle plan. In its gritty reality, nothing at Cowpens was as obvious as Lee painted it.

Morgan, not Lee, once more provided reliable information. He wanted the riflemen to withdraw as individuals to specified places, the conventional militia to withdraw by units. His words were illuminating. He wrote that the first line marksmen completed firing, then "retreated to the Regiments intended for their support."[330] As to the conventional militia on the second line, "The whole of Colonel Picken's Command then kept up a fire by Regiments retreating agreeable to their Orders."[331]

Until 1998, no one seems to have given thought to the manner in which the troops withdrew. Then, Babits noted that "traditional accounts state that the militia ran across the front of the main line and escaped beyond the left flank. As they ran, they were charged by British dragoons from Tarleton's left flank. This makes no sense practically, tactically, or historically for either group."[332] Babits insisted that instead, the Continentals opened up their formation, allowed the militia to pass through,

---

329 As one example among uncounted numbers, see Bartholomees, "Fight or Flee," 121.
330 Morgan to Greene, 19 January 1781, in Showman et al., *Greene*, 7:154.
331 Ibid.
332 Babits, *Devil*, 95.

then reclosed their lines.

The traditional accounts provided the militia were to withdraw around the American left flank. Graham's work is a rich source of traditional oral history. Graham wrote that the riflemen were to withdraw to the main body of conventional militia, who, in turn, were to retreat to the rear of the Continentals, going around their left.[333] Bartholomees agreed, and wrote that the militia were to withdraw around the left flank of the Continentals.[334]

The militia withdrawing to the left has a dedicated following outside the traditional sources. Lieutenant Colonel Moncure is a well-credentialed advocate of the view that the militia withdrew around Howard's left and took a position of safety in his rear.[335]

In contrast, to support the position that the main line separated in order to accommodate the militia retreat, Babits quoted two British sources, one of which asserted the Continentals "suddenly faced to the right, and inclined backwards, a manoeuvre by which a space was left for the front line to retreat," and another, with a very different view, which stated "the second line of the Americans, having opened to the right & left, to afford a passage" for the militia.[336]

The two British accounts were mutually contradictory. One asserted the Continentals faced right, then "inclined backwards," while the other insisted the Continentals opened to the right and left. Selecting one or the other would prove problematic, in that either maneuver would occupy more lateral space than was available on the battlefield.

Babits's second source was the *Annual Register*. As quoted in *A Devil of a Whipping*, the passage read that the American second line "opened *to* the right and left." Actually, it said something completely different. The *Annual Register* stated that the second line "opened *on* the right and left in the wood, as well to lead the

---

333 Graham, *Morgan*, 297.
334 Bartholomees, "Fight or Flee," 121.
335 Moncure, *Staff Ride*, 56.
336 Babits, *Devil*, 95–97. In what must have been a publisher's erratum, Babits's book failed to disclose the identities of the two British sources, Babits, *Devil*, 97n40, 191n40.

victors on, as to afford a clear passage to the fugitives."[337] That is, the American second line did not cover all the lateral space between the forested land on either flank. These two gaps, one on the right and one on the left, provided room for the reserve to advance around the main line, and, in this instance, room for the militia to withdraw.

Babits acknowledged the Continentals lined up two ranks deep.[338] Either of the two moves asserted in the British sources would be impossibly complicated in a double rank of soldiers. Actually, either would be complicated in a single rank of soldiers. These moves, hypothetical in any event, at their most realistic were parade-ground material, and no one would expect soldiers to accomplish this kind of ballet-like precision on uneven ground in the presence of hostile fire.

No American witness supported either British source. Moncure quoted several pension applicants who noted the militia, not following their orders, ran around the left and right flanks of the Continentals to get to safety.[339] No American suggested the Continentals, and their militia flankers, executed a move of breathtaking complexity to allow the militia to pass between their lines. The truth was that the militia, ordered to withdraw to the left, withdrew to both flanks.

Morgan's planning included the secure knowledge the British would charge with fixed bayonets. It was equally secure the militia would run away rather than face bayonets. Charge and withdraw; Morgan accounted for this paradigm by incorporating it into his plan. He wanted a limited number of firings from them. He wanted their shots directed at specific targets. With these tasks accomplished, their duty was fulfilled, and they were to withdraw as heroes, not cowards.

This was new. By using them in a way consistent with their abilities and their inherent deficiencies, Morgan had finally solved the fundamental problem of the militia. He had no illusions that the militia would stand up to the British bayonets. He made it appropriate and acceptable for them to leave before

337 *Annual Register*, 56.
338 Babits, *Devil*, 17, 76.
339 Moncure, *Staff Ride*, 144–145.

they were in bayonet range. He also made them useful. Morgan wanted to reduce the British leadership structure before the enemy reached the critical main American line. The British Army was legendarily disciplined, but it was also led. If he deleted the leadership portion of the equation, he had a better chance of reducing the discipline portion. By using both riflemen and conventional militia to take out British leaders, he could reduce the well-organized and well-led British army into a redcoated mob.[340]

Morgan's strategy was brilliant on many levels. The militia were to evacuate their positions before they were in range of British bayonets. Morgan assured them that in doing so, they were acting bravely, an idea highly appealing to the militiamen. In other battles, the militia, once they started running, often did not stop until they reached home; Camden was an earlier example, Guilford Courthouse a later one. Morgan's plan, by expecting them to run and incorporating this fact into the plan as an advantage, made the militia feel more part of the operation, less likely to run all the way home. The river at the back of the American formation was a final barrier to escaping completely from the battle.

The militia withdrawal brings the story to Morgan's final pre-battle order. He told the Continentals to hold their ground in the midst of the militia retreat.[341] In so doing, he made certain the Continentals would expect the militia to run around them. Anticipated, the militia withdrawal would not initiate a Continental rout.

While Morgan's plan was brilliant, his leadership was unparalleled. Morgan's final preparations with the soldiers were a critical piece of his planning for the fighting.

Graham was careful to preserve the oral history of Morgan on the front lines. With the riflemen on the first line, he insisted they take advantage of the available cover, mostly from trees. As the enemy advanced, he told them to retire, taking cover, but <u>still loading and</u> firing.[342] The personal attention, and encour-

340 Johnson, *Life*, 1:378.
341 Lee, *Memoirs*, 131; Johnson, *Life*, 1:379.
342 Graham, *Morgan*, 297.

agement, to the soldiers was the final piece of Morgan's exemplary performance at Cowpens. He went further: Morgan took advantage of the split among the riflemen between Georgians and North Carolinians to create the spirit of competition: "Let me see which are most entitled to the credit of brave men, the boys of Carolina or those of Georgia."[343]

With respect to the conventional militiamen, Morgan was careful to assert his personal leadership with them, as well. He reasserted his orders to the men. He asked them to retire in good order, in good unit formation, around the left side of the Continentals. He complemented them on their spirit, and expressed solidarity with them in their travails. He expressed his hopes they would add to the reputation they already enjoyed.[344] Although fighting against cavalry and infantry, he reminded them they had the support of similar troops, and the Americans were much better soldiers in any event. He asked for "an ordinary display of manhood" to ensure victory.

At the same time, Morgan was not averse to cracking the whip. He reminded the militiamen that flight would only assure their destruction. While Morgan assured them he had no doubt of a winning result, this would be true only if they performed their duty. He concluded his speech to the militia with a repetition of his orders, and an exhortation with firmness to obey them.[345]

Thomas Young paid Morgan high praise, in declaring that on the night before Cowpens, "I was more personally convinced of General Morgan's qualifications to command militia than I had ever before been." He recalled that Morgan spent the night before the battle with the militia: "he went among the volunteers, helped them to fix their swords, joked with them about their sweethearts, told them to keep in good spirits, and the day would be ours."[346]

Morgan treated the regulars differently. Professional soldiers, they did not need the level of encouragement the militia

---

[343] Ibid.
[344] Graham, *Morgan*, 297–298.
[345] Graham, *Morgan*, 298.
[346] Johnson, *Traditions and Reminiscences*, 449.

required. He reminded them of the plan and his orders. He told them again to expect the flight of the militia, and not to be alarmed by it. He told them not to break and run. If circumstances required a withdrawal, they would rally on the second ridge line. There, with cavalry and militia reserve, victory was inevitable.[347]

With respect to the cavalry, Morgan gave Washington orders to assist in rallying the militia if they ran, or to cover them if they were pursued. Washington's position was advantageous, in that the cavalry was protected from musket fire, but could see the fighting. Morgan wanted Washington in a position to respond as emergencies required.[348]

---

347 Ibid.
348 Ibid.

Chapter 4: The Battle

Cowpens was a resounding victory for the Americans, an unprecedented and unexpected defeat for the British. Since the guns cooled, historians and military strategists have dissected the battle to find the hidden secret of Morgan's triumph. The idea of a lone and terrible secret has eluded the searchers. Cowpens was a perfect storm of many factors, all uniting to create a magnificent result.

Although never yielding the single stratagem that explained the outcome, Cowpens provided a rich trove of stories. The stories, fascinating in themselves, had a point. How did Morgan, with an army mostly of militia, defeat the most feared officer in North America commanding an equal force of professional soldiers? The mystery was multifaceted. Underscoring the whole was the proposition that the fickle gods of war, having allowed Tarleton his way at The Waxhaws, had other plans for him at Cowpens.

The first element in unraveling the mystery of Cowpens was exhaustion, the relative rest or depletion of the soldiers as a way to explain the result. Stedman's account of the British side proved influential. To Stedman, Tarleton could do nothing right. In this instance, in his obsessed pursuit of Morgan, Tarleton drove his troops too hard. Tarleton, uncaring, decided to attack anyway, with soldiers who were cold, starved, and exhausted.[349] Tarleton, smelling blood in the water, started his march toward Cowpens at 3:00 a.m. on 17 January. He relent-

---
349 Stedman, *History*, 320, 322.

lessly drove the men on a "fatiguing march through swamps and broken grounds."[350] These facts would come into focus later, during the fighting. Stedman wrote that Tarleton's infantrymen were unable to take advantage of a break in the American main battle line because they were "enfeebled by their fatiguing march in the morning."[351] Too exhausted to pursue fleeing Americans, they simply stopped in place, a rare event in dealing with British professional soldiers.

Mackenzie, who served at Cowpens, was another author who was no friend of Tarleton. He recalled that "fatiguing marches" occupied Tarleton's forces until 10:00 p.m. on 16 January, when he finally reached the ground Morgan had held the day previously.[352] Then, Tarleton, obsessed with catching Morgan, started at 2:00 a.m. on 17 January. The march "rapidly continued through marshes and broken ground," until the British caught up with Morgan around daybreak.[353] Again, later in the fighting, Tarleton's infantry was unable to pursue the advantage represented by withdrawing Americans. Mackenzie wrote that the British infantry "had been in motion day and night." While he acknowledged there had been many officers in the British casualties, he blamed the infantry's performance on exhaustion: "fatigue, however, enfeebled the pursuit, much more than loss of blood."[354]

It would be inappropriate to rely only on Tarleton's detractors. Lieutenant Colonel Moncure intended his *Staff Ride* to serve as a learning vehicle for other officers, and as such, intended that it remain unbiased and impartial. He agreed entirely with Stedman and Mackenzie. He asserted that before the battle, Morgan's troops had the time and opportunity to prepare their positions, rest, and eat. In contrast, "Tarleton's troops would have none of these advantages," and were "exhausted."[355] Graham, echoing Moncure, made the point that Morgan

---

350 Stedman, *History*, 320.
351 Stedman, *History*, 322.
352 Mackenzie, *Strictures*, 96.
353 Mackenzie, *Strictures*, 96–97.
354 Mackenzie, *Strictures*, 99.
355 Moncure, *Staff Ride*, 45, 58.

ensured his men ate breakfast on 17 January; this was the same time Tarleton flogged his men through the swamps.[356]

Exhaustion was a factor. It does not take an intuitive military mind to understand that soldiers who are rested and fed are more capable of performing than soldiers who are starved and exhausted. It was, however, a minor factor. History is replete with stories of armies who fought to incredible victories with minimal food and rest, or, in some cases, no food and no rest. One of the most famous efforts in the American Civil War was Stonewall Jackson's Shenandoah Valley campaign in 1862. One of its outstanding features was the distance his so-called "foot cavalry" could cover to reach a battle site against Union forces. By most accounts, Jackson's forces marched 646 miles in forty-eight days, defeating three Union armies in the process. No food and no rest did not represent problems. The soldiers loved Jackson and would follow him anywhere.[357] Tarleton's relationship to his men rested on a different footing and led them to a different response.

The tale of Braxton Bragg at Missionary Ridge was another story arising out of the Civil War, divergent from Jackson in the Valley but leading to a similar lesson. In 1863, Ulysses S. Grant was in a duel with Bragg over Chattanooga. Bragg was a martinet whose overwhelming concern was maintaining an intense level of discipline within his army. Everyone disliked him, including, unfortunately for him, his soldiers. He occupied defensive positions on Missionary Ridge, one of the chain of mountains around Chattanooga. All concerned, Grant included, thought his position impregnable. Grant nevertheless attacked the sector that included Missionary Ridge, hoping, at best, to achieve a position on one of its flanks. Instead, almost as soon as the Union forces moved forward, the Confederates abandoned their positions to a man, and ran up the mountain, going south as quickly as they could. Bragg left his tent, an odd thing for him, and intervened personally to stop the rout, but obtained nothing but scorn from the fleeing Confederate soldiers.

356 Graham, *Morgan*, 293.
357 James I. Robertson, Jr., *Stonewall Jackson: The Man, the Soldier, the Legend* (New York: MacMillan Publishing USA, 1997), xi, xiii, xiv.

There was a thread running through the story of Missionary Ridge that the soldiers' dislike of Bragg was so massive, so intense, it overwhelmed any sense of duty. The Confederate Army usually fought against numerical odds, often while unfed and unrested. But here, there was a difference. When Grant attacked, the Confederate soldier's first thought was about Bragg, and what he thought was unpleasant and unsolicitous. He gave short shrift to any idea of defending Missionary Ridge for his uncaring commander, and left.

At the time, the battle for Chattanooga had been going relatively well for the Confederates, which returns the story to Tarleton at the Cowpens. Tarleton's win-loss record was basically unblemished before Cowpens.[358] Everyone loves a winner, an adage especially true for soldiers; a winner is less likely to get them killed. At Cowpens, by the time the infantry was too "exhausted" to take advantage of a break in the American line, the British were in trouble.

Tarleton was a one-man show as a commander. Some commanders are cooperative leaders, glad for input from subordinates with some expertise to offer. Tarleton lived in a different category. His word, and only his, was law. Everyone else was invited to stay out of his way.[359] The soldiers on the ground knew the British trouble was entirely Tarleton's responsibility. As long as he was winning, the soldiers would put up with his

---

358 Blackstock's Farm provided ambiguous data. On 20 November 1780, Tarleton and Thomas Sumter fought, after which both claimed victory. In Tarleton's case, the claim was fictional; Sumter had kept the field and sustained minimal casualties, neither of which was true in Tarleton's case. However, for the rest of his life, Tarleton claimed victory, and the British, including Cornwallis, accepted his view. Many British soldiers fought at Blackstock's, and many more knew one who had. One assumes Tarleton's claim was supported by people other than himself, suggesting the result was equivocal enough that it could look like a British win. The nuances of Blackstock's exceed the scope of this book. As stated in the text, Tarleton's record was *basically* unblemished, Tarleton, *Memoirs*, 181–184; Mackenzie, *Strictures*, 71–78; Ramsay, *American Revolution*, 2:179.

359 One criticism frequently addressed in Tarleton's direction was his failure to bring Majors Newmarsh and McArthur into the decision-making process. Both officers had held commissions since before Tarleton was born, Stedman, *History*, 2:324; Mackenzie, *Strictures*, 108. The British sources spelled the latter officer's name "M'Arthur," while Babits spelled it both "MacArthur" and "McArthur," Babits, *Devil*, 107, 226.

ego and foul temper. In defeat, his soldiers forecast the thoughts of the Confederate soldiers at Missionary Ridge. A push to assist Tarleton was simply not in the cards. If one accepts Stedman and Mackenzie, the British infantry refused to move forward. Exhausted, certainly. Fed up, equally certainly, and more importantly.[360]

Exhaustion was the first of many factors advanced to explain the result at Cowpens. Many blamed Tarleton for moving too quickly. While Stedman saw this as an endemic problem, most saw it only in the minutes preceding the fighting.

Mackenzie described a disaster in the making.[361] His rendition of Tarleton lining up his troops to advance against Morgan screamed at the reader:

> Without the delay of a single moment, and in despite of extreme fatigue, the light-legion infantry and fusileers were ordered into line. Before this order was put in execution, and while Major Newmarsh, who commanded the latter corps, was posting his officers, the line, far from complete, was led to the attack by Lieutenant Colonel Tarleton himself. The seventy-first regiment and cavalry, who had not as yet disentangled themselves from the brushwood with which Thickelle Creek abounds were directed to form, and wait for orders.[362]

What Mackenzie described strikes the reader as impossible. There was no time limitation. The British had plenty of time to arrange their forces for the offensive. Nevertheless, the charge started with an infantry regiment and a cavalry troop entangled in underbrush, completely unprepared for the attack. Who would order these men forward? If one accepted Mackenzie, the answer was *Tarleton*. Despite its seeming impossibility, Mackenzie's view achieved credibility that has lasted hundreds

---

[360] Tarleton complained of his soldiers' fatalism. At the end of the fighting, he tried to rally a cavalry charge, but the men refused to comply; "neither promises nor threats could gain their attention." Afterward, two hundred dragoons "forsook their leader" and left the field against orders, Tarleton, *Campaigns*, 224.

[361] The question of fairness always intrudes in bashing Tarleton. All his enemies wrote with the advantage of knowing that Cowpens was a hopeless disaster.

[362] Mackenzie, *Strictures*, 97.

of years. Mackenzie confirmed the worst suspicions regarding Tarleton's character and performance.

Once again, Tarleton used his memoirs as a vehicle for self-justification. With respect to the charge of exhaustion, Tarleton told the story differently: "The march of the British troops was exceedingly slow, on account of the time employed in examining the front and flanks as they proceeded."[363] This was nonsense. Tarleton flogging his exhausted men through swamps resonated as the Tarleton everyone knew. Taking extra time, enough to delay a major battle, to send out patrols searching for American pickets did not. At Cowpens, American pickets were mostly militiamen, and Tarleton, like most British officers, paid them little heed. With Morgan finally in his crosshairs, he would not delay movement for a few militiamen.

Tarleton overtook an American patrol after crossing Thicketty Creek.[364] Tarleton's detractors insisted he learned from these Americans that Morgan was forming for battle nearby.[365] Tarleton disagreed once again. He received no intelligence from the captured Americans. Instead, he posted Captain Ogilvie with two troops of dragoons in the front of the British formation. Ogilvie soon reported back that he saw the Americans forming into battle lines just ahead. Tarleton asked his Tory guides to describe the terrain, which they did in some detail; the key points were that the woods were open and free from swamps, and the Broad River, six miles to the American rear, ran parallel to the battle lines.[366]

Tarleton then ordered Ogilvie to drive in the American "militia parties who covered the front," to get a view of Morgan's formation.[367] Tarleton saw two lines, militia in front, regulars in back, with cavalry in reserve.[368] With this information, he pre-

---

363 Tarleton, *Campaigns*, 221.
364 Ibid.
365 E.g., Stedman, *History*, 2:321.
366 Tarleton, *Campaigns*, 221.
367 Tarleton, *Campaigns*, 222.
368 Tarleton's statement that he saw the Continental line when reconnoitering the field before the battle appeared in his after-action report to Cornwallis. Babits rejected Tarleton's statement. Babits based his rejection on the basis of "an early-morning battlefield walk in intermittent rain," Babits, *Devil*, 82n6, 83. On this point, one

pared to "undertake those measures which the instructions of his commanding officer imposed, and his own judgment, under the present circumstances, equally recommended."[369] His own judgment dictated an immediate attack.

Tarleton's narrative was devoid of needless haste and confusion. To summarize his orders: the soldiers were to disencumber their gear except weapons and ammunition. He deployed the light infantry on the right, to match the American left flank. The Legion infantry went to the British left. One British cannon started a barrage. The 7th Regiment took a position left of the Legion, and received the other artillery piece to station within its right division. Fifty dragoons each occupied the flanks. He kept the 1st Battalion of the 71st Regiment in reserve, with more cavalry.[370]

Tarleton told a story vastly different from the one told by Stedman and Mackenzie. Tarleton insisted the 7th Regiment was not thrashing in the underbrush with the cavalry, but properly found its place in line. There was no mention of Major Newmarsh posting his officers. As Tarleton told the story, all was appropriately calm.

A third opinion might prove helpful in breaking the tie between Tarleton and his detractors. Lee stands out as an obvious choice. In this instance, Lee, no friend of Tarleton, was only mildly critical. He wrote that "the light and legion infantry, with the seventh regiment, composed the line of battle."[371] He added that Tarleton placed himself in the line, and again mentioned the 7th Regiment: Tarleton had "under him Major Newmarsh, who commanded the seventh regiment." Lee seemed to suggest that the 7th Regiment was in line, properly taking orders from its commander.

Finally, Lee took aim at Tarleton. "The disposition was not completed, when he directed the line to advance."[372] There it

---

disregards contemporary written records at one's peril, and only in the presence of evidence with a force that compels rejection, which this lacks.
369 Tarleton, *Campaigns*, 221–222.
370 Tarleton, *Campaigns*, 222.
371 Lee, *Memoirs*, 132.
372 Ibid.

was: Tarleton advanced before the British line was properly formed. While Lee missed an opportunity bash his adversary mercilessly, he made it clear that Tarleton moved forward before his men were ready.

Historians have grappled with the idea of Tarleton and the 7th Regiment for over two hundred years. There is a split between the traditional British and American views. The British, mortified over the battle's result, have shown no problem blaming Tarleton, and accept the version told by Stedman and Mackenzie.

The Americans traditionally preferred a different solution. William Johnson asserted that Stedman and Mackenzie were confused, and the mistake was theirs, not Tarleton's. Johnson wrote that after Ogilvie reported seeing the Americans, Tarleton, moving forward to reconnoiter, was prevented from doing so by the first line of American skirmishers. Johnson, in the Lee tradition, believed there were three lines of Americans. Tarleton, still arranging his forces for the main attack, wanted to see Morgan's lines, and to do so, sent Ogilvie back to deal with the skirmish line. At this point, the British soldiers were still in motion, and Major Newmarsh was still posting his officers. Johnson reported the skirmishers retired, as ordered, to the second militia line. By this point, all the British units were present and in line. Tarleton, freed of the first line of skirmishers, was finally able to see Morgan's battle lines, and once seen, he could begin his attack.[373] Properly, orderly, and with everyone present.

Johnson was a "booster," that is, a cheerleader, for the Patriot cause. It would not have suited his agenda for Morgan's stellar victory to be the result of a British mistake. Morgan had to win in a fair fight with no deficiencies on the British side. While Johnson's story is engaging, one might enjoy it as a story rather than as history.

Modern historians have abandoned Johnson's boosterism. Babits asserted that Tarleton sent Ogilvie forward to eliminate the skirmishers in the first of three American lines. He failed. As Babits reconstructed the action, Tarleton never saw

---

373 Johnson, *Life*, 1:379.

the American troop dispositions until after he commenced his advance.[374] Buchanan, also in the Lee tradition, wrote that Tarleton advanced, but "did not finish his inspection of Morgan's dispositions" before doing so.[375]

As Johnson told the story, the 7th Regiment's lateness was inextricably enlaced in Tarleton's preparations for the attack. If we disregard Johnson's version of the story, why was the 7th Regiment late? Babits quoted a pension application to the effect that the 71st and 7th Regiments, moving out of the underbrush and toward the line, became entangled. Major Newmarsh, in command of the 7th Regiment, had to post his officers personally.[376]

Babits's pension application presented unreachable hurdles. It was unthinkable that two professional units would dissolve into each other in the presence of the enemy. Moreover, Mackenzie insisted the 7th Regiment was in line, but not ready; it was just the 71st that was mired in underbrush.

As with much at Cowpens, a resolution of this quandary reduces to a contest of credibility. Did Tarleton move too soon? *Yes.* Stedman and Mackenzie had transparent agendas, but even with this consideration, they provided a solid, convincing explanation for these events, as well a forecast of what would follow. One might fairly assert that it was just this kind of event that triggered their agendas. Tarleton, breathing fire, could see Morgan and smell victory. When he gave the order to advance, he knew the first line he faced was militia, and, like all his British colleagues, gave it little thought. The 7th Regiment was in line, but Major Newmarsh was still seeing to positioning. Facing militia, Tarleton did not see this as a problem. The 1st Battalion of the 71st Regiment was still finding its way through the underbrush. This was the reserve infantry, and Tarleton did not anticipate needing it until after he dealt with the militia line. Even so, there was no excuse for forward movement before all the pieces were in place. His thinking, deranged as we might see it presently, is not difficult to intuit.

Tarleton, with some men shuffling, some still disentangling

---
374 Babits, *Devil*, 82.
375 Buchanan, *Guilford Courthouse*, 321.
376 Babits, *Devil*, 83–85.

from underbrush, moved forward. The Americans, waiting in place, experienced those dark thoughts common to all soldiers facing first contact with the enemy.

All battles begin with an artillery bombardment where there is artillery on the field. Cowpens was no exception. However, Tarleton's artillery, for reasons that remain unclear, impressed no one. Bartholomees stood out by mentioning the artillery preparation. He wrote that the British made a "very short bombardment with two small, frame-mounted three pounder cannons."[377] Missing from all accounts is any rendering of the effect of the bombardment. While one may speculate on the reason, guesses of this nature are unhelpful. The only certainty was that the artillery played no meaningful role in the fighting.

Stedman, a minimalist in his prose, described the fighting on the first line in terse words devoid of emotional content.[378] The "first line of Americans being composed of militia, did not long withstand the charge of the British regulars: It gave way in all quarters, and was pursued to the Continentals." Mackenzie, whose primary interest lay in discrediting Tarleton, used language almost as bland to describe a great and powerful engagement: "The military valour of British troops, when not entirely divested of the powers necessary to its exertion, was not to be resisted by an American militia. They gave way on all quarters, and were pursued to their Continentals."[379] Tarleton's detractors, like the British generally, simply credited an easy victory. It was one more example of British regulars fighting American militia, a success in which Tarleton played no part. The Americans saw things differently.

Lee, overflowing with enthusiasm, described the initial fighting in emotion-laden phrases that would have shocked the sober Stedman: "The American light parties quickly yielded, fell back, and arrayed with Pickens. The enemy, shouting, rushed forward

---

377 Bartholomees, "Fight or Flee," 123. Babits, similarly, was not impressed. He asserted that in the opening barrage, shots fell among Washington's dragoons, causing him to order them out of the artillery's target zone. "This might be the only direct effect of the artillery during the battle," Babits, *Devil*, 78.
378 Stedman, *History*, 2:321.
379 Mackenzie, *Strictures*, 97–98.

upon the front line, which retained its station, and poured in a close fire; but, continuing to advance with the bayonet on our militia, they retired and gained with haste the second line."[380] While Lee always made for exciting reading, one cannot ignore Morgan. Morgan reported a fact lost in the Lee version, much to the detriment of the Americans who fought at Cowpens. To Lee, the riflemen on the first of his three lines were posted by Morgan, under orders and within the coherent structure of a battle line. Actually, the riflemen were far more courageous. Morgan insisted that small parties of riflemen began the engagement by detaching and moving against the British, on their own and without the protection or encouragement of the line.[381]

Morgan gave us the most vivid picture of the kind of fight the Americans had anticipated, in fact, desired, and desired intensely. Imagine: an entire line of British soldiers, flanked by cavalry, moving forward at a trot with fixed bayonets against American militia. The Americans, expected by everyone to run in the face of a bayonet charge, instead moved forward directly into the path of the British. This was unprecedented, unheard-of; the stuff of legend. Something new was at work here, something never seen before, and everyone on the ground knew it. The fickle gods of war were at work, and by the end of the day, the British would feel pain.

Morgan wrote that the riflemen gave the British "a heavy & galling fire," after which "they retreated to the Regiments intended for their Support."[382] This had been Morgan's plan all along. The riflemen would engage the enemy, then retire out of bayonet range.

There are divergent legends about Morgan at Cowpens. One odd point that has grown through the accretion of legends concerns Morgan's place in line. Once the fighting started, where was Morgan? James Graham, an admirer, was sensitive to Morgan's reputation as a backwoodsman. While one might

---

[380] Lee, *Memoirs*, 132. Recall that Lee insisted on three American lines of battle.
[381] Morgan to Greene, 19 January 1781, in Showman et al., *Greene*, 7:154.
[382] Ibid. Morgan referenced only McDowell and Cunningham in his report on the "galling fire." It was not clear why he left out the other units on the front line. There is no reason to suspect only two participated, and two sat on their hands.

see such a reputation today as an advantage, Graham took every opportunity to paint Morgan as a gentleman, in the manner of Washington or Hamilton. Graham, determined to prove Morgan's aristocratic *sang-froid*, wrote that once the battle preparations were in place, Morgan "took post in the rear of the main line, and composedly awaited the approach of the enemy."[383] It was highly unlikely Morgan did anything "composedly" while watching the British move forward into his lines, so Graham's version may be disregarded.

Moncure was an exponent of a contrarian view. Moncure wrote that "recognizing in advance that the performance of the militia was important to the outcome of the day, Morgan had positioned himself among them." In short, the opposite of Graham's position. It should be obvious by now the historical records tell us nothing, one way or the other. Moncure wrote that to encourage the militia, he shouted, "they gave us the British halloo, boys, give *them* the Indian halloo."[384] This is largely a quote from Thomas Young in an oral history preserved by Joseph Johnson: "they gave us the British halloo, boys—give them the Indian whoop!"[385] Moncure, placing Morgan at the front, gave credit to Morgan for the order to give the war cry, and being in the front, made it possible for Morgan to give it. Young wrote that Morgan rode up and down the lines of militiamen, encouraging them. Private Young, an eyewitness, put Morgan at the front, indeed the very front, of the American formation.

Once more: Where was Morgan? The answer makes no difference in substance. The course of the battle is a known set of facts, true regardless where Morgan stood. The difference matters only in legend. At the rear, Morgan directed the battle as any great commander of his day, Cornwallis as much as Napoleon. In the front, Morgan was a fire-eater, an American hero defying convention and bullets to lead his men in a win-or-die moment. The question of front or rear turned on which view of Morgan's legend one preferred.

383 Graham, *Morgan*, 299.
384 Moncure, *Staff Ride*, 52.
385 Johnson, *Traditions and Reminiscences*, 450.

Setting aside the preferences of legend, the facts were discernable. To disregard Young is to ignore an eyewitness in favor of a much later, secondary source, an action to undertake only for the strongest reasons. As here. If one deletes Morgan waiting composedly for the British, Graham was right, Young was wrong, and Morgan was in the rear. The legend of the war whoop, fascinating and quite believable, was a spontaneous action by the soldiers. No one needed to order them to give it. But stationing Morgan in the front made no sense. Even Tarleton took his position in the rear of the British formation.[386] This was the traditional station for the commander. There was no reason to suspect Morgan wagered success by putting himself in the front line with the skirmishers. Morgan, a brave and skilled commander, knew better than to make himself an outstanding and obvious target for every British soldier.

As Lee reconstructed the battle, Pickens was next to engage the British. The riflemen "arrayed with Pickens," by which he meant the skirmishers retreated into what Lee described as Pickens's main militia line.[387] The British continued to advance with fixed bayonets, and Pickens, as ordered, took his post on Howard's flank. But, to Lee, this was the right flank. Lee suffered from a kind of military dyslexia. At Guilford Courthouse, among other problems, his *Memoirs* switched the left-to-right orientation of the American brigade commanders on the first line. At Cowpens, he was alone in saying Pickens retreated to Howard's right flank.[388] Lee was incorrect, and there was no doubt Pickens's post was on Howard's left.

Morgan had much more to say about Pickens. Morgan, who planned the battle, was vitally concerned that the plan stay in motion after first contact with the enemy.[389] He asserted that

---

386 Graham, *Morgan*, 300; Morgan to Greene, 19 January 1781, in Showman et al., *Greene*, 7:154.
387 Lee, *Memoirs*, 132.
388 Alone, that is, until William Johnson contracted the condition in 1822.
389 There seems to be a tendency to credit Napoleon with originating every great military aphorism. "No plan survives first contact with the enemy" is another quote Napoleon did not invent. The elder Field Marshal Helmuth von Moltke is the actual source: "No plan of operations can be at all relied upon beyond the first encounter with the enemy's main force." Not the same panache, but at least this one is accurate.

"the whole of Colonel Pickens's Command then kept up a Fire by Regiments retreating agreeable to their Orders."[390]

Lee was not aware of the extent to which Morgan had planned on a militia withdrawal. To Lee, giving up any ground was anathema. He chose to deemphasize this unpleasant news in his otherwise glowing report. In contrast, Morgan saw only two important facts. First, Pickens withdrew by units, and second, the units fired while withdrawing. As far as he was concerned, things could not have been going better; and, of course, he was right. Pickens's militia would not withstand a British bayonet charge, and he had properly planned for this eventuality.

A second disagreement between Lee and Morgan on this point in the battle concerned Pickens's destination. To Lee, Pickens withdrew to Howard's flank. He was wrong. In Morgan's scheme, Pickens started on Howard's flank. When the British drew close enough to put the militia at risk for a bayonet attack, Pickens withdrew to the rear.[391]

Morgan was not the only source for an orderly militia withdrawal. Seymour described the militia delivering a creditable performance. They "stood very well for some time[,] till being overpowered by the superior number of the enemy they retreated, but in very good order, not seeming to be in the least confused."[392]

One further question: Did the militia with muskets follow Morgan's orders for three volleys? The primary sources largely ignored this point. Lieutenant Colonel Moncure asserted "the rebels fired between two and five rounds each and withdrew."[393] He was almost certainly correct. The differentials in reloading times allowed for an array of firings among the militiamen. A dissenting voice was heard from Howard, who asserted that the militia "had not time, especially the riflemen, to fire a second

---

[390] Morgan to Greene, 19 January 1781, in Showman et al., *Greene*, 7:154.
[391] Morgan wrote that once Pickens withdrew, "the Enemy advanced to our Line," meaning the Continentals, standing alone and shorn of Pickens's flank protection, Morgan to Greene, 19 January 1781, in Showman et al., *Greene*, 7:154.
[392] Seymour, *Journal*, 13.
[393] Moncure, *Staff Ride*, 56.

time."[394] Howard, busy with his Continentals, was not the best resource on the travails of the militia. The musketmen had plenty of time to reload.

One final set of questions remains from the first line fighting. How effective was the rifle fire? Did the riflemen select British officers as targets? If so, did this plan have an effect? The use of a full complement of riflemen on the front line was a dramatic innovation. It drew little comment from the eyewitnesses, a concession to necessity. No one was in a position to conduct an interim casualty assessment at the conclusion of the first line fighting.

Mackenzie is the best primary source. At a point later in the battle, after the British engaged the Continentals, he asserted that "not less than two-thirds of the British infantry officers [] had already fallen."[395] Losses of this extreme degree shortly after the first line fighting suggested the riflemen took a heavy toll on the British officers. However, it may have been possible the Continentals killed a large number of British officers early in the second line fighting. Some historians added weight to the discussion. Graham insisted that the first line "opened a close and deadly fire" on the advancing British. "The effect of this and the succeeding discharges told heavily upon their ranks, but particularly so upon their officers."[396] Similarly, William Johnson quoted an unnamed Continental officer, who insisted that the riflemen, not the Continentals, had won the battle. For proof, he pointed to a large number of British officers and noncommissioned officers he insisted had been killed by the riflemen. Here, he said, is where the battle was won.[397]

The record endorsed Morgan's strategy of massed rifle fire. The casualties among the British officers at the conclusion of the first line fighting was unprecedented and revealing. While it may have been technically possible for the Continentals to have been responsible, this notion actually defied common sense. Volleys were not aimed, and relied on mass, not accu-

---
394 Moncure, *Staff Ride*, 128.
395 Mackenzie, *Strictures*, 99.
396 Graham, *Morgan*, 300.
397 Johnson, *Life*, 1:380.

racy. Had Continental volleys caused the British casualties, the effects among the British would have spread equally within the rank structure. Since the effects were felt most noticeably among the officers, the explanation was that accurate rifle fire took out the British leadership, as planned by Morgan. The Continental officer quoted by Johnson was right: the riflemen won the battle. The results validated Morgan's innovation.

The next phase of the battle started with a cavalry attack by the British. Unfortunately, the facts surrounding the attack have become blurred in the mists of legend, complicated by the confusion of multiple versions of the Cowpens story in the literature. Thus far, the bipolarity between Lee and Morgan commanded attention. Going forward, the multiplicity of versions of the fighting proposed by many authors will require analysis.

Stedman provided an appropriate starting point. He asserted that as the militia withdrew, the British pursued the retreating militiamen to the Continental line.[398] The Continentals "maintained their ground with great bravery, and the conflict between them and the British troops was obstinate and bloody." Tarleton sent Captain Ogilvie forward on the British right with a troop of dragoons. The attack on the right put Ogilvie in direct contact with Pickens on Howard's left flank, making Ogilvie's attack an integral part of the pursuit of the retreating first line militia. Ogilvie, however, ran into "a heavy fire," and, in a move that he did not anticipate, a counterattack by Washington's cavalry. While heavy infantry fire stopped Ogilvie, the cavalry pushed him back. Ogilvie, outgunned and outmaneuvered by Washington, retreated.

Mackenzie agreed with Stedman.[399] Ogilvie, whose unit fielded about 50 cavalrymen, attacked on the American left

---

398 Stedman, *History*, 2:321–322. On this point, Tarleton and Stedman agree, Tarleton, *Campaigns*, 223. Babits, in contrast, asserted the move by Ogilvie was part of an attempted double envelopment by Tarleton, Babits, *Devil*, 117–119, 125. The other half of the attempted envelopment was an attack by the British reserve on the American right (*Devil*, 125). At this point, Babits is alone in his assertion of an attempted British envelopment. The eyewitnesses agree that Washington beat back Ogilvie before Tarleton moved his reserve into position for the attack on the American right, e.g., Tarleton, *Campaigns*, 223.
399 Mackenzie, *Strictures*, 98.

flank. Mackenzie was brutal: Ogilvie "cut his way through their line." Cut, literally, in that the saber was the cavalry weapon of choice. He ran into "a heavy fire," and was blindsided by a counterattack by Washington. Ogilvie retreated. Tarleton, who agreed with Mackenzie on very little, told a very similar version of the story: "The British approached the continentals. The fire on both sides was well supported and produced much slaughter: The cavalry on the right were directed to charge the enemy's left: They executed the order with great gallantry, but were drove back by the fire of the reserve, and by a charge of Colonel Washington's cavalry."[400]

Lee saw the opening fight with the Continentals in larger-than-life terms, and his ringing prose went far to explain the immense popularity of his book. "Tarleton pushed forward, and was received by his adversary with unshaken firmness. The contest became obstinate; and each party, animated by the example of its leader, nobly contended for victory."[401] Dramatic, but problematic. Lee made no mention of the cavalry charge. Lee wrote that Washington stayed in reserve until much later in the fighting.[402]

There was a consensus in the primary sources. The militia withdrew to the American left; the British cavalry pursued; they were beaten back by a combination of infantry fire and cavalry counterattack. What was the problem? The problem, of course, was Lee. His influence was so strong that even when he was obviously wrong, as here, later authors felt obliged to defer to his authority.

William Johnson provided an early example of the recurring problem. Johnson's effort amounted to rewriting the original sources. Confusion resulted, a problem in itself, more so in its reverberation through the ensuing years. Johnson wrote that the British cavalry, pursuing the retreating militia, moved forward on the American right.[403] In this, he followed Lee, who incorrectly put Pickens, as well as this part of the battle, on the right.

400 Tarleton, *Campaigns*, 223.
401 Lee, *Memoirs*, 132.
402 Lee, *Memoirs*, 133.
403 Johnson, *Life*, 1:380.

Johnson asserted that Tarleton advanced his reserve to attack on the British left, and in this, Johnson was again incorrect. Tarleton moved up the reserve for the attack later in the fighting, after the Americans had beaten back Ogilvie's cavalry charge.

In Johnson's reconstruction, the British cavalry pursued the retreating American militia on the British left, making the militia's rallying point on the American right, where Lee put it. Johnson seems to have acquired Lee's odd dyslexia, in that he made two contradictory assertions. One, "the cavalry of Tarleton's left wing had poured upon the retreating militia," and two, "Washington was ... vigorously engaged where duty called him on the left." To clarify: Tarleton's cavalry pursued the retreating militia on the American right/British left, while Washington, responding to the incursion, fought on the American left/British right. Washington was successful, and "enabled the militia to regain the tranquillity necessary for returning to a state of order."[404] Washington performed his task well, but there was no way to determine where it took place.

Johnson agreed with the eyewitnesses that the British cavalry continued its pursuit of the fleeing militia to the line of the Continentals. In an *homage* to Lee, the militia in Johnson's version retired to the right. In bringing his tribute to Lee, the narrative became contorted. He agreed Washington counterattacked, and was successful, and in this he was in step with the bulk of authors. But for Lee's incursion, it would all have gone smoother.

Modern historians have not lost their fascination with Lee's narrative. Babis is another historian in the Lee tradition. Writing almost two hundred years after Johnson, Babits interspersed Lee in the tale of Ogilvie's cavalry charge. Babits asserted the militia withdrew through apertures opened by the Continentals in their line. Once through, the militia took positions of safety behind the Continentals. However, "the militia thought they were safe in the American rear, but any impression of security created by Continental bayonets and their steady musket fire was an illusion," because the British cavalry, still in pursuit, got

---
404 Ibid.

behind the Continentals.[405] At this point, Washington counterattacked, and drove the British cavalry back.[406]

Babits drew on Lee, who wrote: "A part of the enemy's cavalry, having gained our rear, fell on that portion of the militia who had retired to their horses. Washington struck at them with his dragoons, and drove them before him."[407] Lee stood in contrast to the eyewitnesses, who painted a picture in which infantry volleys stopped Ogilvie before the line and Washington pushed him back. At no point did the witnesses see British cavalry behind the Continental line.[408]

Lee has never lost his magnetic appeal for American historians. Even where, as here, his views were contrary to the consensus of eyewitnesses, American authors have been unable to disengage from the dashing cavalryman and his enduring prose.

With Lee removed from the picture, Ogilvie's cavalry charge developed simply. The Americans withdrew pursuant to orders. The British saw something else, something they were expecting, another American militia formation retreating in the face of a British bayonet charge. As was their custom, they pursued the Americans vigorously. However, Morgan had planned for the withdrawal. The British encountered two things they had not expected: a high volume of massed infantry fire and a cavalry counterattack. Ogilvie, in command of the pursuing cavalry, called a halt and withdrew. There was no reason to make this episode more complicated.

The next step in the battle was the movement of the British reserve. Tarleton wrote that as soon as Ogilvie returned, he realized he needed help. He called up the reserve, which consisted of the 1st Battalion of the 71st Regiment and two hundred cavalrymen. Tarleton insisted, "no time was lost in performing this manoeuvre."[409] He deployed the 71st in the line to the left of the

---

[405] Babits, *Devil*, 98.
[406] Babits, *Devil*, 99.
[407] Lee, *Memoirs*, 133.
[408] With the possible, ambiguous exception of Howard, who recalled the British cavalry "passes round my left flank," a statement capable of many interpretations, Moncure, *Staff Ride*, 129.
[409] Tarleton, *Campaigns*, 223.

7th Regiment, and ordered the cavalry "to incline to the left, and to form a line, which would embrace the whole of the enemy's right flank." To clarify: he ordered the cavalry to incline to the British left, forming a line intended to enclose the American right flank.

This was the critical moment. Tarleton had passed through the militia line. Both commanders knew the battle would be decided on the Continental line. Tarleton described the fighting: "The contest between the British infantry in the front line and the continentals seemed equally balanced."[410] That is, equally balanced until he advanced the British reserves. The Continentals had no reserves. With fresh troops moved up to the line, victory was so close he could almost touch it. He ordered the 71st to advance. It was make or break time.

Stedman felt the emotion of the moment. Within the next 60 seconds, the British would take the field or lose everything. Tarleton, a gambler, staked everything on the turn of the next card. Stedman wrote that Tarleton ordered the 71st forward, and when the reserve moved, the whole line, acting in perfect unison, moved forward together. The Continentals "no longer able to stand the shock, were forced to give way." He expressed a point manifest to the reader: "This was the critical moment of the action."[411]

The militia had fallen back, and the British no longer saw them as a factor. The Continentals, who had held their own, collapsed under the increased pressure brought by the reserves. All the British needed was to prosecute the advantage of the collapsing American line, and the battle was over. But the gods of war had not finished toying with Tarleton.

Stedman wrote that "the infantry, enfeebled by their fatiguing march in the morning, through swamps and broken grounds, and by their subsequent exertions in the action, were unable to come up with the flying enemy." Moreover, "an order, it is said, was dispatched to the cavalry to charge the enemy ... but if such an order was delivered, it was not obeyed."[412] Everything was in

410 Ibid.
411 Stedman, *History*, 2:322.
412 Ibid.

place, with one exception: Tarleton's soldiers would not move forward. He had gone from the elation of sure victory to the ignominy of a stalled advance in less than a minute.

Mackenzie also believed an order must have been given to the cavalry to charge. It made sense; this was an ideal opportunity for a cavalry charge. Infantry in the open, not in formation, was fodder for the cavalry. "This order, however, if such was then thought of, being either not delivered or disobeyed, they stood aloof, without availing themselves of the fairest opportunity of reaping the laurels which lay before them."[413]

Mackenzie criticized Tarleton for his tyrannical mode of leadership. No one questioned that Tarleton should have ordered the cavalry to charge. In all fairness, each cavalry unit had a commander, and all these officers could see the same thing Tarleton saw: Continentals in retreat. A cavalry charge would have wiped them from the field. Instead, the cavalry stood "aloof," and this word spoke volumes. The cavalry officers, having learned over hard weeks with Tarleton that he did not appreciate anyone else giving important orders, stood by, silently.

Mackenzie again echoed Stedman in his assessment of the British infantry. "The infantry were not in condition to overtake the fugitives … [they] had been in motion day and night… [F]atigue … enfeebled the pursuit."[414]

The British, focused on blaming Tarleton, dissected his conduct but failed to look beyond it to learn if other factors were at work. Therefore, we must turn to the Americans to complete our understanding of the key sixty seconds on the battlefield.

Tarleton gave the American narrative the key, the critical point overlooked by his detractors. In his memoirs, he related that he directed the reserve cavalry and infantry to the British left, which placed them in a position to outflank the American right. If outflanked, this would be an instant and fatal disaster for the Americans. The British failed to appreciate Tarleton's actual tactical skills. Extending the line to the left was an insightful move. On another day, the gods of war might well have given

---

413 Mackenzie, *Strictures*, 99.
414 Ibid.

him the laurel crown of victory, but today was not to be Tarleton's day.

Seymour wrote that his commander, Captain Robert Kirkwood, saw the British in a position to outflank the American right. At this point, "Captain Kirkwood with his company wheeled to the right and attacked their left flank so vigorously they were soon repulsed, our men advancing on them so rapidly that they soon gave way."[415] Disaster converted into victory in one smooth motion.

To make the geometry evident: the British and Continentals formed in straight lines, eighteenth-century fashion. Kirkwood's unit occupied the right end of the Continental line. When Tarleton extended the British line beyond the American right, Kirkwood moved his company like one hand of a clock. The left end stayed in place on the main line, while the right moved forward. The farther right the soldier stood in line at the start, the farther forward he would move by the end. Kirkwood's wheel movement pushed the British back from the extreme right, no longer in a position to outflank the Americans. The move succeeded to the point it started a rout, but this was a bonus. Kirkwood's plan had only been to move the British left backwards a little.

Seymour's story gained no traction with historians or readers. The impediment was a conflicting story by John Eager Howard, a true hero of this battle and the war generally. Seymour's version might have received a better reception had he been in competition with someone less celebrated.

Howard's version of the story has been the foundation for every history of the battle ever written. The two versions can never be reconciled, so to accept Howard is to discard Seymour.

Many years after the war, he provided answers to a series of questions posed by a correspondent working to clarify or reconcile some of the conflicting versions of Cowpens in circulation. In his discussion of pushing back the British left, Howard introduced Captain Andrew Wallace to the world.

Howard asserted Wallace commanded a company of Virginia Continentals. This was a second introduction; the Con-

---

415 Seymour, *Journal*, 13–14.

tinentals thus far had been identified as entirely Marylanders or Delawares.[416] Howard recalled that Wallace's company occupied the sector of the American line on the extreme right flank. The flanks were important positions, which made the story of Andrew Wallace more remarkable.

Howard, normally gracious to a fault, was intensely critical of Wallace. He wrote that Wallace "had formed a connexion with a vile woman of the camp, and the infatuation was so great that on guard or any other duty he had this woman with him and seemed miserable when she was absent."[417] While this was bad, things became worse: "He seemed to have lost all sense of the character of an officer. He was in this state of mind at the time of the action."

Howard knew his right flank was vulnerable. As he told the story, "I attempted to change the front of Wallace's company ... in doing it, some confusion ensued, and first a part, and then the whole of the company commenced a retreat. The officers along the line seeing this, and supposing that orders had been given for a retreat, faced their men about, and moved off."[418]

He explained the move he had wanted Wallace to execute. "To protect the [right] flank, I ordered the company on my right to change its front so as to oppose the enemy on that flank." To clarify the geometry: Howard wanted Wallace to wheel backwards. The leftmost soldier would stay in place in line, the rest would move like one hand of a clock to the rear. The end result would be an "L" formation. The "L" would present a line, the bottom line of the letter "L" toward the British who were moving to outflank the American right. If successful, this move would counter any move to the American flank. The British would simply meet another strong line, not a vulnerable flank.

Something went very wrong. Instead of a single unit wheeling into a flank defense, the whole line faced about and moved back.

---

[416] Babits included Wallace's company of Virginia Continentals in his accounting of Morgan's army, Babits, *Devil*, 28. Actually, given the position Howard recalled for Wallace, it seems likely Wallace commanded a unit of the Virginia militia composed of former Continentals.
[417] Moncure, *Staff Ride*, 129.
[418] Moncure, *Staff Ride*, 127.

This was a disaster of epic proportions in embryo. It would take little for it to erupt into tragedy for the American cause. Who caused this mess? Howard blamed Wallace: "I can account for the retreat but ... as it may involve the character of an officer I wish it to be forgotten." The officer, of course, was Wallace, in the clutches of the "vile woman" who had disordered his thinking.[419]

As Howard recalled the events, he gave an order to Wallace to wheel backwards and provide a flanking defense. "Some confusion ensued," as Howard phrased it, and the Continental line withdrew. The British claimed they saw the Continentals routed, running away. Howard insisted the American officers, mistakenly believing an order to withdraw had been given, faced to the rear and moved the troops back, in line and in order. Morgan saw the same thing. He reported to Greene that the Continentals "retired in good Order about 50 Paces."[420]

The British and American versions cannot be reconciled, any more than the conflicting American versions of Seymour and Howard can be reconciled. One version, the most likely, must be selected from the competitors.

Stedman and Mackenzie were too invested in blaming Tarleton to see other factors at work. They failed to credit Tarleton with nearly outflanking the Continentals. In so doing, they failed to acknowledge the American response. A response would indicate a need to respond, which would suggest a good move by Tarleton, a recognition inconsistent with their agenda. On this point, Stedman and Mackenzie proved too one-dimensional.

Seymour described a maneuver opposite to the one described by Howard. Seymour described a wheel to the front, Howard one to the rear. Viewed from above, Seymour's version presented questions. He maintained Kirkwood wheeled forward, and starting with those on the American right, pushed all the British back. Seymour failed to account for the major problem. The British line was significantly longer than the American. Even on the extreme right, if Kirkwood wheeled forward, he

---

419 Moncure, *Staff Ride*, 129.
420 Morgan to Greene, 19 January 1781, in Showman et al., *Greene*, 7:154.

would have found himself an American island in a sea of the British Army. Isolated, the British would have cut him to pieces. Seymour's version proved insubstantial.

Howard's version succeeded over the others, not merely because the competitors failed. Howard's narrative uniquely accounted for all the events in motion on the battlefield.[421] This fact became clearer as the story moved into its next chapter, Howard's response to the misunderstanding by his subordinate commanders.

Howard wrote that Morgan found him, and ordered him to move back to the area then occupied by Washington's cavalry, a distance of about 100 yards.[422] This is a small matter with large accretions. Several authors offered conflicting views of Washington's position at the time.

There was no question that Washington fought off Ogilvie's cavalry charge against the withdrawing militia on the American left. In Howard's narrative, Washington finished with Ogilvie and returned to the rear. The difficulty with Howard's story was that the battle still raged. Washington was a diligent and aggressive commander, unlikely to sit on his hands while there were British still active on the field.

To give credence to Howard's story, one must pinpoint Washington at the moment of Morgan's order to Howard. As Howard recalled events, Washington was at rest in the rear. In contrast, Lee insisted that "a part of the enemy's cavalry, having gained our rear," was cutting through the massed militia, who had thought themselves safe behind the Continentals.[423] Washington "struck at them with his dragoons, and drove them before him." Who were these British dragoons?

In Lee's narrative, Washington did not fight off Ogilvie in advance of the fighting on the Continental line. Rather, this was Washington's fight with Ogilvie. In Lee's story, the cavalry counterattack took place farther to the rear, actually behind the Continental line, and later in time. The British cavalry in Lee's

---
421 One must remain mindful of some baggage, for example, Howard insisted Tate and Triplett were on his left, Moncure, *Staff Ride*, 48–49, 126.
422 Moncure, *Staff Ride*, 128.
423 Lee, *Memoirs*, 133.

story were Ogilvie's dragoons, a unit everyone else recalled had been driven off by Washington much earlier. Therefore, according to Lee, when Morgan gave Howard the order to form on Washington in the rear, Washington was in the rear, but fighting off Ogilvie. In Lee's version, Washington could not have served as a target to rally the Continentals.

The British narrative, although discredited in broad strokes by Howard, still held potential. Mackenzie wrote that as the Continentals ran away in a disorganized rout, the British stood fast, immobile. Morgan saw the stationary British soldiers, and in these an opportunity. This was the moment he gave Howard the order to reorganize. Morgan ordered Washington forward into the unprotected British. The enemy distracted, Morgan was able to reorganize his forces.[424] Mackenzie's potential manifested as a third point of view. He believed Washington was in front of the Continentals, fighting hard, at the time Morgan ordered Howard to the rear.

Morgan insisted that the Continentals retired in good order, then "Formed."[425] His terse report corroborated Howard, but mentioned nothing about orders to form on Washington.

With the primary sources in conflict, later authors may serve to illuminate some of the darkness. William Johnson provided very little light, but rather a fourth view of the Howard-Washington situation. To Johnson, Morgan saw the Continentals moving back, and assumed it was pursuant to Howard's order. Rather than discuss the matter with Howard, he addressed the Continental officers directly. Morgan told them to halt "as soon as they reached their ground."[426] Johnson did not explain which ground was intended, and context was no help in resolution.

In Johnson's version, Morgan could not have intended forming on Washington in the rear. As Morgan addressed the

---
424 Mackenzie, *Strictures*, 99.
425 Morgan to Greene, 19 January 1781, in Showman et al., *Greene*, 7:154. Two reasons suggest themselves for Morgan's reticence. One is modesty; perhaps he was too self-effacing to take credit in his report for saving the day. A second is prudence. To take credit for saving the day, he needed to report to his commander that the day needed saving, a fact, at bottom, the boss might not need to know.
426 Johnson, *Life*, 1:381.

Continental officers, a messenger arrived from Washington. After pushing Ogilvie back from the Continental line, Washington had decided to pursue him deep into the British sector. Washington was cut off from the American forces. Rather than a disability, Johnson insisted this was a blessing. The messenger reported to Morgan that Washington found the right flank of the enemy open and unprotected. He offered a bargain to Morgan: if Morgan ordered a volley, Washington would charge the vulnerable British right flank.[427]

Where Johnson obtained this story would make a fascinating tale in itself. Johnson was the first to have the records of the southern army as well as Greene's personal papers. One may search these papers at length and find nothing related to Washington and his cavalry, isolated in the enemy's rear, fighting the British by themselves. Moreover, nothing supports the idea that Tarleton left a flank unprotected. Lacking support, Johnson's version fails equally for lack of believability.

In summary, at the time Morgan told Howard to form on Washington, Washington was (1) in the rear, resting; (2) in the rear, fighting; (3) in the front, fighting; or (4) deep inside enemy lines, fighting the British unassisted. With this degree of conflict, looking to one more source may add clarity.

Babits wrote that Morgan saw Howard's men moving back, orderly and under control. In Babits's version, Morgan addressed Howard directly, and "pointing to the rising ground in the rear of the hollow way, informed him that was the ground he wished him to occupy."[428] Babits avoided the question of Washington's location altogether. In Babits's version, Morgan simply pointed to a spot on the ground. Rather than a solution to the quandary, this fifth view added to the conflict: Babits credited Howard as his source. Actually, Howard started this discussion with his belief that Morgan told him to form on Washington.[429]

Some problems never find solutions, and thus it is with Morgan's order to Howard. The point Morgan assigned for the

---

427 Ibid.
428 Babits, *Devil*, 112.
429 Moncure, *Staff Ride*, 128. Moreover, Howard insisted there was no such high ground in the rear, H. Lee, *Campaign of 1781*, 97.

Continentals to rally, as well as Washington's location at the time, will remain uncertain. These deficiencies are not fatal to understanding the battle. At this point, Washington was a sideline. The action focused on Howard, in particular, on what he did next.

Howard's next step was a response to developments on the ground. The Continentals were moving to the rear. They moved under orders in formation. The opposing British accounts describing a disorderly rout have been discredited and written off. Similarly discredited was the insistence by Stedman and Mackenzie that the British soldiers either could not or would not move forward to take the ground given up in the Continental withdrawal. Tarleton's detractors lost credibility in their single-mindedness. The British were some of the finest soldiers in the world, trained to operate through hardship. It defies belief to suggest they simply sat down and failed to move forward in the face of an enemy retreat.

Tarleton related a much more believable story. As the Americans withdrew, "the British rushed forwards."[430] Tarleton finally presented a satisfactory vision of the British response to the Continental withdrawal.

Tarleton confirmed an idea floated by Stedman and Mackenzie. He ordered a cavalry charge. His order made sense. The enemy in withdrawal was a perfect target for cavalry, especially on a field where Tarleton enjoyed a huge numerical advantage over the American mounted troops. If Washington counterattacked, this time he would be contained. At this point, the world turned upside down. Tarleton conveyed a small piece of his shock and dismay at what Howard did next: "An unexpected fire at this instant from the Americans, who came about as they were retreating, stopped the British, and threw them into confusion."[431]

This was the turn of the final card. Tarleton, the gambler, busted. The Americans were not in a rout. At Cowpens, the Continentals never were. They were moving properly under

---

430 Tarleton, *Campaigns*, 223.
431 Ibid.

orders. When they reached the destination selected by Morgan, they halted, turned to face the British, and fired a murderous volley. The British, who had been expecting an easy victory over retreating Americans, were shocked, stunned, and powerless to contest the field.

Howard told the story in its bare bones: "The enemy was now very near us. Our men commenced a very destructive fire, which they little expected, and a few rounds occasioned great disorder in their ranks."[432] Howard, one of the great commanders of the war, left himself out of the story. Volleys issued on order, and there is no doubt Howard ordered these. Morgan said as little as Howard. The Continentals "gave them a fortunate Volley which threw them into Disorder."[433] Fortune had not decided where to stop and when to fire. The deciding factors were Morgan's genius and Howard's ability, working together to destroy a British Army. Lee was one writer who grabbed the emotion of the moment:

> Considering [the main line's] retrograde movement the precursor of flight, the British line rushed on with impetuosity and disorder; but as it drew near, Howard faced about, and gave it a close and murderous fire. Stunned by this unexpected shock, the most advanced of the enemy recoiled in confusion.[434]

"A close and murderous fire:" this was the language that has kept Lee in the forefront since he put pen to paper in 1812. He was right; the volley Howard ordered was massively destructive, and more shocking for its unexpected appearance. The British had sustained casualties in significant numbers to reach this point. In response to the volleys, more fell like tenpins.

Bad as it was for the British, it became worse. Tarleton reported that the British were too shocked to respond. "Exertions to make them advance were useless. The part of the cavalry which had not been engaged fell likewise into disorder, and an unaccountable panic extended itself along the whole line."[435]

---
432 Moncure, *Staff Ride*, 127.
433 Morgan to Greene, 19 January 1781, in Showman et al., *Greene*, 7:154.
434 Lee, *Memoirs*, 132.
435 Tarleton, *Campaigns*, 223.

History offers few parallels to this story. The British Army did not panic, did not fall into disorder, and did not degenerate into a rabble. Except at Cowpens, when the whole machinery of the army stopped working. Tarleton, forced into candor in his report to Cornwallis, followed the story downward into perdition: "The Americans, who before had thought they had lost the action, taking advantage of the present situation, advanced upon the British troops, and augmented their astonishment."[436]

Grim as his report was, Tarleton minimized what was actually a much worse situation. In a bizarre and terrifying reverse of every expectation gained through experience, Howard ordered his soldiers to fix bayonets and attack the British, bayonets forward. Howard reported his order as if it were usual and customary, and not a complete paradigm shift. "I ordered a charge with the bayonet, which order was obeyed with great alacrity."[437] Lee, fortunately, told the story: "Howard seized the happy moment, and followed his advantage with the bayonet. This decisive step gave us the day."[438] Happy moment, indeed. For Lee, who reveled in war, the happiest of all moments. Lee was right. Howard's bayonet charge destroyed the British and guaranteed an American victory.

The British faced two immediate and overwhelming problems. First, they had thought they were pursuing Americans in retreat. Suddenly, they were deep in casualties and mired in confusion after Howard's volleys. Second, they were the ones who used the bayonet. The British were never the recipients of a bayonet charge. This was new, and not good. Tarleton, always getting high marks for courage under fire, could not get them to move: "Exertions to make them advance were useless."[439] Indeed they were; the British were finished. The last turn of the card ended any British hopes at Cowpens.

While the British were finished, the legends of Cowpens were just taking root. One of the most cherished legends arising from the battle was the story of Morgan's envelopment of

---
436 Ibid.
437 Moncure, *Staff Ride*, 127.
438 Lee, *Memoirs*, 132.
439 Tarleton, *Campaigns*, 223.

the British at the end of the fighting. Moncure, as one example among many, described "the envelopment for which the battle has become famous."[440] Famous, certainly. The envelopment was the incentive for Lieutenant Colonel Moncure's tactical study of the engagement.

Envelopment is a Holy Grail among tacticians. Rarely achieved, it means that one side in the battle has encircled, or "enveloped," the opposing force. It is best visualized from above. In this case, one would see American soldiers in front, back, and on both sides of the British.[441] The legend of Morgan's envelopment of Tarleton did not originate with any of the eyewitnesses. It was entirely a creature of later writers.

In his biography of Daniel Morgan, James Graham proved himself an admirer as much as a biographer. He knew that achieving an envelopment of Tarleton would cement Morgan's place in the pantheon of tactical geniuses. Howard had related an unadorned tale in which he ordered his men to stop, face about, and fire a volley into the oncoming British. To Graham, things were much more complicated. He asserted that before Howard opened fire, the militia "opened a galling fire" on the 1st Battalion of the 71st Regiment, the unit leading the move to outflank the American Continental line on the right.[442]

Graham described a world turned topsy-turvy. In a complete reversal of the established pattern, at Cowpens, the militia saved the Continentals. The militia volley pushed back the British infantry, allowing time and space for the regulars to withdraw. At the same time, Washington charged the reserve cavalry, which was also intruding on the American right, and drove them to the point they were no longer a factor in the battle. Washington did not quit, and pursued the enemy cavalry deep into the British rear.

Washington, far behind enemy lines, again perceived his position as an advantage. He delivered a note to Morgan. In

---

440 Moncure, *Staff Ride*, 60.
441 Many sources speak of a "double envelopment." In such a case, the result is the same, an encirclement of the enemy, but achieved by two arms working in tandem, both of which reach behind the opposing force.
442 Graham, *Morgan*, 304.

Graham's version, Washington offered Morgan a bargain, but with different terms than the one described by Johnson. In this version, Washington offered to charge the British line from the rear if Morgan ordered a volley.[443] Morgan, not Howard, gave the order for the Continentals to halt, face about, and fire. Howard, seizing the moment, ordered a bayonet charge.

To the eyewitnesses, Morgan as much as Tarleton, Howard's bayonet charge marked the end of the British efforts. In Graham's version, the British continued. Washington pushed forward until he reached the British line from the rear. To Graham, this was the moment. Graham described the envelopment: "A few minutes before, there was room for their escape by flight. But the defeat and dispersion of their horse left them without protection; and Washington, now in their rear, was advancing with his cavalry upon them at full speed. The greater part of the 7th regiment immediately threw down their arms, and prostrated themselves upon the ground in token of submission."[444]

For readers with a love of stories, this was one of the best. The British "prostrated themselves on the ground in token of submission." Not merely a surrender, but a show of inferiority to their proven and obvious superiors, the least likely of the many possible outcomes. Moncure, normally a sober judge of battle data, conceded ground to the story's allure: "Pressed by bayonet-wielding Continentals to their front, Washington's cavalry on their right and rear, and Pickens' militia on their left and rear, the British crumbled quickly."[445] The story, although greatly appealing, lacked any consistency with the eyewitness accounts. Even Lee, who often disagreed with Morgan, never suggested the Americans enveloped the British.

Moncure described an envelopment of the entire British force, ending the fighting.[446] To Graham, the Americans achieved an envelopment only of the main British line. The British reserve, the 1st Battalion of the 71st Regiment, was still fighting.[447]

---

443 Graham, *Morgan*, 303–304.
444 Graham, *Morgan*, 304.
445 Moncure, *Staff Ride*, 60.
446 Moncure, *Staff Ride*, 61.
447 Graham, *Morgan*, 305.

The 1st Battalion of the 71st Regiment was the reserve unit Tarleton advanced into a position to outflank the American right. It provided the sole reason for the Continentals' withdrawal. It was the unit most decimated by Howard's volleys and bayonet attack. Graham, determined to find an envelopment, saw things differently. The 1st Battalion of the 71st Regiment was the lone British unit still standing, fighting on the American right, facing Pickens's militia front and flank.

Graham's version, although engaging, was impossible. The theme underlying Morgan's plan for the militia was their inability to meet a British unit armed, as here, with fixed bayonets. Graham insisted that Howard "wheeled upon them with the right wing of the American line." As the militia continued to duel with the British, their struggle devolved into hand-to-hand combat. Howard called on the British to surrender, which they finally did.[448] It was the force of Howard's personality more than the mere force of arms that saved the day. Legends, indeed; this was absolutely the stuff of legend.

Howard's rendition of the same events was more grounded. During the bayonet charge, he "was led to the right." Once there, he found himself "among the seventy-first." The battalion was "broken into squads," and as he called on them to surrender, "they laid down their arms."[449]

Howard poured cold water on Graham's narrative. The 71st was broken into squads, not fighting hand-to-hand with the militia. Howard was alone while among the British. He accepted some surrenders, then saw his men following him, a fact that will gain significance very soon. Howard, the very best witness to his own conduct, disagreed with everything Graham asserted.

Graham and Moncure were not alone. Both were part of a long tradition that believed Morgan achieved an envelopment of the British at Cowpens. Graham was part of another tradition of American historians insisting the militia fought off the 71st

---

448 Ibid.
449 Elizabeth Read, "John Eager Howard: Colonel of Second Maryland Regiment—Continental Line," *The Magazine of American History* 7, no. 4, Oct. 1881, In John Austin Stevens, ed., *The Magazine of American History with Notes and Queries, vol. 7*, (New York, 1881), 279.

Regiment, despite the accounts by Morgan and Howard that the Continental volleys, followed by the bayonet charge, finished off all resistance along the British line. Babits, for example, asserted that "the Continentals delivered their bayonet charge on the 71st at the same time Washington's dragoons attacked [the 71st's] left flank and rear... Pickens and his militia chose this moment to reenter the battle... Only after the militia came back on the field did the 71st break."[450] If true, this would mean the 71st had no difficulty holding off both the Continental infantry and the Continental cavalry at the same time, but broke under the force of the militia, a notion that would upend any existing concept of the relative combat power of the two components.

The tradition of the militia breaking the 71st Regiment demonstrates the staying power of a great story. Bartholomees accepted it, but in a reduced form. Bartholomees blended the legend of the envelopment of the British into the legend of the militia fighting the 71st Regiment. He insisted that as the British cavalry stood aloof, and the British infantry fled,

> At this point the militia performed an act heretofore unheard of and counterattacked the left flank of the still resisting 1st Battalion 71st Regiment. Washington, dividing his interests between pursuing the retreating British cavalry, rounding up running infantry, and capturing the British artillery, still had sufficient forces to attack effectively the right flank and rear of this unfortunate unit which then quickly surrendered.[451]

To Bartholomees, the envelopment was of the 1st Battalion of the 71st Regiment, not the main British line.[452] Thus, three authors provided three conflicting envelopments. Moncure: the Americans enveloped the entire British force. Bartholomees: the Americans enveloped only the 71st Regiment. Graham: the Americans enveloped everyone except the 71st Regiment. While

---

450 Babits, *Devil*, 117–119. A similar version was asserted by Buchanan, *Guilford Courthouse*, 325.
451 Bartholomees, "Fight or Flee," 127.
452 One has to be impressed with Bartholomees's confidence in Washington's ability to blanket the entire battlefield in a single moment.

their mutual disagreement suggested a lack of credibility, the fact that all three directly conflicted with the primary sources was sufficient to undercut completely the legend of Morgan's envelopment at Cowpens.

Bartholomees wrote that Pickens's counterattack was "an act heretofore unheard of." He was correct. One may search in vain for another report of a militia unit fixing bayonets and attacking a British battalion, and, then, after some time fighting with weapons, continuing the battle hand to hand. The eyewitnesses—Howard, Morgan, Tarleton,[453] Mackenzie[454]—all agreed the event that decided the battle was the volley, then the bayonet charge, which sapped the British of the will to resist. One disregards a strong consensus of eyewitness accounts only when evidence compels it. The story of the militia breaking the 71st, as with the story of the envelopment, was insufficient.

With the question of the envelopment resolved, it is time to readdress the issue of Washington and the cavalry. When last discussed, Washington eluded placement on the battlefield at the moment Morgan ordered Howard to reform for a counterattack. Washington's role in the final defeat of the British has been a matter of equal contention. The secondary sources were unanimous that Washington was critical to the reduction of some part of the British force. Although unquestionable, which part he reduced is much less clear.

Babits, for example, insisted that Washington charged the 71st from the left flank and rear, just as Howard organized a bayonet attack in the front. This led to the final defeat of the 71st.[455] Buchanan, in partial agreement, asserted that while Howard was charging the 71st from the front, Washington was pursuing

---

[453] Tarleton made it clear that the volley and the bayonet charge formed the breaking point: "An unexpected fire at this instant from the Americans, who came about as they were retreating, stopped the British, and threw them into confusion," Tarleton, *Campaigns*, 223.

[454] Mackenzie was not different from Tarleton: "[The Americans] formed, renewed the attack, and charged in their turn. In disorder from the pursuit, unsupported by the cavalry, deprived of the assistance of the cannon ... the advance of the British fell back, and communicated a panick to others, which soon became general: a total rout ensued," Mackenzie, *Strictures*, 99–100.

[455] Babits, *Devil*, 117–119.

the fleeing infantry, which served to contain the British under Howard's bayonets.[456] While what these historians said made a great deal of sense, what resulted revealed more questions than answers.

As one example among many, if Washington was key to the end of the 71st as a fighting force, where was he for the much larger battle for the main line? James Graham, in his version of the legend of Washington's message to Morgan from behind enemy lines, put Washington directly in the fight for the British main line.[457] As Graham reconstructed the battle, Washington was instrumental in defeating the 7th Regiment.[458] Conversely, Buchanan saw Washington in a side role, and that only in the defeat of the 71st Regiment; he had no role in bringing about the surrender of the 7th.[459]

Rather than analyze more questions, some conclusions are warranted. The best evidence in the historical record is below perfect. Witnesses on both sides agreed Washington fought Ogilvie on the American left at the conclusion of the first line fighting. Defeated on the left, Tarleton pushed his next move on the American right, which served as the focus of the second line fighting. No original source placed Washington in the second line battle,[460] and they must be taken at their word.[461] Washington pursued Ogilvie forward, moving behind the line of British infantry. It took time for Washington to carve out a secure position. Once in place, the second line fighting had reached its bloody climax. Washington turned to running down British stragglers escaping the second line disaster. This was a classic

---

456 Babits, *Devil*, 117–118; Buchanan, *Guilford Courthouse*, 325.
457 Graham, *Morgan*, 303.
458 Graham, *Morgan*, 304.
459 Buchanan, *Guilford Courthouse*, 325.
460 Lee placed Washington's rout of Ogilvie at this moment, and in this he was incorrect. The maneuvers accomplished by Howard—the orderly withdrawal, the rally, the volleys—would have been impossible in the presence of enemy cavalry.
461 Buchanan erred in his contention that Washington's presence while collecting stragglers intimidated the British and held them against Howard's bayonets. The fact there were stragglers established that they were not intimidated from running away. Babits erred in his contention that Howard and Washington worked together. Howard insisted, "Washington's charge had no connexion with mine," Moncure, *Staff Ride*, 129.

cavalry operation, and would have been invaluable at the time. British stragglers covered the battlefield. Washington's role was significant, but not nearly as dramatic as Howard's. The volley and the bayonet charge ended British resistance. Washington, running down the uncounted dozens or hundreds of straggling British refugees from the fighting, played a key role in the American victory.[462]

While the British were finished, Tarleton was not. The British commander made every effort to keep his men in the fight. His efforts failed. He confessed to Cornwallis,

> A general flight ensued... Tarleton sent directions to his cavalry to form about four hundred yards to the right of the enemy, in order to check them, whilst he endeavoured to rally the infantry to protect the guns. The cavalry did not comply with the order and the effort to collect the infantry was ineffectual: Neither promises nor threats could gain their attention; they surrendered or dispersed, and abandoned the guns to the artillery men.[463]

This was a shocking admission from a proud commander. His force was in an orderless panic, and his soldiers no longer cared what he thought. Tarleton had completely lost control. For an officer in command, things could hardly get worse.

Tarleton, not easily discouraged, continued his efforts. "Tarleton made another struggle to bring his cavalry to the charge." The cavalrymen would have none of it. He then made another dire admission: "above two hundred dragoons forsook their leader, and left the field of battle."[464] Everyone, however, did not desert Tarleton or the cause. Fourteen officers and 40 enlisted cavalrymen joined Tarleton in one, final charge against Washington. Tarleton reported some limited success: Washington was "driven back into the continental infantry by this handful of

---

462 This reconstruction does not account for Washington's location at the time of Morgan's order to Howard to reform the Continentals. As stated in the text, some matters are insoluble. The most likely speculation is that Washington did not take all his troops forward to fight Ogilvie. He left a small force in reserve on the hill where he started. This would provide the most credible explanation for Washington's ability to be in the rear and the front at the same time.
463 Tarleton, *Campaigns*, 223–224.
464 Tarleton, *Campaigns*, 224.

brave men."[465] Brave men, indeed. They were fifty-five British soldiers in a sea of Americans, and, against all odds, they had done some work.

Morgan reported the end of the battle quite differently. Given all that Tarleton confessed, one may forgive a few omissions. Morgan wrote that Tarleton did not charge Washington, but rather, attacked some militia riflemen on the left flank of the main line. Washington charged Tarleton, and pushed the British with "such Firmness," that Tarleton did not contest the action, as "one would have expected from an officer of his Splendid Character." Rather, Tarleton "broke and fled."[466] Morgan's version of this event has gained little traction over the years. The reason, once again, was Lee. If Morgan was right in his rendition of the battle's conclusion, it would have cast doubt on the most cherished legend of Cowpens.

Lee told a story distinct from the one related by Morgan.[467] Lee wrote that Washington and his unit had become separated from the main body of Americans. They were fighting by themselves deep behind the British line. Tarleton saw a final opportunity and attacked Washington with elements of the 17th Light Dragoons.[468] Lee distilled the legend to its core: "the American lieutenant colonel was first rescued from this critical contest by one of his serjeants, and afterwards by a shot from his bugler's pistol."

Moncure noted correctly that this became the most famous legend to arise out of the battle. One aspect of the legend was the encounter between the two cavalry officers. Moncure described it as a classic swordfight in the midst of the confusion and death littering the battlefield. To this, he added the second aspect of the legend: "the Virginian may well have been killed were it not for the sure aim of a black soldier who shot one of Washington's assailants."[469] The legend of Washington's brush

---

465 Ibid.
466 Morgan to Greene, 19 January 1781, in Showman et al., *Greene*, 7:154. Contrast Morgan's opaque, awkward syntax with Lee's splendid language.
467 Lee, *Memoirs*, 133.
468 Fortescue, *17th Lancers*, 58; Lee, *Memoirs*, 133.
469 Moncure, *Staff Ride*, 62.

with death has earned great traction over the years. A key piece of it is the soldier of color delivering the fatal shot to the British soldier about to kill Washington.

Lee was an early advocate of the story. But in Lee's version, there was no mention of a person of color. As Lee told the story, the shot that saved Washington was fired by his bugler. In a footnote, Lee related a completely different version of the story, which he credited to John Marshall's biography of George Washington.[470] In Marshall's version, Washington was saved by a shot fired by a waiter. The assumption was that a waiter, in the southern colonies during the era of slavery, must have been a person of color.

There was no way to know the truth of any of this. The details of a small encounter after the conclusion of the second line fighting escaped the notice of British and Americans alike. Lee's bisected account was a poor foundation for the key point, the point that made the story such an important legend, and legacy, of the battle: whether a person of color delivered the final shot.[471]

So things remained for many years, until Lieutenant Colonel Howard answered several questions from a person seeking to remedy confusion about some parts of the action at Cowpens. In his answers, he volunteered that Washington had ridden ahead of his men in pursuing Ogilvie. Unguarded in the enemy rear, Washington drew attention from three British officers, one of whom was, most likely, Tarleton. The three attacked. One approached close enough to strike at Washington with his saber. An American sergeant had caught up with Washington and parried the saber cut. A second British officer struck at Washington, and "a boy, a waiter who had not the strength to wield a sword" drew his pistol and shot the officer.[472]

---

[470] John Marshall, *The Life of George Washington, Commander in Chief of the American Forces, During the War which Established the Independence of His Country, and First President of the United States*, 5 vols. (Philadelphia, 1804–1807).

[471] One of the most famous paintings to come out of the battle was by William Rainey in 1845. It shows a black soldier on the right side of the painting firing the shot that saved Washington, mounted on a white charger in the center.

[472] Moncure, *Staff Ride*, 129–130.

Context made it clear that Howard heard the story from Washington. Howard's account went far to substantiate the legend of the final shot at Cowpens. Whether a person of color fired it, although likely, will remain uncertain.[473]

Tarleton had one last event to recount, and this was a mild success on his part. He reported that a "party of Americans, who had seized upon the baggage of the British troops on the road from the late encampment, were dispersed, and this detachment retired towards Broad River unmolested."[474] He recovered some baggage, and touted this accomplishment.

There was still some of the story left to tell. Howard was the best witness for his actions at the battle's conclusion.[475] As his men moved forward in the bayonet attack, he noticed the British artillery. The cannons were war trophies. Howard set up a challenge between two officers, Captains Ewing and Anderson, to capture the artillery pieces. Anderson took the prize.[476] Tarleton faulted the infantry and cavalry for abandoning the artillery, although the artillerymen hung on.[477] Howard recalled that one British artilleryman refused to surrender his firing match, the match serving as symbolic ownership of the cannon. His men were about to bayonet the recalcitrant soldier, when Howard intervened to prevent it. He surrendered to Howard.

Howard had one tale left in him, and this one might have been the most important.[478] He received the surrender of Captain Duncanson, of the grenadier company of the 71st Regiment. After accepting his sword, Howard tried to depart on his horse, but Duncanson held him in place and refused to let

---

473 But for Howard and Washington substantiating the story, its credibility would border on the ephemeral. If Washington was so far forward he outran his cavalrymen, how did a waiter get so close to him? If we accept Howard, the waiter was not on the front line; he was well ahead of it. The waiter was in the lead, directly behind Washington and dozens of yards in advance of the cavalry troops, an astounding achievement for a noncombatant.
474 Tarleton, *Campaigns*, 224.
475 Read, "Howard," 279.
476 Graham asserted the two prizes were shared, one by Anderson, one by Kirkwood, *Morgan*, 305.
477 Tarleton, *Campaigns*, 224
478 Read, "Howard," 279.

him leave. Howard asked him his reasons. Duncanson said that he saw Howard's soldiers approaching, and this caused him great concern. Duncanson told Howard that the British were instructed not to expect any quarter from the Americans, and accordingly, had orders to give none. Howard noted only that he put Duncanson in the care of a sergeant. Babits asserted that Howard ordered the Americans to give quarter to the British, and in doing so prevented a massacre.[479]

Graham, writing a century before Babits, had arrived at a similar conclusion. Graham insisted the British were in positions of supplication on the ground. The Americans, primed for revenge and "furious at the recollection of their manifold cruelties," maintained the cry of "Tarleton's quarters," a darkly ironic reference to Tarleton's actions at the Waxhaws. Graham asserted "the work of slaughter was about commencing," when Morgan, Howard, and a group of other officers put a stop to it.[480]

At long last, the narrative has returned to its starting point: revenge. Tarleton knew very well what had happened at Waxhaws, and correctly predicted the Americans would be merciless if given the opportunity. Captain Duncanson was right to be worried about his treatment by the advancing Americans; he was probably about to be bayoneted. Only intervention by American officers could have prevented a massacre of the British at Cowpens. The Americans were ready to return Tarleton's treatment to him. It was only by a slender margin that Howard prevented a massive atrocity.

The Aftermath

The casualty figures from the Battle of Cowpens were daunting. Estimates varied widely at the time, but they were hindered by

---

[479] Babits, *Devil*, 122. The story has old foundations. An article appearing in the *Pennsylvania Packet* of 17 February 1781 told of members of the 71st Regiment begging for mercy as they surrendered, stating they given no quarter to the Americans, and had been told to expect none, Showman et al., *Greene*, 7:155n2.
[480] Graham, *Morgan*, 304.

wishful thinking and a dearth of information. Tarleton reported fewer than three hundred killed and wounded on both sides, shared equally between the Americans and British, plus the loss of less than four hundred British prisoners.[481]

Morgan reported ten British officers killed, one hundred British enlisted men killed, and two hundred wounded. He counted 502 prisoners of war. Morgan reported to Greene the American losses were "inconsiderable." He referred Greene to the battlefield returns, but these have not survived.[482] Another contemporary source detailed the American losses as ten killed and fifty-five wounded.[483]

Modern scholarship has not established a consensus on the British casualties. A serviceable estimate is one hundred British killed, two hundred wounded, and six hundred captured. These numbers represent a simplification from a debate without resolution. For example, the American Battlefield Trust put the British killed at 110, wounded at 229, and 529 missing or captured. Buchanan used figures of 110 killed and 712, of whom two hundred were wounded. Saberton advocated much larger numbers, in the range of 977 to 946 total casualties. The American losses have proven less controversial. They were twenty-five killed, 124 wounded, none missing or captured.[484]

After Cowpens, the next move belonged to Cornwallis. History has provided three schools of thought on Cornwallis after Cowpens. One school found roots in a story in which an overwhelmed, emotional Cornwallis broke his sword while listening to reports of the loss at Cowpens. He vowed to recover the

---

481 Tarleton, *Campaigns*, 224. Babits provided extracts from several casualty reports, showing a range between 839 and 957 British casualties in all categories, Babits, *Devil*, 142.

482 Morgan to Greene, 19 January 1781, in Showman et al., *Greene*, 7:154; Showman et al., *Greene*, 7:161n15; cf. Babits, *Devil*, 151.

483 Showman et al., *Greene*, 7:161n15.

484 "Cowpens," *American Battlefield Trust*, www.battlefields.org/learn/revolutionary-war/battles/cowpens.
Buchanan, Guilford Courthouse, 326; Saberton, "Winter Campaign." Saberton's arithmetic is complex and embedded in his article. To simplify his thinking: he used 1,150 as the pre-battle total. There were either 174 rank and file survivors (which he adjusts to 204 to account for officers) or 223 all ranks survivors. Subtraction yields the range in the text.

prisoners held by Morgan.[485] The second school, envisioning a calmer Cornwallis in control of himself, "resolved to prosecute the original plan of the expedition into North Carolina."[486]

The third school of thought adopted elements of the first two. The British government still believed the Carolinas held hidden stores of Loyalists ready to serve the royal cause. As long as the British maintained a credible military presence in the region, the government felt the Tories would rise in support. Cowpens was a disaster for the government's policy. Morgan's militia outnumbered his Continentals. Tarleton's force included a large number of regular British units. It was a worst-case scenario for the British: American militia destroyed an army of British regulars. If the government's strategy was to have any chance of success, the population would have to see Morgan punished and humiliated.

Selecting one of the three would prove futile. Cornwallis's correspondence rested firmly in the second camp, reflecting a calm and rational decision to continue the mission despite setbacks. Human nature, on the other hand, suggests otherwise, and people tend to suspect that beneath Cornwallis's stoic exterior beat the emotional heart of a warrior.

For whatever combination of reasons, reinforced with an infusion of soldiers under Major General Alexander Leslie, Cornwallis began the chase. He commanded a juggernaut of 2700 British regulars.[487] Morgan, realizing he was severely outnumbered, retreated north. This was the first step in the chess game of fire and maneuver termed the Race to the Dan, so-called after the Dan River, the goal of both sides in the con-

---

485 Wickwire and Wickwire, *Cornwallis*, 269.
486 Stedman, *History*, 2:325.
487 As with all troop counts in the southern war, this number is controversial. The debate is beyond the scope of this book. To oversimplify: the second invasion culminated at the Battle of Guilford Courthouse. The official British Army return for the day showed 1,924 men on the field; the U.S. Army figure for British soldiers on the field was 1,900; Buchanan gave us 1,950; Lee famously wrote the "real number" was less than 2,000. The number of British casualties between the start of the invasion and Guilford Courthouse totaled 400. Cornwallis subtracted between 300 and 400 men for baggage guard during the battle. Adding back in these subtractions, we get about 2,700 soldiers at the outset of the move into North Carolina.

test. After considering a number of options, Greene decided to reunite his army. He ordered Brigadier General Isaac Huger to move the eastern wing of the army north, while Greene left to take personal command of Morgan's western wing. Greene led Cornwallis on a chase north in the worst possible conditions. It was winter. Resupply was always questionable. Winter rains swelled the creeks, and made the Catawba and Yadkin Rivers almost impassable. A desperate Cornwallis, in a move emulating Hernán Cortés's invasion of the Aztec empire, burned his supply wagons.

The two halves of the American army joined at Guilford Courthouse on 8 February. The Dan River, flowing near the Virginia-North Carolina border, was the next natural barrier to movement north. Greene sent his quartermaster ahead of his army to requisition every boat he could find, a task at which he excelled. Morgan, debilitated with chronic pain, was sent home, and replaced with Colonel Otho Williams from Maryland. Greene put Williams in charge of a large detachment of light infantry, with orders to harass and delay the British. Greene took the main body of the army north, crossing the Dan on 14 February, followed shortly by Williams, and only hours ahead of Cornwallis's arrival on the riverbank. The British, beaten in time, were also defied by the fact the Americans had taken every boat capable of crossing the river. The Race to the Dan was over, and Greene had won. The Americans gained the time and space to replenish their forces. Both sides were free to prepare the stage for the next phase of the campaign, which followed very soon.

Greene recrossed into North Carolina on 22 February. The two sides skirmished with each other through early March 1781.[488] All the while, Greene received badly needed reinforcements, both militia and Continental regulars. For Cornwallis, there were no new soldiers on offer. On 15 March, the two main armies met for their first and only contest, the Battle of Guilford Courthouse. At Guilford Courthouse, the Americans per-

---

488 The traditional view is that the first skirmish was at Hart's Mill on or about 22 February, the final skirmish at Weitzel's Mill on 6 March.

formed generally well, but at the end of the day, left the field to the British. The victory, though, was too expensive. Cornwallis lost more than one-quarter of his army at Guilford Courthouse. These were losses the British could not replace. Cornwallis, now too weak to fight a rematch against Greene, moved east, first to Cross Creek, then to Wilmington on the coast. After a stay in Wilmington, he abandoned North Carolina altogether and moved north into Virginia.

Cornwallis's move into Virginia, after a few initial successes, led him into disaster at Yorktown. In the meantime, although Greene had lost the field at Guilford Courthouse, he had freed most of North Carolina from British occupation. The only British military presence in the deep south was in half a dozen isolated garrisons such as Charleston and Savannah. The vast swath of the south was Patriot territory.

A Note on Sources

This book is largely about the interplay of what we know, derived from primary source material, and what we think we know, largely derived from secondary sources of all types. The Battle of Cowpens was not inherently complicated. It lasted less than an hour; there was little time for any real complication. Nevertheless, as secondary sources about the battle proliferated over the years, tales and legends grew. Some were fascinating, but sadly, all of them had the potential to confound the casual reader who simply wanted to know what actually happened.

Legendary heroes came wrapped within the legends. Daniel Morgan was a hero, and since Cowpens, has been the subject of legends. While much acclaim was due Morgan, the legendary piece of his fame was problematic for those wanting to learn his real accomplishments.

Hence, this book. I have sifted through the secondary sources, some of which have been both immensely popular as well as incredibly influential, to return the discussion to the eyewitnesses, the soldiers who were at Cowpens and fought the battle.

With these facts in mind, the most important sources are the eighteenth-century officers and soldiers who left us memoirs of what they did and what they saw. Tarleton and Mackenzie from the British side will always figure importantly in any discussion of Cowpens. Stedman, as Cornwallis's staff officer and protégé, reliably reported on what he saw from his position at army headquarters. On the American side, Morgan himself, who left a fine after-action report, has been a valuable, but too-long ignored, resource on the battle. Samuel Hammond, as well, left a wonderful, albeit short, memoir, as did William Seymour.

Much turned on one's views of Henry Lee's contribution to the literature of the battle. Ordinarily, Lee's *Memoirs* have proven an invaluable first-person account of much of the southern campaign. But Lee was not present at Cowpens. His memoir, normally a fine primary source, was the oldest secondary source, and one of the most ill-used. Lee had an enthusiasm for war and a dislike of Tarleton. He loved stories, and loved the soldiers who told them. All of these tendencies came together after Cowpens, and Lee wrote a truly heroic saga of men and war that resonates deeply with us today. There is, of course, one overwhelming problem: much of it is not true. I have referred often to Lee's book, usually to take advantage of his command of the language, his ability to put the reader right there in the saddle, next to him, as he rode into battle. But, at Cowpens, it is dangerous to rely on Lee as a resource for facts. He was much more interested in creating a legend, which he accomplished incredibly successfully.

Another source of both good and bad material was John Eager Howard. A brilliant commander and unparalleled soldier, his prose was not as elevated as Lee's. He left letters and other snippets of work to clue us in on what he did, or what he was thinking. But, overall, he wrote these long years after the war, and much of what he wrote bears the marks of the passage of years. While Howard is a necessary witness, the reader needs to be careful with his writings.

Finally, we have the issue of Revolutionary War pension applications. As I discuss at length in the book, it may be too easy to place reliance on them. The pension enabling acts dated to 1818 and 1832, long years after the war. It was no challenge to embellish, or fabricate, an application for a government pension, either by enhancing one's war record or creating one newly out of whole cloth. People lie for money, and the pension applications are not immune to this sad fact. Lieutenant Colonel Moncure cautioned against them, advising the reader to look at all the facts and circumstances, and decide if an application was believable. He was very helpful in this task, in that he quoted from them extensively, in long segments, which allowed the reader the opportunity to weigh what the applicant said, and how he said it. I disagree with using these applications without this kind of procedural safeguard. Simply footnoting an unquoted pension application provides little value, in that it does not give the reader the means to judge whether the application is worthy of belief.

The secondary sources are available in huge numbers. The important task is selection among the vast array on display. I have limited them to a few, and these, I thought, were important. Buchanan and Babits both wrote important and popular histories, and both were very influential in driving the battle's narrative. In an earlier day, the same was true of William Johnson and James Graham. I like the official histories from the British regiments, as well as those published by the U.S. Army; these all bring some credibility with them, thanks to their sources. By the same token, Bartholomees, later in life to reach a pinnacle of success as a historian for the Army, wrote a key paper on Cowpens that will probably never see an equal.

In the bibliography, I have focused on materials that should be accessible to most people, either through libraries or over the internet. There are thousands of original documents in private collections, but a trip to Maryland to read the Howard papers is probably more effort than the casual reader in North Carolina is prepared to undertake.

Appendix: Morgan's Report

In examining the accretion of legends onto the facts of the Battle of Cowpens, this book has placed great emphasis on Daniel Morgan's report of the fighting. In an odd turn of fate, Morgan's report itself provided a pointed illustration of the way a core of factual events will attract secondary material of arguable value.

The National Archives holds the original report by Morgan to Greene. It begins on page 541 of volume 1 of *Letters from Maj. Gen. Nathanael Greene, 1776–1785*. The letter is a masterpiece of lean prose. It contains not a single wasted word. Here is a transcription of Morgan's original:

Camp near Cain Creek January 19. 1781

Dear Sir,

The Troops I have the honor to command have gained a compleat Victory over a Detachment from the British Army commanded by Lieut. Colonel Tarlton. The action happened on the 17th Inst. about Sunrise at a Place called the Cowpens near Pacolet River.

On the 14th having recieved intelligence that the British Army were in motion and that their movements clearly indicated their intentions of dislodging me, I abandoned my Encampment at Grindales' Ford and on the 16th in the Evening took possession of a Post about 7 miles from the Cherokee Ford on Broad River. My former Position subjected me at once to the Operations of Lord Cornwallis and Colonel Tarlton and in case of a Defeat my Retreat might easily have been cut off. My situation at the Cowpens enabled me to improve any advantages that I might gain and to provide better for my

Security should I be unfortunate. These Reasons induced me to take this Post notwithstanding it had the appearances of a Retreat. On the Evening of the 16th the Enemy occupied the Ground we had removed from in the morning before. An Hour before daylight one of my Scouts informed me that they had advanced within five miles of our camp. On this Information the necessary dispositions were made and from the alacrity of the Troops we were soon prepared to recieve them.

The light Infantry commanded by Lieut. Colonel Howard and the Virginia Militia under Major Triplett were formed on a rising ground. The 3rd Regiment of Dragoons consisting of about 80 men under the command of Lt. Colonel Washington were so posted in their rear as not to be injured by the Enemy's Fire and yet to be able to charge them should an Occasion offer. The Volunteers from N. Carolina, S. Carolina and Georgia under the command of Colonel Pickens were posted to guard the Flanks. Major McDowell of the N. Carolina Volunteers was posted on the right Flank in front of the Line 150 yards, and Major Cunningham of the Georgia Volunteers on the left at the same distance in Front. Colonels Brannons and Thomas of the S. Carolina Volunteers on the right of Major McDowell, and Colonels Hays and McCall of the same Corps on the left of Major Cunningham. Captains Tate and Buchannan with the Augusta Riflemen were to support the right of the Line.

The Enemy drew up in one Line 400 yards in Front of our advanced Corps. The 1st Batt. of the 71t Reg. was opposed to our Right. The 7th Regt. to our left. The Legion Infantry to our Center and two companies of light Troops of 100 each on our Flanks. In their Front they moved two Pieces of Artillery and Lt. Colonel Tarlton with 280 cavalry was posted in the rear of his Line. The Disposition being thus made small Parties of riflemen were detached to skirmish with the Enemy, on which their whole line advanced with the greatest Impetuosity shouting as they advanced. Majors McDowell and Cunningham gave them a heavy and galling Fire and retreated to the Regiments intended for their support. The whole of Colonel Pickens's Command then kept up a Fire by Regiments retreating agreable to orders. When the Enemy advanced to our Line they received a well directed and incessant fire, but their numbers being superior to ours they gained our Flanks which obliged us to change our Position. We retired in good order about 50 Paces, formed and advanced on the Enemy and gave them a brisk Fire which threw them into Disorder. Lt Colonel Howard observing this gave orders for the Line to charge Bayonets which was done with such address that the Enemy fled with the utmost Precipitation.

Lt. Colonel Washington discovering that the Cavalry were cutting down our Riflemen on the left charged them with such Firmness as obliged them to retire in Confusion. The Enemy were entirely routed and the Pursuit continued upwards of 20 miles.

Our loss was inconsiderable not having more than 12 killed and 60 wounded. The Enemys loss was 10 Com. officers and upwards of 100 Rank and File killed; 200 wounded; 29 Com. officers and above 500 Privates Prisoners, which fell into our Hands with two Peices of Artillery, two standards, 800 Musquets, one travelling Forge, 35 Baggage Waggons, 70 negroes and upwards of 100 Dragoon Horses with all their Musick. They Destroyed most of their Baggage which was immense.

Altho' our Success was compleat, we fought only 800 men and were opposed by upwards of 1000 of chosen British Troops.

Such was the Inferiority of our numbers, that our Success must be attributed to the Justice of our Cause and the Bravery of our Troops. My Wishes would induce me to mention the name of every private Centinel in the Corps. In Justice to the [scratched out] Bravery and good Conduct of the officers, I have taken the Liberty to enclose you a list of their names from a conviction that you will be pleased to introduce such Characters to the World.

Major Giles my aid d. camp and Capt. Brooks acting as my Brigade Major deserve and have my thanks for their assistance & behavior on this occasion.

The Baron de Glasbeech who accompanies Major Giles with these Dispatches served with me as a volunteer and behaved in such a manner as to merit your attention.

I am
dr. sir,
Yr. obt. Servt.
Dan Morgan

After Greene received the report, a copyist transcribed the text into Greene's book of orders. The book also survives in the National Archives. The Cowpens report begins on page 39 of volume 1 of *Transcripts of Letters from Maj. Gen. Nathanael Greene, 1780–1784*. Much more legible than its predecessor, the text is identical, with three minor exceptions. First, the copyist corrected spelling errors, most visibly "Tarleton." Second, he used a different scheme of capitalization and abbreviation. Third, near the end, the original reads, "in Justice to *the* Bravery and good Conduct of the officers, I have taken the Liberty to enclose a list of their names." The copy reads, "in justice to *their* bravery and good conduct of the officers, I have taken the liberty to enclose a list of their names." The word forming the focus of the disagreement starts as "the" in both cases. In the original, the "ir" appears to be scratched out, but incompletely. In the copy, the copyist kept the entire word "their" intact. In context, "the" makes more sense.

Morgan's aide de camp, Major Edward Giles, couriered the report to Greene. Greene had the responsibility to report the news to Congress. Rather than prepare a report on his own, Greene sat down with Giles to augment Morgan's original. With Morgan's canvas on his easel, Greene's creativity manifested in his changes.

Greene's editors identified the handwriting in the edited report as Giles's. These historians spent a great deal of time with manuscripts of the age, and were in a position to identify the handwriting of writers in Greene's circle. Here, we accept their expertise.

The handwriting in the edited copy is identical to that in Morgan's original, and must belong to Giles. This development should not alarm. Giles was Morgan's aide, and it would be highly likely he would put Morgan's thoughts on paper.

The edits in the recopied report are substantial. Greene's editors identified both Giles's and Greene's hands at work in the editing process. Presumably, any work by Giles was done at Greene's direction. The edited report shows two paragraphs below Morgan's signature, identified by Greene's editors as Greene's handwriting. In preparing their official transcription of the edited report, the one that went to Congress, the editors declined to include Greene's addendum.

Greene deleted very little, and nothing of substance, from Morgan. Instead, the edits added a huge amount of material, most of it unrelated to the troops on the field at Cowpens. For example, Morgan wrote:

The action happened on the 17th Inst. about sunrise at a place called the Cowpens near Pacolet River.

On the 14th having received intelligence that the British Army were in motion, and that their movements clearly indicated their intentions of dislodging me.

Greene, unsatisfied with such a bare bones approach, believed Congress needed to hear more emphatic language:

The Action happened on the 17th Instant about Sunrise at the Cowpens. It perhaps would be well to remark, for the Honour of the American Arms, that Altho the progress of this Corps was marked with Burnings and Devastations & altho' they have waged the most cruel Warfare, not a man was killed wounded or even insulted after he surrendered. Had not Britons during this Contest received so many Lessons of Humanity, I should flatter myself that this might teach them a little, but I fear they are incorrigible.

To give you a just Idea of our Operations, it will be necessary to inform you, that on the 14th Instant having recieved certain Intelligence that Lord Cornwallis and Lt Colonel Tarlton were both in Motion, and that their movements clearly indicated their Intentions of dislodging me.

Greene made no amendments to the troop deployments or the conduct of the fighting. Nevertheless, he felt compelled to embellish Morgan's original when politics, expediency, or propaganda called. For example, Morgan described the flank protection on the main line of battle as simple facts: "the volunteers from N. Carolina, S. Carolina and Georgia under the command of Colonel Pickens were posted to guard the Flanks." Greene, disappointed in this bland display, gilded the lily: "The Volunteers of North Carolina, South Carolina & Georgia under the Command of the brave and valuable Colonel Pickens, were situated to guard the Flanks."

Troop counts and casualties figured prominently in Greene's editing. The best information available presently elects 23 January as the date Giles arrived at Greene's headquarters with Morgan's report. Six days after the battle, it was possible Greene had better information on the numbers. His edits suggested he had received some information from British prisoners of war.

On the American troop count, Morgan wrote, "we fought only 800 men." Greene expanded Morgan's five words: "From our Force being composed of such a Variety of Corps, a wrong Judgment may be formed of our Numbers. We fought only 800 men, two thirds of which were Militia." Morgan described the British force as "upwards of 1000 of chosen British Troops." Greene added much: "the British with their Baggage Guard, were not less than 1150, & these Veteran Troops. Their own Officers confess, that they fought 1037."

The American casualties in Morgan's report were enumerated succinctly: "Our loss was inconsiderable not having more than twelve killed and sixty wounded." Greene changed this to reflect the fact he had better numbers: "Our Loss is inconsiderable, which the enclosed Returns will evince." The returns have not survived, which suggests he may not have forwarded them to Congress with the edited report.

Morgan's rendition of the British casualties amounted to twenty-nine commissioned officers and one hundred rank and file killed in action. There were two hundred wounded. He captured twenty-nine commissioned officers and more than five hundred rank and file soldiers. He did not separate noncommissioned officers. Greene's version was much less clear: "As I was obliged to move off of the Field of Action on the m[ornin]g to secure the Prisoners, I cannot be so accurate as to the killed & wounded of the Enemy as I could wish. From the Reports of an officer I sent to view the Ground," there were ten commissioned officers killed in action. He enumerated one hundred noncommissioned officers and privates in the tally of killed in action. There were two hundred rank and file wounded. Prisoners of war totaled 502, of which twenty-nine were commissioned officers.

The report as sent to Congress was a near-illegible mass of crossed out sentences and interlineations. The compelling mystery was the reason Greene did not order Giles to prepare a final, clean copy. After all, the original and the edited version were in Giles's handwriting. A clean copy would have been indistinguishable from an original.

The official, final version of the report on the Battle of Cowpens resides in the Library of Congress on microfilm reel 1 of the *Nathanael Greene Papers*. It reads as follows:

Camp near Cain Creek Jan[y] 19[h] 1781

The Troops I have the Honor to command have been so fortunate as to obtain a compleat Victory over a Detachment from the British Army commanded by L[t] Colonel Tarlton. The Action happened on the 17[h] Instant about Sunrise at the Cowpens. It perhaps would be well to remark, for the Honour of the American Arms, that Altho' the Progress of this Corps was marked with Burnings and Devastations & altho' they have waged the most cruel Warfare, not a man was killed, wounded or even insulted after he surrendered. Had not Britons during this Contest recieved so many Lessons of Humanity, I should flatter myself that this might teach them a little, but I fear they are incorrigible.

To give you a just Idea of our Operations it will be necessary to inform you, that on the 14[h] Instant having recieved certain Intelligence that Lord Cornwallis and L[t] Colonel Tarlton were both in Motion, and that their movements clearly indicated their Intentions of dislodging me, I abandoned my Encampment at Grindales Ford on Pacolet, and on the 16[h] in the Evening took Possession of a Post, about seven miles from the Cherokee Ford on Broad River. My original Position subjected me at once to the Operations of both Cornwallis and Tarlton, and in Case of a Defeat, my Retreat might easily have been cut off. My Situation at the Cowpens enabled me to improve any Advantages I might gain, and to provide better for my own Security, should I be unfortunate. These Reasons induced me to take this Post at the Risque of its wearing the Face of a Retreat.

I recieved regular Intelligence of the Enemy's Movements from the Time they were first in Motion. On the Evening of the 16[h] Ins they took Possession of the Ground I had removed from in the Morning, distant from the Scene of Action about 12 miles. An Hour before Day light one of my Scouts returned and informed me that L[t] Colonel Tarlton had advanced within five miles of our Camp. On this information I hastened to form as good a Disposition as Circumstances would admit, and from the alacrity of the Troops we were soon prepared to recieve them. The Light Infantry commanded by L[t] Colonel Howard and the Virginia Militia, under the command of Maj[r] Triplette were formed on a rising Ground, and extended a Line in Front.

The 3rd Regiment of Dragoons under Lt Colonel Washington were so posted at such a Distance in their Rear as not to be subjected to the Line of Fire directed at them, and to be so near as to be able to charge the Enemy, should they be broke. The Volunteers of North Carolina, South Carolina & Georgia under the Command of the brave and valuable Colonel Pickens, were situated to guard the Flanks. Maj^r McDowell of the NC Volunteers, was posted on the right Flank in Front of the line 150 yards & Major Cunningham with the Georgia Volunteers on the left at the same distance in Front. Colonels Brannon & Thomas of the S Carolinians were posted on the right of Major McDowell and Colonels Hays and McCall of the same Corps on the left of Major Cunningham. Cap^{ts} Tate & Buchanan with the Augusta Riflemen to support the right of the Line.

The Enemy drew up in single Line of Battle 400 y^{ds} in Front of our advanced Corps. The first Battalion of the 71st Regm was opposed to our Right; the 7th Regt to our Left. The Infantry of the Legion to our Center. The Light Companies on their Flanks. In Front moved two Peices of Artillery. Lt Colonel Tarlton with his Cavalry was posted in the Rear of his Line. The Disposition of Battle being thus formed, small Parties of Riflemen were dispatched to skirmish with the Enemy, upon which their whole Line moved on with the greatest Impetuosity shouting as they advanced. McDowell & Cunningham gave them a heavy & galling Fire & retreated to the Regiments intended for their Support. The whole of Colonel Picken's Command then kept up a Fire by Regiments retreating agreable to their Orders. When the Enemy advanced to our Line, they recieved a well-directed and incessant Fire, but their Numbers being superiour to ours, they gained our Flanks, which obliged us to change our Position. We retired in good Order about 50 Paces, formed, advanced on the Enemy & gave them a fortunate Volley which threw them into Disorder. Lt Colonel Howard observing this gave orders for the Line to charge Bayonets, which was done with such Address that they fled with the utmost Precipitation, leaving the Field Pieces in our Possession. We pushed our Advantage so effectually, that they never had an Opportunity of of rallying, had their Intentions been ever so good.

Lt Colonel Washington having been informed that Tarlton was Cutting our Riflemen on the left Flank pushed forward & charged them with such Firmness that instead of attempting to recover the Fate of the Day, which one would have expected from an officer of his Splendid Character, broke and fled.

The Enemy's whole Force were now bent solely in providing for their Safety in Flight. The List of their killed, wounded and Prisoners, will inform you with what Effect. Tarlton with the small Remains of his Cavalry & a few scattering Infantry he had mounted on his Waggon Horses made their Escape. He was Persued 24 miles, but owing to our having taken a wrong Trail at first, we never could overtake him.

As I was obliged to move off of the Field of Action in the m[ornin]g to secure the Prisoners, I cannot be so accurate as to the killed & wounded of the Enemy as I could wish. From the Reports of an officer I sent to view the Ground, there was 100 Noncommissioned officers & Privates & ten commissioned Officers killed and two hundred R[ank] & F[ile] wounded. We have in our Possession 502 non C[ommissioned], O[fficers], & P[rivates]. Prisoners independent of the wounded, & the Militia are taking up straglers continually. 29 C[ommissioned] Officers have fell into our Hands. Their Rank &c & you will see by an enclosed List. The Officers I have paroled. The Privates I am now conveying by the shortest Rout to Salsburrey. Two Standards, two Field Peices, 35 Waggons, a travelling Forge, & all their Music are ours. Their Baggage, which was immense, they have in great Measure destroyed. Our loss in inconsiderable, which the enclosed Returns will evince. I have not been able to ascertain Colonel Pickens Loss but know it to be very small.

From our Force being composed of such a Variety of Corps, a wrong Judgment may be formed of our Numbers. We fought only 800 men, two thirds of which were Militia. The British with their Baggage Guard, were not less than 1150, & these Veteran Troops. Their own Officers confess, that they fought 1037. Such was the Inferiority of our Numbers that our Success must be attributed to the Justice of our Cause & the Bravery of our Troops. My Wishes would Induce me to mention the Name of every private Centinel in the Corps I have the honor to Command. In Justice to their Bravery & good Conduct, I have taken the Liberty to enclose you a List of their Officers from a Conviction that you would be pleased to introduce such Characters to the World.

Major Giles my Aid & Capt Brookes my Brigade Majr, deserve & have my thanks for their Assistance & Behaviour on this Occasion.

The Baron De Glaibeeck who accompanies Major Giles with these Dispatches served with me in the Action as a Volunteer and behaved in such a manner as merits your Attention.

I am Dr Sir, Y^r Ob Servt
Dan Morgan

The last two paragraphs that followed Morgan's conclusion, in Greene's handwriting, were a rough draft for his edits on the casualty figures. He started by recopying Morgan's accounting of the American casualties: "Our loss was very inconsiderable not having more than 12 killed and sixty wounded." He then copied the next few sentences from Morgan. Several strike-outs followed, after which he added detail on the casualties and the plunder of war. The wording in the final, edited version emerged from this work.

One sees the accumulation of legend in the mutation of this single document. Greene, who was not present at Cowpens, felt the need, and the entitlement, to change the report of the general on the field. Greene's edits have come down to the present as part of the original report. Therefore, to Morgan's terse and efficient English, one sees added such things as the "brave and valuable" Pickens, as well as talk of "Burnings and Devastations" unrelated to the conduct of the battle. Thus began the addition of legend to the facts. Once down this road, it was a short trip to three lines of battle and a double envelopment.

SELECTED AND ANNOTATED BIBLIOGRAPHY

Books

Annual Register, or a View of the History, Politics, and Literature, for the Year 1781. London, 1782.

The *Annual Register* was an influential London publication digesting current events for a popular audience. Edmond Burke served as its first editor, but he had most likely ceased his association with it by 1781. Those historians accused of plagiarism, such as Ramsay and Stedman, were said to use this reference as their primary resource. During the Revolutionary War, the *Annual Register* reflected the thinking of the British establishment, and serves as a barometer of conventional public opinion at the time. There were imitators with very similar names. The original was published by J. Dodsley.

Babits, Lawrence E. *A Devil of a Whipping: The Battle of Cowpens.* Chapel Hill: University of North Carolina Press, 1998.

Babits's book proved highly influential in the conversation about the Battle of Cowpens. It is a must-read for anyone with an interest in the battle.

Babits, Lawrence E., and Joshua B. Howard. *Long, Obstinate, and Bloody: The Battle of Guilford Courthouse.* Chapel Hill: University of North Carolina Press, 2009.

> This book has become the standard work on Guilford Courthouse, the arguably related successor engagement to Cowpens. Several important issues arose at Cowpens and translated into issues at Guilford Courthouse. Greene, we are told, used Morgan's plan from Cowpens as his template for Guilford Courthouse. So, for example, how many volleys did Morgan want from his militia? How many did Greene? The traditional view tells us that to grasp one is to hold the other.

Black, Jeremy. *Warfare in the Eighteenth Century.* London: Cassell, 1999.

> There are dozens of good books on eighteenth-century tactics. Any serious student of the military engagements of the era will need at least one. I like Black's book for its easy accessibility.

Buchanan, John. *The Road to Guilford Courthouse: The American Revolution in the Carolinas.* New York: John Wiley & Sons, 1997.

> Buchanan's book is a monumental work that takes the reader throughout the southern campaign from its beginning to its climax at Guilford Courthouse. Buchanan enchants the reader with an engaging literary style that makes history read like a novel. This is a key work for the reader interested in putting Cowpens into its historical context.

Fortescue, John W. *A History of the 17th Lancers.* Reprint of the 1895 London edition, Project Gutenberg, 2022.

> Fortescue's book was intended as an official history of the regiment. While it is never risk-free to rely on secondary sources, official sources, with the boost of the organization's institutional knowledge, might enjoy some enhanced credi-

bility. The 17th Light Dragoons, also known as the 17th Lancers, played a significant role at Cowpens, but exactly what role has proven controversial. This book is a huge help in sorting out what we really know, from what other secondary sources have convinced us we might know.

Graham, James. *The Life of General Daniel Morgan, of the Virginia Line of the Army of the United States, With Portions of His Correspondence, Compiled from Authentic Sources.* New York, 1859.

Graham was an early admirer and biographer of Morgan. He was, unfortunately, plagued with the malady that affects so many authors of secondary sources: he had an agenda. He was determined to paint Morgan as a legend. An admirable goal, but one that can make for some questionable history. Graham is an important resource, but the reader always needs to be careful to walk around the pitfalls inherent in his writing.

Graham, William A. *General Joseph Graham and His Papers on North Carolina Revolutionary History.* Raleigh: Edwards & Broughton, 1904.

Joseph Graham was a Revolutionary War fighter, and later in life a militia general during the War of 1812. He is interesting for his contrarian views on almost every engagement that preceded the Battle of Guilford Courthouse. It seems as if every skirmish had an orthodox rendition and a Graham version. In any event, while he was not at Cowpens, he is helpful in his blunt, uncensored views on the militia of his day. A militia officer himself, he spoke with some authority on a touchy subject.

Johnson, Joseph. *Traditions and Reminiscences, Chiefly of the American Revolution in the South: Including Biographical Sketches, Incidents, and Anecdotes, Few of Which Have Been Published, Particularly of Residents in the Upper Country.* Charleston, 1851.

Joseph Johnson preserved a great deal of oral and written history related to the Revolutionary War in South Carolina. It is to Johnson we owe the preservation of Thomas Young's statement and Samuel Hammond's maps. Johnson added nothing of his own; he saw his role as a preserver of history. His book is an essential resource for the Cowpens scholar. Agree or disagree with Hammond's map, it is something everyone studying the battle must deal with.

Johnson, William. *Sketches of the Life and Correspondence of Nathanael Greene*, 2 vols. Charleston, 1822.

William Johnson was a very early biographer of Nathanael Greene. He had unprecedented access to the records of the southern army and Greene's personal papers. He diligently visited the battlefield sites about which he wrote. He was a detailed, thorough historian, and his views on things influenced generations of historians following him.

Lamb, R. *Original and Authentic Journal of Occurrences During the Late American War, from its Commencement to the Year 1783*. Dublin, 1809.

Lamb was a British infantryman who wrote a famous memoir of his experiences in America after the war. Lamb is always interesting for those of us who want to read about the conduct of battles from the ground level. While the officers—Lee, Tarleton, and the rest—wrote of grand strategy and big events, Lamb gave us tales of trudging through mud and wading through freezing water. His tale of Cowpens is short, but he delivered it with punch.

Lee, Henry. *Memoirs of the War in the Southern Department of the United States.* Washington, DC, 1827.

Lee is an indispensable source on any aspect of the southern campaign. He was not an eyewitness at Cowpens, and his rendition of the battle reads more like what he would have done rather than what actually occurred. In this regard, one must be careful with Lee. Usually scrupulous where he was present, he was an admirer of Morgan, and was not averse to adding to the latter's legend. There are many editions of Lee. The first edition appeared in two volumes in 1812. There was a one-volume 1827 edition. The most famous was the 1869 edition, prepared by the author's more famous son, Robert E. Lee.

Lossing, Benson J. *Pictorial Field-Book of the Revolution*, 2 vols. New York, 1852.

Lossing was an early popular history writer, whose book did a great deal to return the Revolutionary War to popularity. For the reader looking to put Cowpens into its historical context, his book is a good choice.

Mackenzie, Roderick. *Strictures on Lt. Col. Tarleton's History of the Campaigns of 1780 and 1781 in the Southern Provinces of North America.* London, 1787.

Mackenzie is one of the necessary primary sources dealing with Cowpens. He hated Tarleton, and his agenda permeated his work. Nevertheless, if the reader keeps this fairly obvious point in mind, his work is valuable as the memoir of an eyewitness to most of the key events in the battle.

Ramsay, David. *History of the American Revolution*, 2 vols. Philadelphia, 1789.

Ramsay's book represented an early effort to put the Revolutionary War into context. He was excoriated for plagiarism in the middle of the twentieth century, but keeping this in mind, Ramsay is interesting for the student who enjoys reading how legends start and develop. For example, it is fascinating to read the course of the battle as told by Ramsay, who wrote his book decades before Lee, then compare it to the battle as reconstructed by Buchanan 200 years later. Their versions reflect intervening scholarship as well as demonstrate the continuing power of the Lee tradition.

Ross, Charles, ed. *Correspondence of Charles, First Marquis Cornwallis*, 3 vols. London, 1859.

Ross compiled a great deal of Cornwallis's correspondence over his long career. Volume one deals with the southern campaign, and for years it served as the authoritative, final word. Ross added very little of his own work, but what he added was a reliable picture of establishment thinking. Ross is still highly recommended for anyone studying the era.

Saberton, Ian, ed. *The Cornwallis Papers: The Campaigns of 1780 and 1781 in the Southern Theatre*, 6 vols. Uckfield, Sussex: Naval & Military Press, 2010.

Saberton represents a recent, successful effort to displace Ross's primacy. Within the field of the southern war, Saberton's work is significantly more inclusive, and preserves hundreds of documents not found in Ross.

Salley, A. S., Jr., ed. *Col. William Hill's Memoirs of the Revolution.* Colombia, SC: The State Company, 1921.

Salley's work is a very short memoir of a relatively obscure South Carolina Revolutionary War figure. With respect to Cowpens, it contains details of the internal workings of the militia. Hill was an acolyte of Thomas Sumter, and Hill's work gains great importance in other battles as Sumter rose to prominence as a militia commander.

Schenck, David. *North Carolina. 1780–'81. Being a History of the Invasion of the Carolinas by the British Army Under Lord Cornwallis in 1780–'81.* Raleigh, 1889.

Schenck is another commonly seen secondary source. Schenck's agenda overwhelmed much of his narrative. He intended to restore North Carolina's reputation in the Revolutionary War, which he believed had been impaired by historians from South Carolina and Virginia. Whether he was right or wrong in his contention, he spent a great deal of effort polishing the role of North Carolina in the southern campaign. Schenck was an engaging writer with an ear for a story, and his book is always interesting reading.

Seymour, William. *Journal of the Southern Expedition, 1780-1783.* Wilmington, DE: Historical Society of Delaware, 1896.

Seymour, like Lamb, was the too-rare enlisted man who was willing to share his experiences in a memoir of the war. Again, like Lamb, while the officers addressed grand matters, Seymour presented a ground-level view of war.

Showman, Richard K., Dennis M. Conrad, Roger N. Parks, Elizabeth C. Stevens, eds., *Papers of General Nathanael Greene, vol. 6: 1 June 1780 –25 December 1780.* Chapel Hill: University of North Carolina Press, 1991.

Showman, Richard K., Dennis M. Conrad, Roger N. Parks, Elizabeth C. Stevens, eds., *Papers of General Nathanael Greene, vol. 7: 26 December 1780–29 March 1781.* Chapel Hill: University of North Carolina Press, 1994.

The Greene papers are an essential, original resource for anyone with a serious interest in any aspect of the southern campaign after Greene took command. The whole series is twelve volumes, of which two, volumes six and seven, relate to the period considered in this book.

Stedman, C. *History of the Origin, Progress, and Termination of the American War,* 2 vols. London, 1794.

Stedman is another indispensable primary source. Stedman was an officer on Cornwallis's staff, and had access to the army's books and records, as well as to Cornwallis personally. Although rightly criticized for plagiarism, the value of Stedman is in his commentary. He was a shrewd observer of people and events, and his book will always provide insight into its times.

Tarleton, Banastre. *History of the Campaigns of 1780 and 1781, in the Southern Provinces of North America.* Dublin, 1787.

Tarleton is an unavoidable resource. He had an agenda after Cowpens, the kind of thing that is always a trap for the unwary. As long as the reader keeps in mind that Tarleton was in deep trouble, needed a way out, and used his book as a way to get it, his narrative is fascinating and valuable. There are two editions of Tarleton, both published in 1787. The Dublin edition lacks illustrations, while the London edition contains sketch maps of the battlefields.

Wright, Robert K., Jr. *The Continental Army.* Washington, D.C.: United States Army Center of Military History, 1983.

The official word by the U.S. Army on its subject. The book is concise, well-researched and well-written. It is highly recommended to anyone with an interest in the Continental Army.

Wyatt, Thomas. *Memoirs of the Generals, Commodores, and Other Commanders, who Distinguished Themselves in the American Army and Navy During the Wars of the Revolution and 1812.* Philadelphia, 1843.

Wyatt is one of the few authors who preserved information derived from John Eager Howard, including his tale of Cowpens. Howard wrote very little, and Wyatt preserved some good information. There is much overlap between him and the other two good Howard sources, Moncure and Read.

Articles

Bennett, C. P. "The Delaware Regiment in the Revolution." *The Pennsylvania Magazine of History and Biography* 9, No. 4 (Jan. 1886): 451-462.

Bennett is one of few good resources on the fate of the Delaware Regiment as it reduced in strength over the southern campaign. The Delawares are a topic unto themselves, so much in Bennett will draw the reader far from Cowpens.

"Cowpens." *The Southern Campaign of the Revolutionary War*, www.battlefields.org/learn/revolutionary-war/battles/cowpens

A quick overlook digesting modern scholarship on casualties during the battle.

Geist, Christopher. "Of Rocks, Trees, Rifles, and Militia: Thoughts on Eighteenth-Century Military Tactics," *Colonial Williamsburg Journal* (Winter 08).

This is one of several accessible overviews on eighteenth-century tactics.

Hagist, Don N. "Untangling British Army Ranks." *Journal of the American Revolution*, May 19, 2016, www.allthingsliberty.com/2016/05/untangling-british-army-ranks/

This is a very good article on its very confusing, and often misleading, subject. Another must-read for the person interested in the military of the period.

Kelleher, J. P., "1781." *The 7th. Royal Fusiliers and Their Part in the American War of Independence 1775–1781 and New Orleans 1815* (n.d.). www.fusiliermuseumlondon.org/download?id=12390

This is the official regimental history, valuable for its treatment of the regiment at the time of Cowpens.

Libby, Orrin Grant. "Ramsay as a Plagiarist," *The American Historical Review* 7(4) (Jul 1902): 697-703.

> Ramsay plagiarized much of his book from the *Annual Register*. Ramsay remains a valuable resource, but his plagiarism makes his work tricky for the unprepared. This article sets out some of the pitfalls in his Ramsay's work.

Maloy, Mark. "Small Arms of the Revolution," *American Battlefield Trust*, www.battlefields.org/learn/articles/small-arms-revolution

> A good source for the burdens and benefits of the rifle and musket, one of several works on the subject, a subject which should have been settled long ago, but still draws controversy.

"Maryland Line," www.encyclopedia.com/history/encyclopedias-almanacs-transcripts-and-maps/maryland-line

> This article provides an overview of the reorganization of the Maryland Continentals after the disastrous loss at Camden.

National Park Service, "British Units at the Cowpens," www.nps.gov/cowp/learn/historyculture/british-units-at-the-cowpens.htm

> This is the official National Park Service word on its subject. While many may disagree with it, it provides an interesting, if somewhat superficial, treatment of its subject.

National Park Service, "Forty-Eight Hours After the Battle of Cowpens," www.nps.gov/cowp/learn/historyculture/forty-eight-hours-following-the-battle-of-cowpens.htm

> This is one of the most readily accessible resources on the legend of a distraught Cornwallis breaking his sword while learning of the disaster at Cowpens.

Newmyer, R. Kent. "Charles Stedman's *History of the American War.*" *The American Historical Review* 63(4) (Jul 1958): 924–934.

> Newmyer is the source for the criticism of Stedman as a plagiarist. Newmyer is essential for anyone wanting to rely on Stedman as a resource. Because Stedman is largely unavoidable, Newmyer's article is an important addition to the discussion of the southern war.

Read, Elizabeth. "John Eager Howard: Colonel of Second Maryland Regiment—Continental Line," *The Magazine of American History* 7, no. 4 (Oct. 1881). In *The Magazine of American History with Notes and Queries, vol. 7,* edited by John Austin Stevens, 276–282. New York, 1881.

> Read is another author who preserved some writings from Howard, making her work an essential component of any study of the southern war, Cowpens included.

Saberton, Ian. "Cornwallis and the Winter Campaign, January to April 1781," *Journal of the American Revolution,* April 28, 2020, www.allthingsliberty.com/2020/04/cornwallis-and-the-winter-campaign-january-to-april-1781/

> This article is valuable in its treatment of the British Army numbers in and around the time of Cowpens.

Shaw, Travis. "The British Army in the American Revolution," *American Battlefield Trust,* www.battlefields.org/learn/articles/british-army-american-revolution

> This article joins the discussion of the size of British regiments, a topic that has unfortunately given rise to uncertainty.

Wright, John W. "The Rifle in the American Revolution," *The American Historical Review* 29 (no. 2, Jan. 1924), 293-299.

This is an excellent resource on the rifle versus the musket in the war. The question is especially visible at Cowpens, where so many sources disagree on the numbers of riflemen fielded by the Americans.

Wright, Robert K., Jr. "The Colonial Military: Warfare in the Eighteenth Century," *The Society of Colonial Wars in the State of Connecticut*, www.colonialwarsct.org/colonial_military_warfare.htm

Another good source on its topic, focused on such things as the Continentals and their formations in depth.

Theses and Dissertations

Bartholomees, James Boone, Jr. "Fight or Flee: The Combat Performance of the North Carolina Militia in the Cowpens-Guilford Courthouse Campaign, January to March 1781." PhD dissertation, Duke University, 1978.

This is still the standard work on its subject, the difference in the heroic performance of the North Carolina militia under Morgan at Cowpens, as opposed to its poorer showing under Greene at Guilford Courthouse.

Pearson, Jesse T. "The Failure of British Strategy During the Southern Campaign of the American Revolutionary War, 1780-81." Master's thesis, U.S. Army Command and General Staff College, 2005.

This article discusses its topic well, although its level of detail may frustrate casual readers.

Published Papers

Johnson, Todd J. "Nathanael Greene's Implementation of Compound Warfare During the Southern Campaign of the American Revolution." Fort Leavenworth, Kansas: School of Advanced Military Studies, United States Army Command and General Staff College, 2007.

> A very advanced treatment of Greene's use of both conventional and unconventional warfare in the southern campaign.

Moncure, John. "The Cowpens Staff Ride and Battlefield Tour." Fort Leavenworth, Kansas: Combat Studies Institute, United States Army Command and General Staff College, 1996.

> Moncure is valuable for several points. He preserved long tracts of Howard's writings. He also made good use of Revolutionary War pension applications, by quoting from long excerpts of them as opposed to either short snippets, or simply footnoting to them without quotes. He was careful to caution that there was a possibility the applications might not be reliable, and encouraged people to make their own decisions.

Raddall, Thomas H. "Tarleton's Legion." *Collections of the Nova Scotia Historical Society* 28 (1949). Halifax, Nova Scotia: Nova Scotia Historical Society, 1949, Mersey Heritage Society, 2001, www.mersey.ca/tarletonslegion.html

> A highly specialized treatment of Tarleton's Legion, by a Canadian historian who saw Tarleton as a war hero and honored forebear, and not as a malevolent actor.

Significant Websites

American Revolutionary War: 1775 to 1783, *American Revolutionary War Continental Regiments*, "List of American Regiments in the Revolutionary War," www.revolutionarywar.us/continental-army.

> Discusses strength of Continental Army units, a subject of all-too frequent debate.

"A Brief History of the Regiment between 1688 and 2009," *The 16th Regiment of Foot*, www.bedfordregiment.org.uk/history/16thfoothistory.html

> The official history of the regiment, valuable within its subject area.

Southern Campaign American Revolution Pension Statements and Rosters, www.revwarapps.org/

> For those who want to delve into pension applications, this site is the master resource.

Documents

Morgan's report to Greene. National Archives, *Letters from Maj. Gen. Nathanael Greene, 1776–1785*, vol. 1, 541–544.

Greene's orderly book copy of the Cowpens report. National Archives, *Transcripts of Letters from Maj. Gen. Nathanael Greene, 1780–1784*, vol. 1, 39–47.

Greene's report to Congress. Library of Congress, *Nathanael Greene Papers*, microfilm reel 1.

Maps

The following maps are available on the companion website to this volume: blackwaterpress.com/cowpens.

Hammond map. Reprinted on pages 529 and 530 of Joseph Johnson's *Traditions and Reminiscences*.

Clove map. Preserved in the National Archives, microfilmed as M859, located in Record Group 93, War Department collection of Revolutionary War records, entry 6, Numbered Records. The Clove map is manuscript 23813.

Pigree map. Preserved in the National Archives, microfilmed at M859, located in Record Group 93, War Department collection of Revolutionary War records, entry 6, Numbered Records. The Pigree map is manuscript 28475.